WOMEN EMPOWERMENT
Issues and Challenges

WOMEN EMPOWERMENT

Issues and Challenges

Dr. C. PARAMASIVAN
M.Com., M.A., M.B.A., M.Sc., M.Phil., Ph.D.
Assistant Professor
PG and Research Department of Commerce
Periyar E.V.R. College
Tiruchirappalli (T.N.)

REGAL PUBLICATIONS
New Delhi - 110 027

WOMEN EMPOWERMENT
Issues and Challenges

ISBN 978-81-8484-127-5

Typeset by
RAHUL COMPOSERS
358, Pocket-B, Phase-2, Sector-16 B, Dwarka, New Delhi - 110 075

Printed in India at
MAYUR ENTERPRISES
WZ Plot No. 3, Gujjar Market, Tihar Village, New Delhi - 110 018

Published by
REGAL PUBLICATIONS
F-159, Rajouri Garden, New Delhi - 110 027 • Phone : 45546396
E-mail : regalbookspub@yahoo.com

Contents

PART II

EDUCATIONAL EMPOWERMENT

PART III

SOCIO-ECONOMIC EMPOWERMENT

Preface

A woman is a powerful segment of the society who contributes more on the development of civilized society of the country. Women become useful resources; we can achieve the socio-economical goal with sustainable manner. Hence, every part of the world, women issues become popular and concentrate more to their socio-economic, political and legal empowerment. Women development activities are witnessed and implemented with innovative strategies to attain the almost achievement of women society. The country can be full-fledged and independent when the women development programmes are successfully implemented and evaluated.

Empowerment is about people—both women and men—taking control over their lives: becoming conscious of their own situation and position, setting their own agendas, creating space for themselves, gaining skills, building self-confidence, solving problems, and developing self-reliance. It is not only a social and political process, but an individual one as well and it is not only a process but an outcome too. Empowerment of women is a pressing need of the day. Unfortunately, it is least understood. It is therefore very essential to define empowerment for the benefit of all partners.

Empowerment is a process, by which women gain greater control over material and intellectual resources which will assist them to increase their self-reliance and enhance them to assert their independent rights and challenge the ideology of patriarchy and the gender-based discrimination against women. Women empowerment consists of the following components:

Social empowerment—to create an enabling environment through various affirmative developmental polices and programmes for development of women besides providing them easy and equal access to all the basic minimum services so as to enable them to realize their full potentials.

Economic empowerment—to ensure provision of training, employment and income generation activities with both forward and backward linkages with the ultimate objective of making all potential women economically independent and self-reliant.

Educational empowerment—develops the personality and rationality of women-qualifies them to fulfil certain economic, political and cultural functions—improve their socio-economic status.

Political empowerment—is participation, right to vote, contest, campaign, party membership and representation in political affairs at all levels and effectively influences decisions thereby leading to political empowerment.

This book mainly focuses on the women empowerment through education, economic activities and problems faced by the women related with their empowerment in general. There are 34 articles received from the academician and researchers across the country and edited on the basis of the interrelated parts.

I am thankful to Dr. T. Subramanian, for having kind cooperation and encouragement for all kind of my academic occupation and I wish to thank all the contributors for sending their articles in a reasonable time period. My special thanks to the Regal Publications for publishing this edited book as a gorgeous style in a short period.

Dr. C. PARAMASIVAN

List of Contributors

A. Sulthan Mohideen, Lecture in Commerce, Sri Venkateswara College, Peravurani, Thanjore District (T.N.).

B. Rajamani, Research Scholar, Annamalai University, Annamalai Nagar (T.N.).

C. Paramasivan, Assistant Professor in Commerce, Government Arts College, Chidambaram (T.N.).

D. Sureshkumar, Ph.D. Research Scholar, Department of Commerce, Karpagam University, Coimbatore (T.N.).

Dr. C. Madhavi, Professor of Business Administration, Annamalai University, Annamalai Nagar (T.N.).

Dr. Chitra Sivasubramaniam, Assistant Professor (SS), Department of English, Avinashilingam Deemed University for Women, Coimbatore (T.N.).

Dr. G.D. Kharat, Associate Professor in Economics, M.G. Vidyamandir's Arts and Commerce College, Yeola, Nasik (Maharashtra).

Dr. Harish Adke, Arts, Science and Commerce College, Manmad, Dist. Nasik (Maharashtra).

Dr. J. Senthil Velmurugan, Asst. Professor, PRIMS, Periyar University, Salem (T.N.).

Dr. K. Arulselvam, Associate Professor, Department of Economics, Avanshilingam Deemed University for Women, Coimbatore (T.N.).

Dr. K. Krishnakumar, Assistant Professor in Commerce, Department of Commerce, Periyar University, Salem (T.N.).

Dr. K. Rajmohan, Assistant Professor, Post Graduate Department of Commerce, Jawaharlal Nehru Rajkeeya Mahavidyalaya (Govt. College), Port Blair.

Dr. S. Rajamohan, Professor, Alagappa Institute of Management, Alagappa University, Karaikudi (T.N.).

Dr. K. Suriyan, Assistant Professor, Sociology Department, Annamalai University (T.N.).

Dr. M. Ketharaj, Assistant Professor, PG Department of Commerce, Sethupathy Government Arts College, Ramanathapuram (T.N.).

Dr. P. Palanivel, Professor and Controller of Examination, Karpagam University, Coimbatore (T.N.).

Dr. R. Annapoorani, Professor of Economics, Avinashilingam Deemed University for Women, Coimbatore (T.N.).

Dr. R. Rathidevi, Assistant Professor, Department of MBA, Mahendra Institute of Technology, Namakkal Dt. (T.N.).

Dr. R.D. Bhosale, Head of the Department of Economics, Arts & Commerce College, Yeola, Nasik (Maharashtra).

Dr. S. Arulkumar, Assistant Professor in Business Administration, Directorate of Distance Education, Annamalai University, Annamalai Nagar (T.N.).

Dr. S.B. Sanap, Head of Department, Department of Commerce, S.P.H. Mahila Mahavidyalaya, Malegaon Camp, Nasik (Maharashtra).

Dr. T. Subramanian, Professor, Department of Management Studies, Vidhya Vikas College of English, Tiruchengode (T.N.).

Dr. T. Sundara Raj, Assistant Professor, Department of Sociology, Periyar University, Salem (T.N.).

Dr. T. Vijayaraghavan, Assistant Professor, Department of Humanities, PSG College of Technology, Coimbatore (T.N.).

Dr. Yathish Kumar, Selection Grade Lecturer, Department of Commerce, University College, Mangalore (Karnataka).

E. Murugesan, JRF (Doctoral) Scholar, P.G. Department of International Law, T.N. Dr. Ambedkar Law University, Chennai (T.N.).

G. Gnanarubi, Research Scholar, Department of Economics, Avinashilingam Deemed University for Women, Coimbatore (T.N.).

G. Jayalakshmi, Lecturer, Department of Commerce, Vidhya Sagar Women's College, Chengalpet (T.N.).

G. Ravi, Assistant Professor of Commerce, Dr. Ambedkar Government Arts College, Vyasarpadi, Chennai (T.N.).

K. Krithiga, Research Scholar, Annamalai University, Annamalai Nagar (T.N.).

K. Sivakumar, Assistant Professor, Department of Commerce, Aringar Anna Arts College, Karikal, Puducherry (T.N.).

M. Chandrasekaran, Asst. Professor, Department of Management Studies, Kathir College of Engineering, Coimbatore (T.N.).

M. Julius Prasad, Research Scholar, Annamalai University, Annamalai Nagar (T.N.).

N. Ramani, Lecturer in Commerce, Chellammal College for Women, Guindy, Chennai (T.N.).

P. Baby, Ph.D. Research Scholar (RGNF), Department of Commerce, Periyar University, Salem (T.N.).

P. Ganesan, Assistant Professor, Sociology Department, Annamalai University (T.N.).

P.M. Sugavnaswari, Ph.D. Research Scholar, Department of Commerce, Periyar University, Salem (T.N.).

R. Srinivasan, Lecturer in Commerce, Sengunthar Arts and Science for Women, Tiruchengode (T.N.).

S. Jayasankar, Lecturer in Commerce, Vivekananda College of Arts and Sciences for Women, Tiruchengode (T.N.).

S. Sivakumar, Assistant Professor, Department of Commerce, Karpagam University, Coimbatore (T.N.).

Sonawane Dnyaneshwar, N., Lecturer in Econimics, M.S.G. College, Malegaon, Distt. Nasik, (Maharashtra).

U.K. Teke, Assistant Professor, Department of Commerce, S.P.H. Mahila Mahavidyalaya, Malegaon Camp, Nasik (Maharashtra).

PART I

WOMEN EMPOWERMENT—AN OVERVIEW

1

Status of Women and Empowerment

J. SENTHIL VELMURUGAN

STATUS IN THE FAMILY AND SOCIETY

In the current social climate, the significance of family is vital for women, particularly for poor women in the rural areas. The prevailing attitude to women is still conditioned by religious symbolism which highlights the self-sacrificing, self-effacing pure image of women and the preferred role of a woman as a faithful wife and devout mother, whilst at the same time emphasizing the subordination of women, i.e., a daughter or wife is a commodity or possession.

Women's survival is not socially conceivable without the family. Motherhood is the only acceptable social goal to which she can aspire. Her worth as a 'reproducer' confers some status on her. At the same time, the social value placed on the role of women in the family is also responsible for her subordination to men and for her lack of access to economic and political resources, even where she contributes equally or more to the family economy.

Women face considerable insecurity in the patriarchal family structure. Sent as a young bride into a strange household (in Tamil Nadu the average age of marriage is 20 years), contact with her natal home is discouraged. At the same time, a woman is never a permanent member of her husband's family—she may have to leave if she does not satisfy. This fear frequently encourages a woman to relinquish her rights to a share (legal coparcenary rights) in the parental property in favour of her brothers in order to enjoy the 'affection' of the brothers and to ensure a welcome in case she has to fall back upon them if her marriage breaks down.

ECONOMIC ROLE OF WOMEN

The position of women in the social structure affects the way they are regarded in their economic roles as well. Firstly, it has resulted in a pervasive sexual division of labour, which reinforces the notion of the male having more power and relegates low status occupations to women. In so doing it leads to a waste of female potential and ignores individual differences in capacities and abilities within each sex. Once occupational or task segregation takes place, it tends to be retained against all other rational criteria.

Secondly, through defining women as solely responsible for family care, their incursion into the labour market, made inevitable by inadequate incomes of males or absence of male earners, is at certain levels seen as deviant behaviour and results in the pervasive notion of the woman worker as a supplementary earner irrespective of the total resources contributed to the household or the time and energy spent. Thus, a woman who earns as much as 50% or sometimes 100% of the household income is still regarded as a supplementary earner. And almost in all cases and in all levels (except to a large extent in the organized sector which accounts for a very small percentage of women) they do not get equal wages for equal work, nor do the conditions of work offered to them take into account their dual roles. The need to combine productive work with her reproductive role and family responsibilities means that a woman's choice of work is often dictated by what is feasible and easily available, and this need for flexibility is frequently exploited by the labour market and is easily used as another excuse to pay *low wages to women.*

Women are principally engaged in agriculture or in the unorganized informal sector as construction workers, petty hawkers and vendors and in traditional home-based occupations such as basket and mat-weaving, bidi-making, lace-making, agarbathis, etc. Women are also involved in marketing in certain traditional areas. Marketing of agricultural products, however, is traditionally undertaken by men. Women are involved in fish trading, vegetable and flower vending and other areas of petty market trading. Similarly, women involved in handicraft occupations such as basket-making, etc., will frequently market their products in the local shandies (bazaars).

WOMEN IN AGRICULTURE

Women carry out the bulk of the work in agricultural production. Around 70-80% of all field work is done by women whilst most post-harvest and processing tasks are solely their responsibility. There is, however, strict sexual division of labour in agricultural work. All operations involving machinery and draught animals are performed by men. Thus, men are responsible for all ploughing, harrowing and leveling, for irrigation using bullock bailing, for threshing where animals are used and for spraying. All activities involving direct manual labour are assigned to women. These include sowing, transplanting and weeding. Women also play an important role in harvesting and processing work, which has not been mechanized. This particularly applies to harvesting, threshing, winnowing, dehusking and grinding of millets. Rice, on the other hand, is now mostly de-husked by rice mills.

Women are also heavily involved in animal husbandry. Whilst the care of draught animals tends to be the man's responsibility, care of milch animals, sheep and goats are the woman's preserve. In this connection, women are involved in the collection of fodder from the forests and other communal areas.

WOMEN IN THE INFORMAL SECTOR

Women's involvement in the informal sector is characterized by a high incidence of casual labour with women mostly doing intermittent jobs at extremely low wages or working on their own account for very uneconomical returns. There is a total lack of job security and social security benefits. The areas of exploitation are high resulting in long hours, unsatisfactory work conditions and health hazards. In addition, the women are exposed to financial exploitation by traders and middlemen who provide credit or raw materials and take back the finished product, cheating the women through providing insufficient or sub-standard raw materials and then making unreasonable deductions for poor quality. The organized sector takes advantage of this vulnerable position of the labour force in the informal sector and large industries are now finding it advantageous to decentralize production to make use of workers in the informal sector.

ACCESS AND CONTROL OVER INCOME AND PARTICIPATION IN DECISION-MAKING

Although many families can only survive through the contributions made by women to the family income, women generally have little control over family income and expenditure decisions. As a rule, the men consider their wages as their own income and they give only a certain part to the women for family needs. Wages for agricultural work, even when paid to the women, are usually taken over and controlled by the household men. The squandering of income by the men on drink, etc. is a major concern of many women, who criticise the fact that the so-called breadwinners consider their income to be private property whilst they are left to manage the household as best they may. However, where the women have some control over the money they earn, they usually spend the bulk of it on the family's basic needs, especially food. Hence, the issue of control over household income is a crucial factor affecting nutritional levels of women and children.

Various studies have revealed that children's nutritional shortfalls in agricultural labour households are much more closely linked to whether or not the mother was employed, than to the father's employment; daughters in particular were left much worse-off than the sons on the mother's non-working days.

Women, in addition, have virtually no control over the family assets. In the majority of cases land is in the name of the male head of the household. The women also have no control over, or access to, other means of production necessary for agricultural operations like wells, ploughs and draught animals which are the men's possessions. The same is true of other agricultural implements and tools, like harrows, sowers, carts, etc. The only tools and implements in the possession of women are sickles, baskets and winnowing fans. Furthermore, there is a qualitative difference between the tools controlled by men and those in the control of women. Whereas men's tools are usually based on the use of other-than-human sources of energy, women's tools are usually dependent on their own physical energy. Thus, women's tools imply more labour-intensive work than those of men and as a result, women's work is considered less productive than men's work and is consequently lower paid. Thus, wages for women in agriculture are only around 50-60% of those of men.

FEMINIZATION OF POVERTY

Poverty and unemployment have the worst effect on women leading to the phenomenon of feminization of poverty. Wide inequalities exist in the distribution of the burden of poverty between male and female household members in the male headed households. Women are discriminated against in access to basic necessities such as food and medical care. When the family resources are meager, the shortfall in the women's food intake is likely to be twice as high as for the male members of the household. Amongst children, consistently higher proportion of girls is found to be *malnourished*, with the situation particularly acute amongst the landless families. Given the link between nutritional deficiency and susceptibility to infection, this leads on to a *higher incidence of illness* amongst female children, which coupled with less access to medical treatment for girls, results in higher mortality rates for young girls than for boys.

Amongst adults, a greater percentage of women than men receive no medical treatment in the event of illness and among those treated, the reliance on traditional medicine is higher amongst women whereas men receive more expensive modern medical treatment. Indian women have a lower expectancy of life than men and the difference between male and female life expectancy has been increasing consistently since 1921 when female life expectancy exceeded that of males by 1.5 years. Now the position is reversed and male life expectancy exceeds that of females by 1.7 years.

The few time allocation studies undertaken in India indicate that rural women of poor households put in long hours of work, often longer than men, when domestic work, other home-based work and labour outside the home is counted. Anecdotal evidence also indicates that rural men have more leisure than rural women who can rarely enjoy 'leisure' in any real sense due to their sole responsibility for child care. The burden of women's domestic work, particularly their specific responsibility for collecting fuel, fodder and water has increased under conditions of increasing deforestation and ecological deterioration requiring them to walk longer distances and spend longer hours in acquiring the family's needs. Where these can no longer be met, changes in consumption patterns occur involving a decrease in the number of cooked meals which adversely affects the nutritional quality of the food intake of the family.

Women are particularly affected by seasonal variations in poverty particularly where food-at-work as part of the wages is a significant factor in women's overall intake of food. Women's employment is much more seasonal in nature than men's due to the greater task-specificity of women's work. This means that female agricultural labourers have access to income only in certain times of the year and during the slack period they are exposed much to the risk of undernourishment and starvation.

The major problem for the bulk of rural families is the availability of employment. The pressure on land, the extinction of certain handicrafts, etc. have contributed to migration from the rural areas. 77% of all migrants are females.

FEMALE HEADED HOUSEHOLDS

Female headed households are predominantly to be found amongst the poor where they constitute a much more marginalized group even amongst the 'poorest of the poor'. Women headed households are the result of widowhood, migration, desertion or illness, unemployment or the addictive habits of their husbands. They suffer a high incidence of poverty and occupy the bottom rung of society. At the same time, the delivery structures of credit, technical advice, etc. do not reach them as institutions are slow to recognize women as heads of households. In Tamil Nadu, 15% of the households are headed by women compared with 10% for India as a whole but this is acknowledged to be a gross underestimate, failing to take due account of the *de facto* female headed households where women are the effective supporters of the family, due to the inability of male members to provide for the family. Amongst all the States, Tamil Nadu has the fourth highest percentage of female-headed households in the country.

Various studies of female headed households (FHHs) indicate that compared to male-headed households (MHHs), a significantly higher percentage of FHHs are in the higher age groups (over 60 years), depend on wage labour as opposed to self-employment in non-agricultural activities and have a low education level and high illiteracy rate. Amongst cultivating households, FHHs tend to be concentrated amongst the smallest holding size of less than one acre. Thus overall, FHHs have poorer survival chances given their lower control over land resources and their greater dependency on wage income, their higher rate of involuntary unemployment and the lower levels of education and literacy of the household heads. The smaller size of FHHs also implies a lower availability of household labour. This can negatively affect the ability of female heads to be successful in self-employment ventures. All these factors indicate that female-headed households are more poverty-prone.

THE IFAD EXPERIMENT AND THE TAMIL NADU EXPERIENCE

It is in this context that the TNWDP experiment becomes relevant. This early pioneering effort was aided and enhanced by assistance of the International Fund for Agricultural Development, through the Tamil Nadu Women Development Project (TNWDP) taken up for implementation by the Government of Tamil Nadu through the Tamil Nadu Corporation for Development of Women Ltd. (TNCDW) in eight Districts (then five districts) of Tamil Nadu in 1989-90. The prime objectives of the project were to improve the social and economic position of women below poverty line, through the formation of *Self-Help Groups* of poor women in these districts with active assistance and supervision of NGOs. The results of the project speak for themselves.

Financial discipline inculcated through *internal rotation of savings* and introduction of best practices like double-entry book-keeping helped in building capacity of the SHG members. Training in SHG management, skill development, etc., also played a very important role in empowering poor women. An interim evaluation report by ORG clearly points out how the standing of SHG members in their families and neighbourhood and participation of women members in decision-making in their families and community have improved significantly, pointing to successful achievement of social empowerment of women. Credit goes to Indian Banks in joining this massive effort and supporting credit-worthy groups with timely doses of credit, while subsidy was provided by TNCDW. It is a matter of great pride that so far Rs. 48.16 crores have been disbursed as credit and Rs. 32.33 crores as subsidy, totaling Rs. 80.49 crores to 87,541 SHG members, with an average repayment of 85% till date. 5207 SHGs with 1,20,960 women-members having a total savings corpus fund of Rs. 22.89 crores are proof of the successful partnership between TNCDW, NGOs, Indian Banks and NABARD. IFAD funding came to a close on 31.12.98, with post-project activities, including continued credit support under progress.

TNWDP has effected a sea change in the living conditions of poor rural women. NGOs have played a key role right from formation of women Self-Help Groups to attainment of women empowerment, by providing necessary training and other inputs. The average repayment level of IFAD loans is above 85% consistently and is one of the key indicators of success of IFAD Project. Efforts have also been made to make all IFAD groups sustainable. The need for sustainability and *strategies for sustainability* have been impressed upon SHG members to make groups self-reliant in the long-run.

The ultimate objective of the intervention is to leave behind self-reliant and *sustainable SHGs*, through a process of careful and slow withdrawal by NGOs and TNCDW in a phased manner, has been achieved with a large majority of groups reaching this stage.

Considering the meritorious features of this unique project, similar Projects with IFAD funding have been launched in other states. This project has also become the role-model for emergence of lot of Self-Help Groups in both IFAD and non-IFAD districts of TN, on their own. Tamil Nadu Women Development project has been the main source of inspiration for formation of thousands of groups by Arivoli Iyakkam, TANWA, SGSY, Banks, TNINP, and NGOs.

A Gender Impact Assessment study made as part of the IFAD Completion Evaluation Mission indicates substantial improvement in women's access and control to resources, increased mobility, increased self-confidence, increased voice of women in household and community decision-making.

MAHALIR THITTAM

These groups would to begin with be involved in savings and credit activities. Later on they would not only engage in productive economic and social activities, but also function as important *sustainable, democratic and women-managed institutions.* These SHGs would be instrumental in assimilation and dissemination of knowledge about health, nutrition, literacy, womens' rights, child care, education, adoption of new agricultural practices, farm and non-farm sector economic activities, etc., and pave the way for increased participation of women in decision-making in households, community and the local democratic set-up besides helping to prepare women to take up leadership positions.

Mahalir Thittam—A Women-centric Approach to Development

- Development of strong, cohesive, Self-help Women Groups, through *inculcation of the spirit of Mutual Help, Self-help and team spirit.*
- Reduced vulnerability to crisis by *inculcating habit of regular savings.*
- Getting out of money-lender's clutches, by regular *savings and internal rotation of savings.*
- Increased asset-base and income, through access to *inexpensive and timely credit.*
- Improved access to vital credit for economic activities by *making SHGs credit worthy and bankable.*
- Making SHGs credit worthy *by making SHGs adopt principles of financial discipline (of timely savings and prompt loan repayments).*
- Financial self-sufficiency and sustainability *by building up of SHG corpus and building ability to meet SHGs costs on their own, over a period of time.*
- Increased access to financial resources through linking and encouraging need-based *tapping of alternate credit delivery systems*—like NGO funds, HDFC housing loans, RMK, etc.
- Improved access of SHG members to various governmental, development schemes and bank credit, by *forging sustainable linkages of SHGs with banks, Government departments,* etc.
- Self-confidence building and improved communication skills through *training, increased mobility, exposure and collective action.*
- Increasing Social Awareness, through *motivation, intermingling, networking, exposure and participation in Social Action/Reformation Programmes.*
- Improved Status of women in the family and society,

through access to credit, increased control over resources, improved skills and collective action.

- Bringing out hidden talents *by constant motivation and providing opportunities.*
- Improved opportunities for self-development by *breaking social and cultural barriers and inhibitions.*
- Improvement in Health and Family Welfare, through *awareness, training and exposure.*
- Improved Functional Literacy (incl. numeracy) through *training, exposure and practice.*
- Awareness of Legal rights and legal aid access, through *networking and training.*
- Overall *leadership development,* through *exposure to SHG management by conscious rotation of responsibilities.*
- Change from worker status to worker-manager status, by *motivating them to assume control over their lives.*
- Development of business competence, through *entrepreneurship training, facilitating participation in exhibitions, collective negotiation/bargaining, facilitate emergence of structures like marketing unions and dissemination of information on markets.*

References

www.google.org

DRDA Office, Dharmapuri.

Muttram, Monthly Journal of Women Empowerment.

Mangathai, R.A. (2001), "Together We Stand (Success Story)", *Kurukshetra,* November, 50. 30-31.

Nair, Tara S. (1998), "Meeting the Credit Needs of the Micro Enterprise Sector : Issues in Focus", *The Indian Journal of Labour Economics,* July-Setember, 41.3:531-538

Narashimban Sakunatala (1999), "Empowering Women: An Alternative Strategy for Rural India", New Delhi, Sage Publications India Pvt. Ltd.

www.tnwdc.org

Women Empowerment

N. Ramani and G. Ravi

INTRODUCTION

Women constitute almost 50% of the world's population. As per as their social status is concerned, they are not treated as equal to men in all the places, though in the western countries women are treated on par with men in most of the fields, their counterpart in the east suffers from many disabilities. The disabilities on the one hand and the inequalities between men and women on the other, have given rise to what is known "Gender problem". All one the world and particularly in South and East Asia and Africa the gender problem has assumed importance during the recent years, the gender issue has become virtually a crucial point of argument. It is now widely believed that empowerment of women, i.e., providing equal rights, opportunities and responsibilities to women will go a long way in removing the existing gender discrimination. Women empowerment in contemporary Indian society in forms of their work, education, health and media images in the forms of their work, education, health and media images in the context of lineage, rule of residence and household chores, their context of lineage, rule of residence and household chores, their participation in social and political activities, their legal status in terms of marriage, divorce and inheritance of property, seeking wealth care should be taken into consideration. Empowerment in terms of knowledge and awareness of ones own life and society including legal raise their status with regard to the lives.

ROLE OF WOMEN IN DEVELOPMENT PROCESS

The principal of gender equality was recognized in the United Nations Charter in 1945 and the UN Declaration of Human Rights in 1948, the majority of development planners did not fully address the role of women in development process. In 1975, the first UN Conference of Women and Development was held at Mexico City under the motto, "Equality, Development and peace". The need to integrate women into development was internationally proclaimed in the 1995 Beijing Conference. The Economic Survey (1999-2000) used an entire section on gender inequality. It began with a reminder of the commitment made in the ninth plan document of allocating 30 per cent of resources for women's development schemes through "Women's Component Plans". According to Menon and Probhu (2001), there was a strong plea for investing in women's equality on the ground that this made economic sense and spoke of "the social rate of return on investment in women" being greater that the corresponding rate for men. According to Paten (2002), women's development can be attained by improving here status and bargaining power in the economy.

Sushma Sachay (1998) argues that approaches and strategic for women empowerment could be possible by outlining the mechanisms and tools that till influence for women empowerment. Decisions-making process, multidimensional processes that are enabling worn to realize their full identity and powers in all walks of life.

Empowering may be understood as enabling people, especially women to acquire and possess power resources, in order to make decision on their own or resist decisions that are made by others that affect them. A person may said to be powerful when he/she has control over a large portion of power resources in society. The extent of possession of various resources such as personal wealth, such as land skills, education, information, knowledge, social status, position held, leadership trains, capabilities of mobilization.

The National Policy on Education (1986) suggested certain strategies to empower women. Accordingly, women become empowered through collective reflections and decision-making enable them to become agency of social change. The global conference on Women Empowerment (1988), highlighted empowerment as the best way of making own partners in development, the Development of Women and Children in Rural Areas (DWCRA) program was initiated as a sub-scheme of the national-wide poverty alleviation program i.e., the Integrated Rural Development Program (IRDP). It aims at imparting self-reliance to rural areas through income generating skills along with group organization skills. Keeping this in view the year 2001 was celebrated as "The Women's Empowerment Year". Human resource development and empowerment of women unlock the door for modernization of society, Instead of remaining as passive beneficiaries, women must become active partner. Participation and control over resources of power are considered as the critical indicators in the process of development discharged women especially in rural areas possess the least proportion of these resources and as a result they are powerless and dependent on the powerful and wealthy.

ROLE AND EMPOWERMENT

We will now realize the vital importance of the terms such as role, empowerment and function for an understanding of society. These terms tell us how individual and groups organize themselves as well as relate to each other. Very simple, role tells us about what is expected from individuals in a particular situation. While empowerment deals with her or his expectation arising out of the situation. Similarly, a role deals with duties and obligations while empowerment deals with rights. For instance, it is commonly assumed that the most is a woman, a wife a cook, a teacher of her children and daughter-in-law and so on. What happens when the mother is also the principal of the local village school? Not only does she have to deal with a range of roles and empowerments, but also with the tensions that may rise out of her role as mother and her role as an administrator.

"Woman reposes more closely on the central surface of life, while man hunts it in the boundaries of existence, always concerned to overcome, and in the last analysis, to kill. A woman has a secret alliance with eternal life and man with the principle of death. Woman wants to embrace the contradiction of life and to reconcile them in the act of degree so. Men on the other hand release the tension between opposites by annihilating one of the sides, the one he finds unpleasant. He seeks the solution not in love and reconciliation, but in over-coming and annihilation. He has a militant and not an erotic manner. The male principle borne of isolation, makes solitude thermal, seeks being in itself and disturbs life as a wholes his being is battle and self-service, his will-to-life is concerned with ascertaining his own person or overthrowing that of the stranger until the motive of salvation kindles within him. Woman with her sustaining constitutions is at one and is harmony with the basis of the world. But man wants to change the world to bring it forward to overcome it".

WOMEN'S EMPOWERMENT IN CONTEMPORARY INDIA

Contemporary Indian society has been exposed to the broad processes of social transformation, agricultural modernization and economic development, urbanization and globalization. However, these processes have generated regional imbalances, sharpened class inequalities and augmented the gender disparities. Hence, women have become critical symbols of these growing imbalances. All these have affected adversely the various aspects of women's empowerment in the contemporary Indian society. The family and women's work is not enough to say that any society consists of men and women. It is equally important to look at how the two groups of people interact, as well as at the role and exceptions each group has of the other. Such roles and exceptions are a product of the stereotypes of each gender. By gender stereotype we mean attributes and qualities commonly associated with a gender. Thus, the first idea on gender role differences, which a child acquires, is that of women of one's family marrying and leaving their homes to leave with different groups of people. Secondly, men appear to exercise far greater influence in decision-making and are far more visible and audible than their wives. Third, most of the tasks within the home are done by the mother, grandmother, sisters and so on. At meal times they carry food to the fields for the men. All these tasks, which consume time and energy, are not counted as work and there is no payment involved. In western countries, women's groups, politicians and other concerned individuals have been arguing for payment for house work and childcare. In India, the question of payment for household jobs has not really been an important issue or demand. As we shall see, there are many other issues, which require urgent attention. At the same time, it is important for us to remember that non-payment should not also mean non-recognition. The fact that women are expected to perform all these tasks as a part of their conventional roles and on special merit is awarded to them for these tiring and tiresome jobs.

WOMEN'S WORK PARTICIPATION

As per to 1981 figures 19.7 per cent Indian women were recorded as paid workers. Of whom over 87 per cent were in the unrecognized or informal sector of the economy. The work participation rate of woman in 1991 and 2001 was 22.3 and 25.7 per cent respectively. The increase in the work participation of women during the decade 1991-2001 is mainly due to the increase in the proportion of marginal workers (6.3 per cent to 11 per cent) in total female work force. It is held by many observations of Indian economy that without women's paid or unpaid labour the Indian agricultural economy would not be able to function. In the informal sector, there are no legal redresses for problems; no maternity or other leave benefits and little security of service. Working long hours as domestic servants, stitching clothes for the garment export industry, working on the assembly line of small electronics manufacturing units or the beedi, tobacco, cashew nut factories. A woman lives in fear of retrenchment, exploitation and low wages.

WOMEN'S SELF-PERCEPTION

According to Maithreyi Krishna Raj that though women were concerned about continuing their jobs, they were not looking for better prospects nor have they begun with a long-range carrier strategy. Once in a job, women rarely attempted to acquire further qualifications was by no means clear-cut. T.S. Papola's study of workingwomen, which covered a range from those in supervisory post in industrial establishments to unskilled workers, showed that women were more different than men in respect of their promotion prospects.

EMPLOYER'S ATTITUDE

Papol's study showed that women were discriminated against at the time of promotions tended to be crowded into lower status electrical and primary school jobs. They were rarely promoted to executive and supervisory posts. As regards employment and promotion to supervisory category, male employers defend themselves by pointing out that women did not come forth to be recruited or promoted.

TRADITIONAL POSITIONS OF AUTHORITY IN URBAN AREAS

In the urban areas, the working class, and men in particular have a wide range of job options available to them. The study by Leela Kasturi shows that when unemployed weavers from Tamil Nadu migrant to Delhi, the women folk found jobs only as domestic servants. While men become mechanics, cooks or drivers. The shift in residence meant a severance with an established way of life and the support of the extended family.

WORKING CONDITIONS

For the majority of working class women, a job is essential. In relation to the limited chances for occupational mobility, when men and women work in the same occupation, female tasks are often the more arduous and time consuming. For instance, in paddy cultivation they spend long hours in sowing, weeding transplanting. In Kerala the extraction of the cashew seed from a corrosive liquid is women's work. Again when both sexes do identical jobs, women often get paid less than man. Protests are rare, apart from ignorance of legal and other rights; there is a fear of exploitation and sexual harassment by the landlord or contractor.

CONCLUSION

Irrespective of social class there is at the level of belief, widespread commitment to the nation that a woman's job just not interfere or compete with her primary role of wife and mother. There is also concern with her physical safety and the respectability of the occupation. Clearly, working class familiar are far less able to ensure circumstances. NGO's, SHGs have been working to promote women more viable towards social, political, economic and cultural development micro finance is a significant factor and accessible to small and micro enterprises, socio-economic progress of poor women. Education and training also plays a major role in changing the life of poor women. The several institutions have been extending all types of vocational training, income generating activities and self-employment activities for poor women.

Empowerment of women is mainly related to their participation in decision-making with regard to raising and distribution of resources, i.e., income, investments and expenditures at all levels. Even though the Government of Karnataka has formulated and implemented various schemes of the social, economic and overall development of the rural women, when the present position of women is taken into account these schemes do not appear effective in enhancing the confidence and capability of the women.

References

Chiranjeevulu, T. (2003). Empowering Women through Self-Help Groups—Experiences in Experiment, *Kurukshetra*, March.

Gopalan, Sarala (2002). Towards Equality—The Unfinished Agenda. Status of Women in India, National Commission for Women, New Delhi.

Kapadia, Karin (2002). The Violence of Development: The Politics of Identity, Gender and Social Inequalities in India, *Kali for Women*, New Delhi.

Krishnaraj, Maithreyi (2002). Growth and Rural Poverty, *Economic and Political Weekly*, September 21.

Manohar, Sujatha (2002). Women's Empowerment—Law and Gender Justice. Paper Presented in the International Women's Day, 8th March 2001, Department of Women and Child Development, New Delhi.

Sarkar, C.R. (2004). *Poverty, Education and Economic Development.*

3

Women Empowerment

Special Reference to India

HARISH ADKE

INTRODUCTION

Empowerment is a social action process that promotes participation of people, organization and communities in gaining control over their lives in their communities and larger society. Empowerment in its simplest form means the manifestation of the redistribution of power and challenges, patriarchal ideology and the male dominance. Barbara Israel (1994) has specifically emphasized process and outcome activities at the three different levels of empowerment—individual, organizational and community. Major factors determining participation were immediate material and social benefits, and symbolic benefits such as increased status. Empowerment is a construct that assumes a productive approach to life, a psychological sense of efficacy and control, socio-political activity and organizational involvement.

PREAMBLE

Ours is the large populated and oldest democratic country at the map of the world. It is large oldest and ideal democratic country having 28 states and 7 union territories. The education is imparted by a roundly 24 regional languages and 2 national languages.

In present political and economical environment, every know and then we are reading and using the words like women empowerment, women representation gender equity, gender-base budgeting, etc.

We are trying to achieve equity on the aspect of male-female development. The constitution Amendments 72, 73 for women representation and pending Lok Sabha bill on women reservation gives more light on subject.

We were taught by our forefathers that Mother is Mata; Shakti (Power) is Devi. The Laxmi, Saraswati, Durga, Kali, Parvathi are at highest place of our heart. Our tradition of Rakhi shows immense importance to Brother-Sister relationship. My dear bothers and sisters at Chicago catch the eyes and years of world. The Rani Laxmi Bai, Jija Mata, Indira Gandhi, Sonia Gandhi formed place at the top of world map.

Various Government efforts directed through plans programmes policies are helping for women empowerment. But still we are not active the gender equity, empowerment. The society is tide by various laws derived from traditions and drive by superstition. Sea-change is requiring in the area of women development and empowerment. The dowry cases, attempted rape, rape, workplace harassment, illegal women trafficking cases are recorded now and then.

NATIONAL POLICY FOR WOMEN DEVELOPMENT

The Policy announced in 2001 by Government of India emphasis on following points:

(1) Creating an environment through positive economic and social policies for full development of women to enable to realize their full potential.

(2) The *de-jure and de-facto* employment of all human rights and fundamental freedom by women on equal basis with men in all sphere—political economic, social cultural and civil.

(3) Equal access to participation and division-making of women—in social, political and economic life of the nation.

(4) Equal access to women in health care quality education at all level, carriers and vocational guidance, employment, equal remuneration occupation, health and safety, social security and public office.

(5) Strengthen legal system aimed at elimination of all forms of discrimination against women.

(6) Changing societal attitudes and confine practices by active participation and involvement of both men and women.

(7) Mainstreaming and gender perspective in the development process.

(8) Elimination of discrimination of all forms of violence against Women and Girl Child.

The policy adopted for women empowerment aims at creating conclusive atmosphere for gender equity. The need-based programmes are chalk out for this purpose. The equal participation is required in decision-making at public and personal life. The legal system will be framed to insured ending of violence of any form against the women. The change in attitude of society is expected. As the women are backbone of family she should be empowered and developed to upliftment of family. If women develops the family will develop automatically the nation. Women including girl child constitute 48% of total population.

Separate Ministry of Women and Child Development were established from 31.1.2006. The vision of this ministry is to ensure survival, development and protection of women of the country to enable them to lead productive and wholesome lives as citizens. The ministry is engaged in formulating policies, programmes, action plans for advancement of women.

WOMEN EMPOWERMENT—WHAT I UNDERSTOOD

There are so many barriers to development for women in India. These are social family, cultural dependency. Their participation in decision-making is negligible. They are driven by forced traditional bondage, cultural compulsion; they totally depend on society and family. A girl child depend on brother or father. A wife depends on husband and mother depends on son. There are economical barriers too. They are not supposed to become economically strong and independent.

The ending of all barriers is the empowerment, increasing the political, social, economical strength, power is the women empowerment. They must be free for decision-making as well as access to political system and decision-making, education, economical resources, family development, etc. There must be equality with men in all aspects of life. It is arrangement of resources, allocation of resources, opportunities which will help to make women politically, economically, spiritually strong, stable and confident.

BARRIERS TO WOMEN EMPOWERMENT

(1) Social Barriers

The society is still not in position to digest the concept. The son is for life time asset and daughter is life time liability is the thinking style. The women are for family work like kitchen, cleaning, washing clothes, etc. They are not openly and freely access to education, society and other such aspects.

(2) Dominating Male Attitude

Often male members of family are in higher position women are dominated on various grounds like gender, economic, decision-making, participating in rights and family work.

(3) Political Parties

The agenda of political parties on paper and in practice differs. The women representation is not equal to share age. Lok Sabha seats was merely 6 up to 14th Lok Sabha.[2]

(4) Up Keeping of Girl Child

The girl child is always neglected while up keeping. She is organized the housework and which is taught her that it is the first priority and responsibility. Education is not on priority list.

CONSTITUTION AND WOMEN EMPOWERMENT

The constitution has rightly provided for women empowerment—

(1) Article 14 of Indian Constitution provides for equality before to law.
(2) Article 15(1) states that there should not be discrimination by state on the grounds only of religion, race, caste, sex, place of birth.
(3) Article 15(3) refers to special provision for women and children.
(4) Article 16 is for equality of opportunity for all citizens in matters relating to employment and appointment to any office under state.
(5) Article 39(9) is to secure men and women equally the right to an adequate mean of livelihood. Equal pay for equal work for men and women.
(6) Article 42 is specially for maternity relief and good working conditions.

Apart from this there are several Acts, like

- Immoral Traffic Prevention Act, 1956.
- Dowry Prevention Act, 1961.
- Prohibition of Child Marriage Act, 2006.
- Protection of Women from Domestic Violence Act, 2005.
- Commission of Sati (Prevention) Act, 1987.

GOVERNMENT SCHEMES FOR WOMEN DEVELOPMENT

After Independence so many schemes are floated by Government of India for women empowerment. Before independence the social reformers like Rajaram Mohan Roy, Mahatma Jyotiba Phule and Others tried their level best for the noble Job.

Special Training and Employment Programmes (STEPs)

(1) Special training and employment programmes were launched by Government of India. The training area was from the area of Animal Husbandry, Fisheries Handicrafts Dairy, and Handlooms, etc. It is Support to Training and Employment for Women (STEP). The central scheme started from 1987.

(2) Government of India started the scheme of family counseling under the title of Family Counseling Central Programme. The Ministry of Child and Women Development is taking care of the scheme. The total beneficiaries of the schemes are 1,11,250 families up to Dec. 2009. The sanction amount for this scheme is Rs. 1696.92 Lakhs. The total units established under this scheme are 890.

(3) The Swayamsidha Scheme is especially designed for the women. It is applied practice through self-help groups. The aim is to provide credit facilities and to make aware them for personal finance.

(4) The Swadhar scheme is started in 2001. It is for holistic and integrated service. Under this scheme the women prisoners are released from various jails and rehabilitation were made. The women are trained to protect themselves from trafficking and sexual abuse.

(5) To encourage the women for development and social work the Government of India started awarding *Sree Shakti Puraskar, Devi Ahilya Holkar Puraskar, Mata Jijabai Puraskar, Rani Laxmi Bai Puraskar.*

Needed Agenda

(1) Education

Special primary to post graduation education institutions must be established for women and girl child. Education will bring empowerment. The Hostel facility along with placement center is needed. The seats in professional and vocational courses must be reserved for girls and women.

(2) Imparting Empower Education

The secondary level of schooling may include the lessons for empowerment for women and the importance

(3) Social Reforms

The process of social reforms, education, and true knowledge about tradition should be properly introduced. Any negative traditional bondage should be challenged.

(4) Strict Compliance of Law

The law machinery should be properly geared up for effective implementation. Any crime against women must be brought in light and speedy trial is to be made.

(5) Political Will

All political parties must make up the mind for women representation.

(6) Efforts for Female Literacy

Efforts should be made for increase in rate of female literacy. It is showing sufficient inequality.

(7) General Sex Ratio

The all India average of female to male ratio is 933. Some states like Punjab, Haryana, Uttar Pradesh records very low general sex ratio.

The efforts are needed to strictly ban sex determination at clinics.

(7) Increase in Family Welfare Expenditure of Central and State Government

The Central Government must increase the expenditure on family welfare, it is at 0.50% of total expenditure. It must be at least of 2% of total expenses.

CONCLUSION

Women are backbone of family. Family is unit of country. If all families are develop we can developed out country. Learn and teach women empowerment.

Women Empowerment Programmes in India
Concerns and Strategy

G. Jayalakshmi

INTRODUCTION

The empowerment of women is one of the central issues in the process of development of countries all over the world. Tamil Nadu has a glorious tradition of recognizing the importance of empowering women over several centuries. Self reliance as well as speeding women's freedom of selection by themselves. Some adherents consider empowerment as increasing the participation which is one of the factors of facilitating the empowerment.

In recent years women empowerment has become a subject of great concern for the nations all over the world especially in poor and developing countries. The impact of globalization is seen eventually on position of women in some form or other in most of the developing countries with the variation of degree. The United Nations has also strived hard in an incredible way to draw the due attention of the World Community on this issue in the past years.

The number of women in training and extension programmes should be increased, especially in posts from which they have been excluded until now. The contents and subjects of training and extension programmes should be expanded so that the role of women in production, processing, and marketing can also be taken into account. The present paper is based on women's empowerment programmes and its implementation and utilizations.

THE ROLE OF GOVERNMENT OF INDIA IN WOMEN EMPOWERMENT

The first few plans followed a welfare approach and treated women as recipients of aid. The First Five Year Plan focused its attention on the problem of high infant and maternal mortality and thence undertook steps to develop school feeding schemes for children and creation of nutrition sections in the public health departments and maternity and child health centers. The focus of second plan was on the problems of women workers. Hence, policies were initiated for equal pay for equal work, provision of facilities for training to enable women to compete for higher jobs and expansion of opportunities for part time employment. The main thrust of the third plan was the expansion of girls' education. On the social welfare side the largest share was provided for expanding rural welfare services and condensed courses of education for adult women. The fourth plan continued to emphasize women's education. The fifth plan gave priority for training of women in need of care and protection, women from low income families, needy women with dependent children and working women.

It is only during the fifth plan a separate Bureau of Women's Welfare and Development (WWD) was set-up in 1976 as part of the erstwhile Department of Social Welfare in order to intensify the country-wide efforts launched during the International Year of the Women. The sixth plan for the first time in India's planning history contained a separate chapter on Women and Development. To make the International Women's Decade a success it emphasized on three strategies viz. economic independence, educational advancement and access to health care and family planning. Hence, variety of programmes was taken up under different sectors of development to ameliorate the socio-economic status of women. In the rural development sector the IRDP gave priority to women heads of households and about 35% of total number of beneficiaries under TRYSEM was women. During the seventh five year plan an integrated multidisciplinary approach was adopted covering employment education, health nutrition, application of science and technology and other related aspects in areas of interest to women. It is only during the seventh plan 'Women Development Corporations' were established for promoting employment generating activities for women.

Thus with the beginning of International Women's Decade in 1975 a number of schemes were introduced and earnest efforts were made by the government to improve the status of women. In spite of implementation loopholes these policies strive their best to integrate women into the mainstream of society. Thus the Department of Women and Child Development being the national machinery for the development of women plays a vital role assisted by the Central Social Welfare Board and the National Institute of Public Co-operation and Child Development. While the Central Social Welfare Board is an apex body with state level branches to encourage voluntary effort in the field of women's development NIPCCD is an advisory-*cum*-research-*cum*-national level training institute in the field of child development with a separate division for women's research and development. In India, legislations and programmes favouring women had never been wanting. But unfortunately the spirit behind these policies is hardly appreciated by the implementing authorities.

ECONOMIC EMPOWERMENT OF WOMEN

1. Poverty Eradication

Since women comprise the majority of the population

below the poverty line and are very often in situations of extreme poverty, given the harsh realities of intra-household and social discrimination, macro-economic policies and poverty eradication programmes will specifically address the needs and problems of such women. There will be improved implementation of programmes which are already women-oriented with special targets for women. Steps will be taken for mobilization of poor women and convergence of services, by offering them a range of economic and social options, along with necessary support measures to enhance their capabilities

2. Micro-credit

In order to enhance women's access to credit for consumption and production, the establishment of new and strengthening of existing micro-credit mechanisms and micro-finance institution will be undertaken so that the outreach of credit is enhanced. Other supportive measures would be taken to ensure adequate flow of credit through extant financial institutions and banks, so that all women below poverty line have easy access to credit.

3. Women and Economy

Women's perspectives will be included in designing and implementing macro-economic and social policies by institutionalizing their participation in such processes. Their contribution to socio-economic development as producers and workers will be recognized in the formal and informal sectors (including home-based workers) and appropriate policies relating to employment and to her working conditions will be drawn up.

4. Women and Agriculture

The programmes for training women in soil conservation, social forestry, dairy development and other occupations allied to agriculture like horticulture, livestock including small animal husbandry, poultry, fisheries, etc. will be expanded to benefit women workers in the agriculture sector.

5. Women and Industry

The important role played by women in electronics,

information technology and food processing and agro-industry and textiles has been crucial to the development of these sectors. Women at present cannot work in night shift in factories even if they wish to. Suitable measures will be taken to enable women to work on the night shift in factories. This will be accompanied with support services for security, transportation, etc.

SOCIAL EMPOWERMENT OF WOMEN

Special measures will be taken to eliminate discrimination, universalize education, eradicate illiteracy, create a gender-sensitive educational system, increase enrolment and retention rates of girls and improve the quality of education to facilitate life-long learning as well as development of occupation/vocation/technical skills by women.

1. Health

Women's traditional knowledge about health care and nutrition will be recognized through proper documentation and its use will be encouraged. The use of Indian and alternative systems of medicine will be enhanced within the framework of overall health infrastructure available for women.

2. Nutrition

In view of the high risk of malnutrition and disease that women face at all the three critical stages viz., infancy and childhood, adolescent and reproductive phase, focused attention would be paid to meeting the nutritional needs of women at all stages of the life cycle. This is also important in view of the critical link between the health of adolescent girls, pregnant and lactating women with the health of infant and young children.

3. Housing and Shelter

Women's perspectives will be included in housing policies, planning of housing colonies and provision of shelter both in rural and urban areas. Special attention will be given for providing adequate and safe housing and accommodation for women including single women, heads of households, working women, students, apprentices and trainees.

4. Environment

Women will be involved and their perspectives reflected in the policies and programmes for environment, conservation and restoration. Women will be involved in spreading the use of solar energy, biogas, and smokeless chulhas and other rural application so as to have a visible impact of these measures in influencing eco-system and in changing the lifestyles of rural women.

IMPLICATION AND UTILIZATION OF GOVERNMENT PROGRAMMES

The empowerment of Rural Women is crucial for the development of the Rural Bharat. Bringing women into the mainstream of development is a major concern for the Government of India, which is why 2001 has been declared as the *"Year of Women Empowerment"*. The Ministry of Rural Development has special components for Women in its programmes and funds are earmarked as "Women's Component" to ensure flow of adequate resources for the same.

The major Schemes, having Women's Component, include the Swarnajayanti Gram Swarozgar Yojana (SGSY), the Jawahar Gram Samridhi Yojana (JGSY), the Indira Awas Yojana (IAY), the National Social Assistance Programme (NSAP), the Restructured Centrally Rural Sanitation Programme, the Accelerated Rural Water Supply Programme, the (erstwhile) Integrated Rural Development Programme (IRDP), the (erstwhile) Development of Women and Children in Rural Areas (DWCRA) and the Jawahar Rozgar Yojana (JRY). The brief details of the Schemes are as follows:

(a) *SGSY*: The Swarnajayanti Gram Swarozgar Yojana, which has been launched with effect from April 1, 1999, is a holistic programme covering various aspects of self-employment, such as organisation of the poor into self-help groups, training, credit, technology, infrastructure and marketing. It is envisaged that 50 percent of the Groups formed in each Block should be exclusively for women who will account for at least 40 percent of the Swarozgaris. Under this Scheme, women are encouraged in the practice of thrift and credit which enables them to become self-reliant. Through assistance in the form of Revolving Fund, Bank Credit and Subsidy, the Yojana seeks to integrate women in the economy by providing increasing opportunities of self-employment.

(b) *JGSY*: The Jawahar Gram Samridhi Yojana (JGSY) has been launched with effect from April 1, 1999, with the twin objectives of creation of demand-driven community, village infrastructure and the generation of supplementary employment (for the unemployed poor) in the rural areas. Wage-employment under the JGSY is extended to below poverty line families. It is stipulated that 30 percent of the employment opportunities should be reserved for women.

(c) *IAY* : The Indira Awas Yojana (IAY) aims at providing assistance for the construction of houses for people 'Below the Poverty Line' in rural areas. Under the Scheme, priority is extended to widows and unmarried women. It has been laid down that IAY houses are to be allotted in the name of women members of the household or, alternatively, in the joint names of husband and wife.

(d) *NSAP*: The National Social Assistance Programme (NSAP), which came into effect five years back represents a significant step towards introducing a National Policy for Social Assistance benefits to households 'Below the Poverty Line', with a major focus on women. The NSAP has three components, namely, the National Old Age Pension Scheme, the National Family Benefit Scheme and the National Maternity Benefit Scheme. The National Maternity Benefit Scheme is exclusively aimed at assisting expectant mothers by providing them Rs. 500 each for the first two live births. Under the National Old

Age Pension Scheme, Central Assistance of Rs. 75 per month is provided to women and men who are 65 years of age and above and have little or no regular means of subsistence from their own sources of income or through financial support from the family members. Women are also beneficiaries under this Scheme.

(e) *CRSP*: The Restructured Centrally Sponsored Rural Sanitation Programme (RCRSP), which was launched with effect from 1st April, 1999, provides for the construction of sanitary latrines for rural households. Where individual household latrines are not feasible, provision exists for construction of village sanitary complexes exclusively for women, to ensure privacy/ dignity. Upto 10 percent of the allocated fund can be utilized for construction and maintenance of public latrines for women.

(f) *ARWSP:* Under the Rural Water Supply Programme, training is being afforded to women to enable them to play an active role in using and maintaining handpumps for the supply of drinking water. Women are also represented in Village Level Committees and are actively involved in the selection of sites for handpumps and other sources.

(g) The erstwhile Scheme of Development of Women and Children in Rural Areas (DWCRA), now merged with the SGSY, was intended to raise the income level of women of poor households so as to enable organized participation by them in social development for economic self-reliance. The primary thrust was the formation of groups of 10-50 women from poor households at the village level for delivery of services like credit and skill training and cash and infrastructure support for self-employment.

CONCLUSION

Now we are living in the modern and technological world. The Effective Implementation and Utilization of Women Empowerment Programme in government of India to safeguard the interests of women authorizer to bring the effective implementation and utilization of social, economic and political status of women in India. The paper concludes the details of woman's empowerment in some specific challenges faced by the women according to the effective utilization of empowerment program

References

Dr. Jaya Kothai Pillai, 1995, Women Empowerment, Gyan Publishing House, New Delhi

Dr. Anita Arya, 1963, Indian Women, Volumes I, II and III, Gyan Publishing House, New Delhi.

Tandon, R.K., 1998, Women in India, Indian Publishers & Distributors, Delhi, 1998.

Agarwal, C.M., 2001, Indian Women, India Publishers & Distributors, Delhi.

Saraswathi Mishra, Status of Indian Women, Gyan Publishing House.

5

Women Empowerment in India

A. SULTHAN MOHIDEEN

INTRODUCTION

One of the thrust areas of development strategy is the focus on empowerment of women. As half of the population in the world comprised of women and perpetuity of the human race depends upon them, the status of women is a crucial determinant in the present context of population policy. Amid the current important of emancipation of women, the role of women as a mother and how this influenced her status, all the more becomes an important factor worth studying. The international community has realized that social and economic goals cannot be sorted out without advancement of women. Empowerment of women has emerged as an important issue in our country. The role of women in the development of nation is very important nowadays. So women should be respected both in the society as well as in the family. To empower women government has taken initiatives like introducing various schemes such as DWCRA, TRYSEM, and SGSY.

One among them is Self Help Groups. This programme is mainly meant for the rural poor who are living below the poverty line or under vicious circle of poverty. This programme is for pooe women, marginalized women and so on. Its main aim is to alleviate poverty among the poor. Micro-credit is an effective tool in this Endeavour which leads to peaceful development. Micro-finance helps the poor people to meet their needs for easy credits and financial services. The International Fund for Agriculture Development (IFAD) declared 2005 as International year of micro-finance. In India Micro-credit programmes are implemented through group structure which is know as "Self Help Groups". It finance to a group. There is sufficient evidence of the effect of the degree of equality between women and men on reproductive behaviour but emphasis is often laid on achieving progressive urbanization, education and economic stability—all attributed to men. Today, the situation is completely changing; the greatest revolution which is in the new relationship that is developing between men and women.

The present day world has come to know that the ultimate demographic equation of human history depends upon the quality and nature of the changing status role-relationship of women, particularly that of women. It is this light that there has been a conscious effort on the part of the government to implement programmes, formulate policies to improve the status of women in terms of health, nutrition and education. In order to actively associate women in development process, participation in Panchayat Raj Institutions (PRI) is being encouraged. Interest in the welfare of women is not confined to Government along voluntary Agencies, NGOs and other institutions are also actively involved in the process of empowering women increasing participation of women in economic activities offers challengers and opportunities to Governments both at Centre and State.

"Status of women" as implying the extent to which women can exercise their personal autonomy and have access to knowledge, to economic resources and to political power as compared to men. The status of women can be broadly classified into three categories—the ideal, high and low status.

Ideal status prevail in a society where legal sanction for equality with men in matters of personal autonomy and choices and options exit. In such a society, responsibilities will be shared equally by men and women, as a way of life. High status implies a society where women are in a position to exercise their economic, social and political rights in society. Empowerment is a process, whereby women become able to organize themselves to increase their own self-reliance, to assert their independent right to make choices and to control resource, which will assist in challenging and eliminating their own subordination. Empowered programme for women have been found to be successful in improving her status in family and society, while giving a feeling of self-worth and esteem. In this context the Tamil Nadu Women Development Project taken up for implementation under the name of Mahlir Thittam covered about 1,97,152 poor women of the state. The scheme is intended to promote economic development and social empowerment of the poorest women through network of Self Help Groups formed with active support of NGOs.

EMPOWERMENT OF WOMEN

Self Help Groups are small economically homogeneous groups. The size of the groups consists of 15-20 members who are financially weak. There should no discrimination among group members based on caste, religion or political affiliations. They come together for the purposes of solving their common problems through self-help and mutual help who do not have access to formal financial institutions. The meetings will be held weekly, fortnightly or monthly. These group members save small amount of money which depends on their capacity and they kept the money in the bank. From the savings they use to take loan from the group itself. The rate of interest is not too high. Even these groups will also get help from the NGOs, Government, Banks, and Co-operatives.

All these members are actively participate in all the activities. Small loan and small savings are very helpful for the poor, even to have their own job, where they are able to improve their lifestyle or towards socio-economic activities.

With the help of the Anganwadi teacher these members are able to maintain their attendance registers, minute books, account books, pass book. Self Help Groups enhance the equality of status of women as participants, decision-makers and beneficiaries in the democratic, economic, social, and cultural spheres of life. The objectives of SHGs are to save their income avail the loan from the common fund of the group, create confidence and capabilities of the members, help the members in decision-making, motivate the members by taking up of the social responsibilities to discuss the women-related issues.

SHG helps the women in uplifting their living conditions and also encompass the social, economic, educational level to improve their empowerment level. The components of empowerment of women are: (a) Access to economic resources, (b) Participation in economic decision-making, (c) Opportunities for self-development, (d) Participation in socio-political decision making, (e) Scope for skill development, and (f) Impact of general welfare of the family and community.

STEPS TO BE TAKEN TO IMPROVE THE STATUS OF WOMEN

A woman has great capacity to work, but they do not find proper avenues. There is a lack of confidence in her, which is mainly the result of environment factor. What is needed today is to restore the confidence of women in their own capacity and to provide a sense of security, the problem is a very complicated and comprehensive one. It needs an integrated approach for tackling the problem by different agencies.

For uplifting status of women in India, some concrete issues should be considered an implemented: 1. There is a need to create awareness in society about social ills. 2. The law enforcement agencies should be made more effective and suitable to tackle the problems in right perspective. 3. To make necessary changes in the procedure and approaches of Judiciary administration so as to get the desired results. 4. To provide social-economic security to women. 5. Women's reproductive rights include the right to knowledge regarding their own bodies and right to make decisions regarding fertility and seeking health care. 6. Women's full participation in planning, implementation and evaluation of maternity care programmes, in their communities is essential. 7. Maternal mortality reduction is supported by gender equity in access to education, income and decision-making in the community. 8. There are a need of creating socialization, social awareness and motivation among women on war footing basis. 9. There are urgent needs to educate women with the co-operation of men in removing female illiteracy. 11. There is need for change in social attitude for achieving this target mass media has to play a crucial role.

There is a need for spiritual revolution. The religious leaders and religious organizations have to play a pioneering role to mould public opinion in ameliorating the condition of women. The programmes, policies and laws meant for women's development and welfare have to be comprehensively codified in simple language and be distributed widely to the rural, hilly, backward and tribal areas. There is need for mobilization of public opinion and effective community participation against eradication of social evils, through constant education there is a need for active involvement of voluntary organizations, Panchayat Raj Institutions and women's organizations for upgradation of standards of living of women especially those working in the unorganized sectors. The basic idea of equality, peace and development must be given shape through practicability measures suited to local needs and requirements.

The problems facing women have to be tackled against rural-urban background in the context of the problems of educated and uneducated women and unorganized and organized sectors of employment. Formulate time-bound targets and concrete actions to improve the basic health, nutrition, education and social status of the girl child and to launch effective public information and communication programmes to create awareness about vulnerability of the girl child and her special development needs.

CONCLUSION

Empowerment of women is therefore the processes of

controlling power and strengthening of their vitality. Of the three broad categories of empowerment viz., economic, social and political, the first is the key and may lead to other kinds. Efforts are being made through special development programmes with greater gender sensitivity. However, the programmes of women being holistic and integral approach are the need of the hour to articulate their hopes and aspirations. The potential of the women at present is not fully tapped and utilized for the community. If the woman is given the proper role in the various activities of the community namely, social, economic, and political fields women will be able to plan, mould and activate various programmes for the betterment and the development of the community. She has a positive role in social welfare activities in health care, in economic progress, if the present political mindset is to be changed. Women must be encouraged to participate in the political activities right from the village level to nation level if women participants in the legislate bodies. Many of the social problems with regard to women can be curbed or removed.

References

Gupta, M.L. (2006) "Economic Empowerment of Women through SHGs", *Kurushetra*.

Swamy Vigneswara, P.M. (2006) "Self Help Groups and Women Empowerment", *Journal of Development and Social Change*, Vol. 3, Nos. 3 and 4.

Vinayagamoorthy (2007) "Women Empowerment through Self-Help Groups—A Case Study in the North Tamil Nadu", Vol. 34, No. 1.

Dwivedi, Archana (2008) "SHG's and Micro Credit", *Yojana*, Vol. 52.

Prof. Satish Taneja and Dr. S.L. Gupta, Entrepreneurial Development, Galgota Publishing Co., Karol Bagh, New Delhi.

Pradeep Kashyap, "Marketing Strategies for Success in DWCRA", NIRD, Hyderbad.

District Rural Development Agency; The Report of Project Director, DWCRA, Guntur, 2004-07.

Empowerment of Tribal Women in India

G.D. KHARAT

INTRODUCTION

India is the second largest country in the World after S. Africa Continent in terms of tribal population and communities. There are 370 million Indigenous people in some 90 Countries in the World. Share of tribals in the global population is about 6%.[1] Tribal population of India is 84.3 million and its share to the total population is 8.26% as per the Census of 2001. As per the Article 342 (1) of our Constitution tribals are known as Scheduled Tribes. There are near about 700 Scheduled Tribes in India of which most of overlapping.[2] Total and tribal population of Maharashtra is 9,68,78,627 and 85,77,276 respectively as per the Census of 2001. The share of tribal population of Maharashtra is 8.9% to the total population. Share of Maharashtra to the total tribal population of India is 10.17%. There are 45 Scheduled Tribes in Maharashtra as per the latest notification of the Government.[3] Mizoram, Nagaland, Meghalaya, Arunachal Pradesh, Lakshadweep, Dadra Nagar Haveli are the Tribal States/Union Territories in India. India started its tribal development program through TSP from 1974-75.[4] TSP (Tribal Sub-Plan) Strategy seeks to ensure adequate flow of funds for tribal development from the State plan allocations, schemes and programmes of Central Ministries and Departments besides financial and developmental institutions in proportions to tribal population. Madhya Pradesh, Maharashtra, Orissa, Gujarat and Rajasthan are the main TSP States having the largest share of tribal population in India.[5]

Tribal women are the backbone of socio-economic and cultural tribal life. Women contributes loins share in the rich cultural tribal life.[6] They play the vital role in all the activities. Family life management of tribal women is noteworthy. Considering their role and contribution, empowerment of tribal women is the basic criteria of tribal development in India. Unfortunately, their contribution has been neglected and they didn't have the proper place in the development. The task of tribal development is challenging and it will be not possible without empowerment of the tribal women.

RESEARCH METHODOLOGY

This Paper highlights the state of tribal women and suggests solutions for their empowerment. Information and Data about the paper has been collected from the various Secondary sources such as Websites, Research articles and Reports, Journals and Reference Books.

OBJECTIVES

(1) To study the state of tribal women.
(2) To focus on health and education of tribal women.
(3) To study the problems of tribal women.
(4) To suggest the solutions for the empowerment of tribal women.

STATE OF THE TRIBAL WOMEN IN INDIA

Share in Tribal Population

Share of women in tribal population is near about 50% in India. Maharashtra's men and women tribal population is 4,34,754 and 42,29,522 respectively.[7] According to population figures, tribal women represents the tribal communities equally in India.

Sex Ratio

Tribals have the better sex ratio than the main society. General and tribal Sex ratio in India is 933 and 978 respectively.[8] Tribal Sex ratio shows proper direction to the modern society. The general and tribal sex ratio in Maharashtra is 922 and 973 respectively.[9] These figures explain that tribal women got better social status than general women in India. Culture, social and religious customs have given the tribal women much more importance in society as compare to main society. There is no gender discrimination in tribal society at social level. They follow the principle of equality.

Literacy

Tribal women got the place in society but they are still ignored in education. The overall tribal literacy of India is 47.10%. The male and female literacy is 59.17% and 34.76% respectively. Rural and Urban tribal women literacy is 32.44% and 59.87% respectively in India.[10] Literacy of tribal women is comparatively low and varied according to various States in India. PVTG (Primitive Vulnerable Tribal Groups) women are neglected in the process of education. Maharashtra's total, male and female tribal literacy is 55.31%, 67.02% and 43.08%.[11] Tribal women are on the back foot in terms of development due to illiteracy. There is a paradoxical situation about tribal women literacy. Tribal States like Manipur, Mizoram and Sikkim got the highest literacy while Bihar, Orissa, UP are the lowest literacy States in India.

Place in Tribal Economy

Tribal economy is still away from the market economy. Agriculture, Agricultural labour and collection of MFP

(Marginal Forest Produce) are the main components of tribal economy.[12] Tribal women are the invisible hand of tribal economy. Women contribute in each and every economic activity. Agricultural work, collection of tendu patta and other forest produce are the activities of tribal women while managing the family. Tribal men are comparatively lazy and most of the responsibilities bear by the women. Women have to sell the MFS in the market for the livelihood of family. They are cheated in the market by traders and others due to illiteracy and lack of market knowledge. Due to family responsibility and economic burden they have no time to care about themselves which resulted in their bad condition and other problems.

Health

Illiterate and engaged tribal women are not aware about health. Due to physical hard work, malnutrition they face so many health problems and lived in miserable condition. Women are not interested in modern health facilities because traditional customs. Poor health condition, hunger and poverty are the causes of illness and diseases.

Education

Most of the tribal women have not seen the door of school. Due to family responsibility and poverty they have to work for livelihood instead of schooling. Stagnation and dropout are the main hurdles of female education.[13] Tribal women won't get many opportunities in the process of welfare and development. Insecure surrounding of Ashram schools has prevented tribal girls from the schooling. Sexual exploitation of Ashram school girls is the burning issue in Maharashtra. Exploitation by teacher, school peon and schoolmate in Nasik District are the latest incidence. Educational backwardness has blocked their empowerment.

Political Representation

Political representation means stage for decision-making. There are 47 Parliamentary and 554 Assembly seats reserved for Scheduled Tribes in India.[14] Share of tribal women in these respective seats is nominal. They got respective share in village politics due to constitutional provision and amendments. So many women's are the Sarpanch in villages but used as a rubberstamp. Due to marginal political representation, they did not find the place in policy-making.

Social Status

Tribal women got equal social status but they face inequality in terms of rights. They face economic discrimination such as low wage, less development weightage. As per the social custom, there is a tradition of bride prize which is known as "Dej".[15] Following and attachment of main society is crashing this tradition and the tribal grooms are interested in dowry. Tribal women have to perform several duties but they are denied rights. Only few tribes such as Khasi, Garo and Mezzo offer land and other property rights to women.[16] Social and family burden, sexual and economic exploitation, early marriages and child birth, victims of alcoholism, traditions and ill-treatment from main society are the alarming problems of tribal women.[17]

SUGGESTIONS FOR THE EMPOWERMENT OF TRIBAL WOMEN

- Central Government should fund 100% for Ashram Schools and Hostels. Tribal Entrepreneurship development program should be introduced.
- New higher educational schemes for the tribal's announced by Government should be implemented with priority to women.
- Facility of primary health centre with adequate staff and medicine, family welfare schemes should be provided. Tribal women's should be encouraged for modern medical facilities through awareness and consultation.
- Tribal women should get the share in Tribal Sub-Plan as per their population proportion. Special development schemes should be introduced for the rural and urban tribal women.

- Self-help groups for processing, marginal forest produce marketing should get preference in tribal area.
- Existing development schemes such as tailoring should be modernized and grants should be increased.
- Primitive Vulnerable Tribal Group Women are in worse condition and struggling for survival. They should be attached with the developing society through special provision and programmes.
- Reservation policy, legal provisions should be implemented properly for the betterment of tribal women.
- Atrocity Act should be implemented strictly to avoid exploitation of tribal women.
- Tribal women should get importance in social banking.
- Moneylenders and landlords should be removed through tribal co-operatives. Tribal women should get the membership of these societies for their self-reliance.
- Displacement and migration problems should be solved through proper rehabilitation and self employment. Tribal women should get the importance in rehabilitation benefit.
- Special Central Assistance schemes for empowerment of tribal women should be renewed and amount for the said scheme should be increased.
- Marketing knowledge and facilities should be spread among the women. TRIFED (Tribal Co-operative Marketing Federation of India), NSTFDC (National Scheduled Tribe Finance and Development Corporation) should provide the marketing and self-employment stage for tribal women.
- ITDP's (Integrated Tribal Development Project) should encourage tribal women for the benefit of various development schemes.
- NGO's (Non-Government Organization) working for tribal women should be supported and encouraged for working in remote area.

CONCLUSIONS

Tribal women's contribution in socio-economic and cultural tribal life is vital and important. The issue of tribal women empowerment is a challenging task due to illiteracy and negligence. After the completion of 63 years of Independence, we are unable to solve the problem of tribal development. Planners have adopted the TSP strategy for tribal development but empowerment of tribal women is still not the serious issue of their agenda. Empowerment of women is the basic need of overall tribal development. Proper implementation of development schemes with the concentration on women is the need of hour. Health and education, removal of exploitation and special attention in development scheme will change the traditional picture and give them opportunity to self-reliance with dignity.

NOTES AND REFERENCES

1. 2009, "The State of the World's Indigenous Peoples", Dept. of Economic and Social Affairs, Division for Social Policy and Development, Secretariat of The Permanent Forum on Indigenous Issues, United Nations, New York.
2. 2008-09, "Annual Report", Tribal Affairs Ministry, Government of India, India.
3. http://www.trti.mah.nic.in/staticpages/frmstlist.html
4. 2003, Varma, R.C., "Indian Tribes through the Ages", Publication Division, Ministry of Information and Broadcasting, Government of India.
5. www.tribal.nic.in
6. 2002, Mukhopadhyay Lipi, "Tribal Women in Development", Publication Division, Ministry of Information and Broadcasting, Government of India.
7. Economic and Statistical Directorate, Government of Maharashtra, Maharashtra.
8. 2001, "Census of India", Office of the Registrar General of India, India.
9. 2001, "Maharashtra ST Highlights", Census of 2001, Office of the Registrar General of India, India.
10. 2001, "Census of India", www.planningcommissionofindia.

11. 2008-09, "Tribal Sub-Plan Report", Tribal Development Department, Government of Maharashtra, Maharashtra.
12. Planning Commission, Government of India, 11th Plan, Vol. 1, Chapter 6, Social Justice.
13. 2007, "SARVA SHIKSHA ABHIYAN", Tribal Development Plan, Department of School Education and Literacy, Ministry of Human Resource Development, Government of India, New Delhi.
14. 2009, "General Election", Reference Book, Ministry of Information and Broadcasting, Government of India, India.
15. 2002, Gare Govind, "Scheduled Tribes in Maharashtra" (Marathi Book), Continental Publishing House, Pune.
16. 2004, Bose, Nirmal Kumar, "Tribal Life in India", revised by Tripathi, C.B., National Book Trust, India.
17. 2008, "A Shadow Report to the UN Committee on Economic, Social and Cultural Rights", The Problem of Non-implementation of ESC Rights in India by National Committee for Human Rights Treaty Monitoring in India, Secretariat—AITDN, Janakpuri, New Delhi. May 2008.

PART II

EDUCATIONAL EMPOWERMENT

7

Women Empowerment Through Education

K. Rajmohan

INTRODUCTION

In India, the position of women has always been a rather ambivalent one in our culture. On the one side, she has been raised to the status of divinity and on the other side; she has been exploited as somebody lower in status to men in every walk of life. Fortunately for us, from the middle of the nineteenth century, consciousness raised in our country to eradicate this dichotomy from her existence. Social reformers rose especially in Bengal, like Vidya Sagar and Raja Ram Mohan Roy, founder of the Brahmo Samaj who advocated education for girls, marriage after adolescence and the right to widow remarriage. In the North, the Arya Samaj movement led by Swami Dayanand Sasraswathi also wanted to purify Hinduism by preaching education of girl children as well as improvement in the status of women. Towards the end of the nineteenth century, it would be true to say that women have started coming out of their homes for education. When our Constitution was passed in 1950, it stressed on the equality of sexes in Articles 15, 16 and 39 and empowered the government both for preventing discrimination against women as well as undertaking affirmative action to improve their situation.

Today, the women's concern in all sectors—education and literacy, health and nutrition, training and income generation, legislative and judicial reforms—has been flag-marked. The challenge lies in converting these concerns into reality. Strategies for empowering women and rural women in particular would have to be sharpened to be effective.

WHAT IS EMPOWERMENT?

The definitions of empowerment range from increasing the choices available to and capacities of the poor, to transforming the power structure of the society. At its core, empowerment means having more control over the forces that shape ones life.

According to one dictionary, to empower means "to enable", or "to promote the self-actualization or influence of oneself".

Women constitute one-half of the world's population and a visible majority of the poor. Women either solely or largely support an increasing number of families. Projects aiming to improve the living conditions of the poor cannot, therefore, be effective unless women participate in their formulation and implementation, as contributors as well as beneficiaries.

The term empowerment consists of a very conspicuous word 'power' which means control over material assets, intellectual resources and ideology. The process of challenging existing power relations of gaining greater control over the sources of power may be termed as empowerment. Empowerment is an active multidimensional process which enables women to realize their full identity and powers in all spheres of life. Power is not a commodity to be trans-located, nor can it be given as alms. Power has to be acquired and once acquired; it needs to be exercised, sustained and preserved.

EDUCATION AND EMPOWERMENT

Considering education as one of the most important means of empowering women, many programmers, schemes, awards and facilities have been initiated by the Central Government and State Governments to promote girls and women education. The Government of India has taken recourses to comprehensive literary drive for girls related to poor and socially weaker sections of the society.

NATIONAL GIRL'S EDUCATION PROGRAMME, 2004

The aim of the programme is to provide extra facilities and financial help to motivate the girls for education at primary level, in this programme, emphasis is being laid on the construction of models schools, provision of text books, stationary, uniform and other necessary inputs for education of girls, thereby burden of education of poor class can be reduced. It is well known fact that the girls of poor families are deprived of education because of economic burden of education. Widespread poverty and discrimination cultural practices and the prime cause for the gender gap in education. This programme is intended to remove these barriers, thus promoting girls' education.

LITERACY AWARD SCHEME

Central Government has launched a scheme of "Decadal Literacy Award and Decadal Female Literacy Award" for those who have done a pioneer task in the field of education. Because of the active involvement of Central and State Government in women's education, the enrolment of girls in schools has increased remarkably. The attempt that has been made so long is the United Nations Charter of Human Rights. This could be the basis for surveying the status of women with regard to her rights. But then the basic indignation for the concerned may not prove helpful for the purpose envisaged. Yet the fact remains, the woman is no longer prepared to compromise on this issue and will continue to fight for her rights which is her right.

EMPOWERING WOMEN THOROUGH EDUCATION

The 2/3 of the world's illiterate population of 876 million people are women. The World Education Forum (26-28 April, 2000) identified the following goals and made a commitment to attain them:

- Ensuring that by 2015 all children, particularly girl, children in difficult circumstances and those belonging to ethnic minorities, have access to and complete free and compulsory Primary Education of good quality.
- Achieving a 50% improvement in levels of adult literacy by 2015, especially for women, and equitable access to basic and continuing education for all adults.
- Elimination gender disparities in primary and secondary education by 2005, and achieving gender equality in education by 2015, with a focus on ensuring girls full and equal access to and achievement in basic education of good quality. Education is the most important tool for development and empowerment of women given in the programme of Action, 1992.
- Enhance self and self-confidence in women.
- Building a positive self-image of women by recognizing their contribution to the society, polity and economy.
- Developing ability to think critically.
- Foster decision-making and action through collective process.
- Enable women to make informed choices in areas like education, employment and health especially reproductive health.
- Ensure equal participation in the developmental process.
- Provide information, knowledge and skill for economic independence.
- Enhance access to legal literacy and information related to their rights and entitlements in the society

with a view to enhance their participation on an equal footing in all areas.

- The implementation of the Programme of Action (POA-1992) enunciated in the NPE-1986, along with the multifarious efforts towards adult and non-formal education has helped in increasing the female literacy. It has improved from 7.93% in 1951 to 39.29% in 1991, i.e. an increase of 31 percentage points. The corresponding change in male literacy is from 25% to 64%, i.e. an increase of 39% (NPPW, 1988). It becomes imperative therefore to design strategic policies and programmers for promoting literacy which is pre-requisite for women's equality and empowerment and for their well-being. In order to make women economically independent, the curriculum must be reshaped and made vocational within the school system. A good number of girl students drop-out from school at secondary level especially in the rural areas where home related work is given much preference. So, for the empowerment of such rural women, open and distance education can play a very important role.

It is a known fact that Indian women have played a very significant role in the independence struggle and did occupy prominent positions in the Indian Government. The Indian constitution gives equality to women in politics by legitimizing their roles for participation in public life within the formal and legal framework. Further, reservation of seats for women guaranteed the election of good number of women in Government. But, we all know that presence of women in politics is not satisfactory.

There are many factors on which this poor situation of women in politics is based. Our culture accepts woman's role as that for family and home only and the domination of man over the woman. Women have also been forced to have this opinion that politics is meant for males only and is unfeminine, unethical and does not go with their roles at home. Many factors are responsible for the non-enrolment and high drop-out rates of girls.

1. Poverty is attributed as one of the main cause of deprivation of girls from education.
2. Early marriage of girls is also a factor responsible for the high drop-out rate of girls.
3. Conservative attitude and social traditions are also responsible for the withdrawal of girls from schools.
4. Inadequacy of infrastructure facilities like toilets, drinking water, transport and hostel facilities in schools is also responsible to the high drop-out rate of girls.
5. The fear of sexual harassment deters the parents to send their daughters to the schools and a factor responsible for high drop-out rates of girls.

It is a well known fact that problems of adult women are more acute and more complex. They are engaged in household chores, rearing children and fields work continuously and little time is left for education. So, special measures should be taken to spread literacy among these illiterate women.

To achieve the goal of 100% female education, the following measures should be adopted by the Government in collaboration with NGO's and community. Some of these are as follows:

1. Promotion of education and awareness among men and women.
2. Strengthening adult literacy programmes and freeing the illiterate women from their home management occupations are necessary.
3. Providing project opportunity guidance to enterprising women.
4. Promotion of women specific clusters, Self Help Groups and area programmers for women.
5. Consensus building developing system for power sharing and active participation in socio-political system.
6. Strict implementation of gender budgeting by all the ministries in Central and State Governments.
7. Poverty eradication programmes should also be

specifically addressed to the needs and problems of women.

8. Special attention for Reproductive Rights of Women needs be given as per the needs of women and girls at all the stages of lifecycle by providing quality health care and reducing malnutrition, reduction of Maternal Mortality, Death Rate, etc. These spheres need be accorded priority to achieve the goal.
9. The change in the society and human values would play an important role in changing the old age and outdated customs. Both men and women have to join hands to light against the detrimental established practices in the society. The evils like dowry, child marriage, girl feticide, *parda* system or subordination of women in society need to be eliminated by creating social awareness.
10. There is need for 33% reservation of women in parliament and State Assemblies to give fillip to the empowerment and leadership of women. Women need to be oriented towards politics as a career.
11. Orientation programmes need be organized for women to handle different situations in different fields.
12. There is need to coordinate gender balance in government, administration, private sectors and other spheres.
13. Women and men together must then negotiate a new institutional setting that provides space for both the groups.

CONCLUSION

The empowerment of women makes them self-confident and self-reliant. To empower women is to increase their control over the decisions that affect their lives both within and outside the household. Women should be encouraged to bring their vision and leadership, knowledge and skills, views and aspirations into the development agendas from the grass-roots to international levels. Women should be assisted in conflict situations and their participation in peace processes supported.

Different types of academic plans should be formulated in order to empower women so that they have more control over their lives and play an affective role eliminating or reducing gender bias and discrimination in the society. In brief, it can be said that women must be empowered in order to have a safe environment, economic and social justice, adequate reallocation of resources, and the survival of all species and the common goal of healthy plant in which the future generation can flourish. Women empowerment is no gratis but a right denied so long and fight will continue o achieve it.

8

Education—A Key for Women Empowerment

K. KRISHNAKUMAR AND P. BABY

INTRODUCTION

Every girl is able to exercise her right to get education, beyond their attainment of individual rights; girls' education has also proven to be a remarkably effective catalyst for social development and economic growth in developing countries like India. Education is capable of facing the challenges of life at varied fronts and is empowered in the true sense of functionality, in which girl can make informed choices and take action without being scared. From this point of view, a woman is "empowered" when she is literate, educated, and has productive skills, has access to capital and self-confidence. This view of empowerment as individual self-reliance is considered not to recognize nor question how a woman can gain increased access to resources if the hurdles of gender bias remain in place. It leaves out the political and ideological dimensions of women's struggle. Empowerment would become more relevant if women are educated, better knowledgeable and can take rational decisions. A woman needs to be physically, and mentally well, so she is able to take challenges of equality.

Before thinking about the Women Empowerment, one needs to understand the exact meaning of the word empowerment. According to Cambridge English Dictionary empowerment means "to authorize". In the context of the people they have to be authorized to have control over their lives. When applied in the context of development the particular segment of population, the poor, the women, the vulnerable, the weak, the oppressed and the discriminated have to be "empowered" to have control over their lives to better their socio-economic and political conditions. But the questions raised are, who empowers them and how to empower them? Ideally speaking, no one empowers any one, the best way is 'self-empowerment', by the segments of population mentioned above are handicapped both structurally and culturally to empower themselves without any outside help and affirmative action by the state and others. But still as long as these segments of population does not make any effort at self-employment. It would be long and tough task and process for the outsiders to empower them.

POSITION OF WOMEN IN INDIA

It is important to say that the Constitution of India grants equality to women in various fields of life. Still a large number of women are either ill-equipped or not in a position to drive themselves out of their traditionally unsatisfactory socio-economic conditions. Female infanticide continues to be common. Statistics also show that there is still a very high preference for a male child in states like UP, MP, Punjab, etc. The male to female ratio is very high in these states. Domestic violence is also widespread and is also related with dowry. Women in India feel proud to display that they are well protected and pampered by their husbands without realizing that they are making themselves helpless. Such women's economic literacy is so low that they cannot play any role in family's decision regarding family's budget, savings and investments. To such women, the national budget discussion is for men only and soap operas are for them. Such women suffer a lot if something inconvenient happens to their husbands. Dependant women are not empowered women. If modern women think that they are empowered, it's a myth for them. Empowerment means to inspire women with the courage to break free from the chains of limiting beliefs, patterns and societal or religious conditions that have traditionally kept women suppressed and unable to realize their true beauty and power. They should have political, legal, economic and health awareness. They should have knowledge about support groups and positive attitudes towards life. They should get goals for future and strive to achieve them with courage. Jawaharlal Nehru had said, "You can tell the condition of the nation by looking at the status of women."

The grade of women in India has been subject to great many changes over the past few millennia. From a largely unknown status in ancient times through the low points of the medieval period, to the promotion of equal rights by many reformers, the history of women in India has been eventful. But even today Indian women have a status that is mostly subordinate to men, from birth to work to even death. Some scholars believe that in ancient India, the women enjoyed equal status with men in all fields of life. However, some others hold different views. Works by ancient Indian grammarians such as Patanjali and Katyayana suggest that women were educated in the early Vedic period Scriptures such as Rig Veda and Upanishads mention several women sages and seers, notably Gargi and Maitreyi. According to studies, women enjoyed equal status and rights during the early Vedic Period.

EDUCATIONAL POSITION OF WOMEN IN INDIA

Though it is gradually rising, the female literacy rate in India is lower compared to the male literacy rate. Compared to boys, far fewer girls are enrolled in the schools, many of them drop-out. This is the major drawback of our society. According to the National Sample Survey Data of 1997, only the states of Kerala and Mizoram have approached universal female literacy rates. According to majority of the scholars, the major factor behind the improved social and economic status of women in Kerala is literacy. Under Non-Formal Education programme, about 40% of the centers in states and 10% of the centers in UTs are exclusively reserved for females. As of 2000, about 0.3 million NFE centers were catering to about 7.42 million children, out of which about 0.12 million were exclusively for girls. Currently, in engineering, medical and other colleges, 30% of the seats have been reserved for females.

Unfortunately, girls still face discrimination in our society. Participation of girls in education also suffers because of societal attitudes. New initiatives have, therefore, become necessary to give the girl child her due, and to empower her for a life of equality and dignity. Despite the immense diversity of cultures, the challenges confronting women in fighting the problems are often unusually the same. In addition to facing discrimination due to their society, members of lower caste face lot of difficulties ranging from causing poverty in education, employment and everyday life. Women particularly from remote, rural areas, where they lack infrastructure and access to larger markets are still fighting it out from being discriminated. Years of discrimination have spread many women in rural and remote areas into poverty, thus further damaging their chances at empowerment and opportunities to improve their situation. However, recent changes in the societal attitude, government policy and women rights movement have set the ball in motion and sooner or later the cultural discrimination against the women will come to an end.

CONCEPT OF WOMEN EMPOWERMENT

Empowering may be understood as enabling people, especially women to acquire and possess power resources, in order to make decision on their own or resist decisions that are made by others that affect them. A person may said to be powerful when he/she has control over a large portion of power resources in society. The extent of possession of various resources such as personal wealth, such as education, information, knowledge, social status, position held, leadership trains, capabilities of mobilization, etc.

The concept of women empowerment was introduced at the international women conference at NAROIBI in 1985.

Women Empowerment has five components:

- Women's sense of self-worth.
- Their right to have and to determine choices.
- Their right to have access to opportunities and resources.
- Their right to have the power to control their own lives, both within and outside the home.
- And their ability to influence the direction of social change to create a more just social and economic order, nationally and internationally.

THE OBJECTIVES OF WOMEN'S EDUCATION

It was also necessary to clarify the goals of women's education. The participants agreed that the more important objectives are:

- To eliminate illiteracy;
- To develop self-esteem and self-confidence;
- To have knowledge about their bodies and sexuality;
- To have the ability to make their own decisions and negotiate;
- To raise the women's awareness of their civil rights;
- To provide skills for income generation;
- To make participation in Community/society more effective; and
- To prepare them to be good women leaders.

Crucial to education work are other complementary activities such as those in the areas of legal reform, transformation of international economic and political relations, action-oriented research and networking. It was stressed that it is equally important to convince men that better education of women will be beneficial to the entire family and the society as a whole.

WOMEN ARE EMPOWERED THROUGH EDUCATION

Are women empowered through education? Women's marginalization shows that participating in male dominated society including education systems, benefits only a tiny percentage of women who are able to succeed with the chances stacked against them.

However, this remarkable educational attainment is not automatically translated into better jobs or into personal, social and political power for women, who remain at a disadvantage when compared to their male counterparts. Income disparities are considerable, and women have less access to political and economic power. For example, they are underrepresented in parliament, local government and the judiciary. In other words, the positive development for women in the educational field over the past three to four decades has not been matched by greater empowerment. This situation is motivated by economic globalization processes. Women in the adult education system are increasingly being threatened by younger graduates, equipped with new skills. A woman's family responsibilities very often prevent her from taking advantage of the opportunities for continuing education. They also have less time to dedicate themselves to adult continuing learning. A constant problem in education is the separation of the curriculum according to fairly strict and traditionally accepted gender boundaries.

- Women are still concentrated in the so-called "soft subjects", qualifying them for low paying and low status jobs.
- Women with so-called "soft skills" such as sewing and hospitality management form the bulk of the unemployed labour force.
- Within the academic track, men predominate in physics, while women prefer biology, integrated science, the humanities or the arts.

This situation should be changed. Very rare women made achievement in different difficult fields in our country. This is possible only through proper education for women. They should motivate in all different fields for further developments.

ROLE OF EDUCATION FOR WOMEN EMPOWERMENT

Education is the key for women to participate in all fields. The overall global trend in education shows that women's literacy rate has improved, particularly in developing countries. The gap between female and male literacy is narrowing. The situation is the same for secondary and tertiary education. The number of women entering tertiary education has also improved in many countries, but this is closely related to the wealth of the society in which they live. The education for women has greatly improved their entry into new technology jobs and into the urban economy. Education is a key and cross-cutting factor in empowering women and increasing their competitiveness with men for employment opportunities and for starting their own business. There is a clear relationship between education and starting entrepreneurial activities. For example, in high-income countries, 57 per cent of those who start an entrepreneurial activity have a post-secondary degree as compared to 38 per cent in a middle-income country, and 23 per cent in low-income countries.

(1) Education is landmark of women empowerment, because it enables them to responds to the challenges, to confront their traditional role and change their life. Empowerment is an active and multidimensional process which enables women to realize their full identity and powers in all sphere of life. Empowerment of women is very much essential to achieve sustainable development. Quoting UNFPA report, "the state of world population 1992", the News of Bernard Van Leer Foundation says that there can be no sustainable development without development of women, because it is women who contribute most for development for children.

(2) Education is highlight of women empowerment because it enables them to responds to the challenges, to confront their traditional role and change their life.

So that we can't neglect the importance of education in reference to women empowerment. Education is the first step towards empowerment and the most crucial factor in overall development of the individual as well as nation. Literacy sets one free from ignorance, exploitation and poverty. It liberates the minds, opening up new horizon, new hope/ opportunities and self-confidence further equipping them with the knowledge, skills, self-respect and freedom to participate sustain and excel in their life. Illiteracy on the other hand, breeds ignorance, which leads to exploitation, poverty, neglect crimes and number of social evils.

(3) Literacy withdraws women from all opportunities and further prospects of leading a meaningful life and enjoying good standard of living. Education is an effective instrument for social and economic development and national integration. Education enables women to understand their social and legal rights, become economically independent, acquire a voice in the affairs of the family and the community. Education is a gateway to information, opportunities and empowerment.

STRATEGIES TO BE FOLLOWED FOR EMPOWERING WOMEN THROUGH EDUCATION

Literacy Programme to Rural Areas

Literacy Programme is very important in the process of women's empowerment. It is a base for any educational programme. It enables rural women to acquire new knowledge and technology required for improving and developing their tasks in all fields. Literacy helps rural women to bring up their children and carry out the responsibility of motherhood.

Non-Formal Education

Non-Formal Education (NFE) is an effective method of women empowerment in rural areas. Due to some constrains like lack of sufficient time and higher level of age, it is very difficult to provide formal education to rural women. Therefore, non-formal education is the best vehicle in transferring new knowledge and technology to them. NFE for empowerment means people gaining an understanding of and control over social, economic and/or political forces to improve their standard in society.

Some indications of the effect of NFE for empowerment are:

- Increase access to resources,
- Increase collective bargaining power,
- Improved status, self-esteem and cultured identity,
- Ability to reflect critically and solve problems,
- Ability to make choices,
- Legitimization of peoples' demands by officials, and
- Self-discipline and ability to work with others.

MOBILIZATION OF WOMEN AND COMMUNITY

Mobilizing of women and the community at the village level and our country should take part in educational planning for improving enrolment, retention and educational achievement of girls.

Interacting with Media

Development of messages and themes relevant to promotion of girls' education and positive self-image particularly amongst those from deprived groups.

Awareness Programme

- Arranging Awareness Programme for women empowerment through education.
- Knowing special schemes about women education.
- Educational rights for women.

Effective Extension Educational Methods for Rural Women Like

- Mobile courses instead of women's training centre.

- Utilization of educated girls and widows as female extension workers.
- Education of women through negotiation between husband and wife or inter-spouse communication.
- Tours and visits organized by women's group or organization (cooperatives etc.).
- Set-up extension organisation for rural women like Pakistan, Sri Lanka and Bangladesh.
- Encourage make extension agents to work with women's group.
- Post-female extensionists in their local areas or close to their husband's workplace.
- Working women extensionists in pairs (husband and wife as extension workers).
- Encourage and support the establishment of women local groups and organisations to take up responsibility of communicating new science and technology to rural women.

COMMUNITY EDUCATION

Community education is an integral part of community development and community empowerment is a way by which people involve in-group efforts to identify their problems, analyse their cultural and socio-economic roots of problems, and develop strategies bringing positive change in their lives and in their communities. It is an ongoing process that demands time and continued commitment towards better quality life and justice for community.

Community education can uphold their effective involvement of rural women in building community through collective action. This type of education gives them the power to participate in all aspects of community development and be active citizens. This education will also tackle social and cultural barriers which restrict the participation of rural women in social activities.

ADULT EDUCATION

Adult education is another type of non-formal education

which is an effective strategies intervention for empowerment of women. This will lead the community to have same impression about the necessity of women's empowerment and pay attention to their gender specific needs. Older people have a lifetime experience, knowledge and wisdom to offer to others in their community. In view point, girls' education in some countries where there are social and cultural barriers for educating females, community level work may help parents understand the value of educating girls. Adults' education classes provide one such opportunity for influencing the thinking of parents.

ACCESS TO COMMUNICATION MEDIA

Access to communication media prepares women for improving their communication and mediation skills to strengthen their capacity to contact and mediate with external world. Consequently, the employment of this skill will prepare the way for transaction of their own experiences, knowledge and work skills with other persons and increase their awareness about the women's rights, allocated facilities, and resources by government or other organisations.

ACCESS TO APPROPRIATE TECHNOLOGY

Experience show that the technology can be appropriate for rural women when it has the following characteristics:

- Based on their needs and problems,
- Cheap, simple and small scale,
- Harmonise and compatible with local materials, resources and cultures,
- Locally available skills and knowledge,
- Labour and time saving, and
- Access and control of rural women.

Due to some implements like, lack of access to land, credit, education, lack of recognition and their contributions to village life, rural women don't have suitable access to and control over new technology.

CONCLUSION

At present when we talk about 21st century, and women empowerment, we feel very upsetting when we see a woman in a very pitiable condition in our society on the other side we feel very proud when gains highest position represent our nation. If we want to realize women empowerment, firstly, we will try to minimize the literacy gap between man and woman and give priority to educate a women. So that education plays a crucial role in accelerating the women empowerment. Thus education seen as "Unique investment" in present and future in reference to Women Empowerment. The National Policy on Education states that Education will be used as driving force of basic change in the status of women in society.

References

Akthar, Najma, "Higher Education in Future", Manak Publication Pvt. Ltd., New Delhi 2000.

Anand, S. and A. Sen (1995): "Gender Inequality in Human Development: Theories and Measurement", in Fukuda Parr and A.K. Shiv Kumar (eds.) Readings in Human Development, OUP, New Delhi.

Bardhan, K. and K. Stephan (1999): "UNDP's Gender Related Indices: A Critical Analysis.

Barkat, A. (2008): "Women Empowerment: A key to Human Development.

Blumberg, R.L. (2005): "Women's Economic Empowerment as the Magic Potion of Census of India (2001): Government of India, New Delhi.

Chattopadhyay, R. and E. Duflo (2001): "Women's Leadership and Policy Decisions: Commissioner, New Delhi.

Das, Suranjan, "The Higher Education in India and the Challenges of Globalization", *Social Science*, Vol. 35, Nos. 3-4, March-April 2007. Department of Economics, Universidad Carlos III de Madrid.

Desai, N. and U. Thakkar (2007): "Women and Political Participation in India" : Empowerment as a Variable in International Development", Unpublished Paper for the World Bank. www.unicef.org/pubsgen/humanrights-children/index. html. Visited on 11th January, 2008, at 5 p.m.

Empowerment through Local Governance organized jointly by Institute of Social empowerment.htm. Visited on 10th February 2008 at 10 a.m.

Empowerment Qualitative Health Research, Vol. 5, No. 1.

Evidence from a Nationwide Randomized Experiment in India, Indian Institute of Evidence from the NFHS", *Economic and Political Weekly,* Vol. XXXIX, No. 7.

Figueras, I.C. (2008): "Women in Politics: Evidence from the Indian States".

G.O.I. (2002): National Human Development Report, 2001, Planning Commission.

G.O.I. (2005-06): National Family Health Survey-III, Ministry of Health and Family Welfare, New Delhi.

Government of Assam (2003): "Women : Striving in an Unequal World" in *Assam Human.*

Janaki, D., "Empowerment of Women through Education : 150 Years of University Education in India", *University News,* Vol. 44, 480, Nov. 27-Dec. 03, 2006, pp. 82-84.

9

Women Educational Programmes in Tribal Areas

An Overview

G. JAYALAKSHMI

INTRODUCTION

The tribal societies have their own tradition of living. They manage their affairs in their own social structure. Long before they chiefly depended upon hunting and good gathering but with pressure of their population they gradually trade to agriculture and they started cottage, industries. After independence, when many industries were established in the tribal areas they also got employment opportunities in these industries as unskilled labours. Education is a potent tool in the emancipation and empowerment of women. The greatest single factor which can incredibly improve the status of women in any society is education. It is indispensable that education enables women not only to gain more knowledge about the world outside of her hearth and home but helps her to get status, positive self-esteem, and self-confidence, necessary courage and inner strength to face challenges in life.

THE TRIBAL EDUCATION IN INDIA

Under different five-year plans, a number of programmes were launched for the socio-economic development of tribals in view of the Directive Principles of the constitution of India. But these programmes, which were implemented by the states and the central governments, have not yielded the desired results in view of the constraints involved in the development of tribals. The seventh plan noted the constraints, which impede the goals of development of tribal. The main noted point is low literacy among tribals, heavy dependence on agricultural and forest products, isolated habitations with no infrastructure, 'is lands of poverty', represented by tribal hamlet with the developed area, pod cultivation, etc., so this paper to highlights the importance and position of education.

The ministry of education has, ear-marked Rs. 11.35 crores for the past merit scholarships for scheduled tribes and awarded permission to open 3,178 schools and 395 hostels particularly to tribal students. During third plan, a number of hostels, Ashram schools and book banks were established and efforts were made to provide remedial coaching counseling and guidance to tribal students. During the sixth plan emphasis was laid on the universalization of elementary education and spread of non-formal education among tribals. Female literacy rate was given priority to primary education of tribals was given. Following the national policy of education 1986, District Primary Education Program and mid-day meal programmes were introduced during eighth five year plan. The goal of the ninth five year was to make the nation fully literate by the year 2005.

EDUCATION DEVELOPMENT PROGRAMMES

The educational programmes of the central government include award of post-metric scholarships, provision of grants, hostels, pre-examination training centres, and coaching-*cum*-guidance facilities to tribal students appearing for several competitive exams and overseas scholarships, funds exemption from tuition fees, mid-day meals. Building for school completes of which about 59% was specify on educational institutional 18% on post-metric scholarships and 9% in building for school complexes, 6.19% for residential schools, each 2.03% on educational infrastructure and pre-metric scholarships. It is very clear from the above the analysis reveals that the India is interested to develop the tribal education in order to encourage the students to join the schools, government has introduced post-metric scholarship to the students belonging to scheduled tribes from 1948-49, the years of inauguration of the scheme hostel facilities were also provided to attract the scheduled tribes students to the hostels.

THE ROOT CAUSES FOR LOW LITERACY AMONG WOMEN IN INDIA

Women education is a multi-dimensional phenomenon. No single factor or cause can be held responsible for very low literacy rate of women in India. Subsequently, it is associated with combination of many factors including social, cultural, economic, educational, demographic, political and administrative and so on. The following are some of the important factors which could be attributed for the present poor state of affairs of womenfolk in education.

1. The Lower Enrolment

The lower enrolment of girls in schools is one of the foundational factors which stand as stumbling block for women empowerment in India. Reliable sources indicate that more than 50% of the Non-Starters (those who have never been to school) are girls. According to the latest statistics, two out of every ten girls in the age group of 6-11 are still not enrolled in schools.

2. Higher Drop-out Rate among Girls from Schools

The incidence and prevalence of drop-outs among girls especially in rural, tribal and slums areas seem to be quite high.

According to available sources, occurrence of drop-out and stagnation amongst girls is nearly twice that of boys all over India

3. Girl Child as Second Mother

In many families girl children play the role of second mother by shouldering the responsibilities of household work such as looking after the sibling, fetching water, collecting firewood, bringing fodder for cattle, cleaning and cooking, etc. In rural India especially in poor families this traditional sex rôle makes girl child handicapped and conditioned by the attitude of mother and the family and discourages girl child to go school as it becomes secondary

4. Bonded Labour System

This social evil is a quite discouraging phenomenon which stands as barrier for girl's education in rural areas for the underprivileged families of washermen and agricultural labour, scheduled caste and scheduled tribès.

5. Cast System as a Barrier

Children belonging to low caste families are forced to learn skills and work ways and not encouraged to go to school due to various factors in the sphere of strict instruction/threat from high caste communities for their selfish motives of keeping them as domestic servants and child labourers in the farms or factory.

6. Dowry as Cordon

Dowry system and other social practices act as main causes of the neglect of the girl child and discrimination against girl child including the deprivation of right of education. In many families especially poor and down-trodden think that if their daughters are educated more, they have to accumulate more assets and properties to provide as dowry in large proportion at the time of marriage, so prefer rather to either stop their children with average education and so on but never higher education. This prevails more in underprivileged families and communities

7. Child Labour Practice

A large segment of child population in India is engaged in child labour practices. According to UN sources India is the most child labour populous nation in the globe with more than 50 million child labourers indulged in beedi works, carpet-making, bricks, mining, quarrying, glass, bangles, match and fireworks, gem polishing, handloom works, zari, embroidery, coir industry, domestic works, construction, etc. In most of these industries girl children are preferred for high productivity and low cost.

8. Poor School Environment for Girls

In general the school environment for girls in India is not really interesting and encouraging. The subjects taught in schools are also not related to the environment of girl children. The methods of teaching are mostly out-dated, rigid and uninteresting. There are still hundreds of schools with poor basic amenities such as drinking water, latrine and toilet facilities, improper building, and inadequate number of teachers especially female teachers preferable for any parents for safety of their girl children from different types of exploitation and abuse.

9. Female Age at Marriage

There is high association of female literacy with female age at marriage. By and large the female age at marriage of 18 (recently 21 years) as prescribed by various legislations not at all followed in India. It is very much ignored and neglected by the families of parents with low literacy and illiteracy background. This obnoxious practice discourages female children to continue their schooling and higher education as they enter into family life at the early age which is not advisable from the physical and mental health point of view and also of social development.

10. Inferiority, Subservience and Domesticity

The female child in Indian culture especially in rural, tribal and poor families is expected to develop the qualities of inferiority; subservience and domesticity which place severe limitations on her education and development.

11. Poverty as a Barrier

In much poverty stricken families, children especially girls are considered as economic assets as they bring income for livelihood as well to save from economic crises due to death or incapacity of parents (sick/handicapped/aged).

12. Ineffective Law Enforcing Machinery

Indian constitution and various legislations pertaining to education to children assure free and compulsory education to all children of this nation but unfortunately the enforcement machinery fail to discharge its duties and responsibilities to the satisfaction of the public interest and welfare of women.

13. Demographic Factors

The high population growth rate, rapid urbanization, migration, etc. also attribute immensely for the poor literacy level of women and girls in India

14. Political Will and Conviction

Government officials, policy-makers, politicians, etc. of our country have neither political will nor conviction for the empowerment of women in general.

REMEDIAL MEASURES FOR IMPROVING THE LITERACY LEVEL OF WOMEN IN INDIA

The following measures can be considered for bringing phenomenal change in the plight of women's education and empowerment in India.

- The Ministry of Education both at Centre and State-level should work out strategic steps to stop firmly the ongoing high drop-outs among girls especially in rural, tribal and slums areas with the serious involvement of voluntary organizations in every locality to realize zero drop-out among girls.

- The poverty stricken families can be identified through proper research and necessary poverty alleviation services be provided to strengthen the income thereby to enable the families to send their children to schools and colleges without much financial difficulties.
- Appropriate steps should be taken by the educational authorities with the participation of communities in order to bring the girl children to the mainstream of education and development at every level including family and community.
- The female child in every Indian family irrespective of socio-economic status should be molded to overcome the challenges of inferiority; subservience and domesticity which place severe limitations on her education and development. Every family irrespective its socio-cultural and economic background can take it a challenge to bring up their girl children as dignified human being with empowerment in physical, mental, economic and social dimensions of life.
- The Mid-day meal scheme and other educational supportive services like free text books, Note books, Free uniforms, Free Bicycles, scholarships, Free bus pass and so on as done in the state of Tamil Nadu can be provided in all states and union territories to lift up the literacy level among girls.
- The electronic and print media can play significant role in building a good and positive image about girls and women in general in the society by giving no focus for such advertisements and news fetching commercial gain at the cost of depicting women as an object. This would help in changing the society's attitudes towards girls and their roles to treat every girl or woman as human being with self-respect and dignity.

REFERENCES

N.L. Gupta (2003), *Women's Education Through Ages*, Concept Publications Co., New Delhi.

R.K. Rao (2001), *Women and Education*, Kalpaz Publications, Delhi.

Hamilton Roberta (1978), *Liberation of Women*, London, George Allen Publishers.

Jaya Kothai Pillai (1995), *Women and Empowerment*, Gyan Publishing House, New Delhi.

Government of India, *Census of India, 2001.*

10

Progressive Development in the Socio-demographic Status of Women Through Education

Chitra Sivasubramaniam

INTRODUCTION

It took icons for women to come out of their pre-ordained duties, to pfove that they are worthy equals during the freedom struggle. They stood shoulder to shoulder, enduring the tyranny and sacrifices for the sake of the motherland. From then, it has been a long and strenuous journey to attain the position at which they are now at the pinnacle of every single path of their choice. But this does not make them any different from their male counterparts. Actually it is the obstacles and sometimes in harsh reality, the ridicule, that they are subjected that makes them yearn for a chance to excel and prove their capability.

What helps her to stand out in the crowd in this appalling situation would make a very interesting question, the answer to which lies in one single word—"EDUCATION". Empowerment and education go hand in hand: "It helps an individual to focus on strength and self-confidence to gain control over available resources and to exercise their right to obtain quality of life for themselves and their family (Moyle, Dollard & Biswas, 2006)". A truly empowered woman should be characterized by high self-esteem and spectacular decision-making ability. Self-esteem refers to an individual's judgment of self-worth, which is derived from self-evaluations based on competence or on attributes that are culturally invested with a certain value (Bandura, 1997). Self-esteem can also facilitate the empowerment process because it relates to an individual's sense of value or worth and is 'a favourable or unfavourable attitude toward the self' (Rosemberg, 1965).

Decision-making ability is all about defining an individual's goals and striving to achieve it on his/her own terms. This requires immense levels of determination, perseverance, and passion to achieve an empowered status. But the inception to this path lies in the realization of the situation that has been thrust upon women. In other words, they must realize that they have every right to control their own lives. The current scenario is one where there is lack of control due to the archaic and baseless yet existing social structure bound by asinine superstitions.

In terms of socio-demographic status, education is considered as the key factor to increase women's empowerment by increasing their self-confidence and understanding of how to operate in the world. In India, right to education is a basic fundamental right provided by the law. Unfortunately, it is very scantily, rather seldom recognized as a fundamental right. This is mainly the scenario in the families of workers in agricultural workers and blue-collared jobs.

There are many obstacles in trying to impart education to girls and the first hurdle commonly observed is when education is ignored in the process of rearing a child. It is daunting to know that children belonging to the low-income families are never sent to school but to work with the rest of family members in construction or household work. Sometimes they are the only earning members in the family, not to mention at a tender age as early as 3-5 years old.

The second most horrendous obstacle is when parents think of easy money by holding their children at stake. The parents brutally forget their responsibility to provide and care for their wards. They think of their kids to be a quick means to attain a paltry sum of money and sell them to human traffickers. The misery and sufferings that these children face is deplorable beyond doubt. They are subjected to sexual abuse and physical torture. It is unbelievable that even 3-year olds are not exceptions. These indicate that though a woman is no longer seen as a child-bearing machine, she is still considered apathetically as an object of desire, with their rights denied, opportunities curtailed and voices silenced.

However, it is partly due to the women's subordinate nature and acceptance of situation in the name of fate that impedes their literacy rate. This reflects either upon their poor self-esteem or stunted interest in education. Limited social interaction allied with submissiveness further makes them believe that that learning is not one of their innate talents and hence, they feel useless and worthless. The next dimension in the hurdles takes the form of poor health due to frequent pregnancies, physical violence or bodily abuse. Then there are the intangible barriers that precipitate a state of apathy.

Thus, it is only education that can be the door to the alluring yet palpable thought of equality and respect. This can be challenging in many ways. Tamil poet Kaniyan Poogundranar in his work *Purananuru* says, *Yaadum oore, yavarum kezhir*, which means "I'm a world citizen and every citizen is our kith and kin". An initiative must be taken by every individual to make the importance of education and its impact on the future of the child felt among the parents. Secondly, there should be ways and means to provide these children with education and safety.

For instance, an organization run by Dr. Sunita Krishnan rescues victims of human trafficking and sexual abuse, trains them in various fields ranging from carpentry to welding and resuscitates their hope to sustain and survive. So far, more than 3200 persons including women and children have been rescued.

Women should be given training based on their work as it imparts integrity and sense of belonging. Thus the major fields that should be a part of curriculum include training in planning, management and entrepreneurship. It is also of primary importance to discuss how well we are equipped to make women outstanding in the chosen fields. All in all, empowerment of women can be said to have taken place if they are able to handle complex issues at the domestic and societal level.

The recruitment of women teachers in school will have a great impact. This will lead to increase in the number of girls' enrolment. It can also have other positive changes regarding the improvement of girls' education. Women teachers make for excellent advocates of issues and needs of the girls. They understand how important it is to have a safe and secure environment for teaching girls. They also make themselves available in case of any personal assistance required by girls.

Information technology is also said to have an important role in catalyzing the literacy rate of women. They can make the course material more true-to-life and be used as a mnemonic device to enhance the learning process. It brings down all the social, cultural, personal barriers regarding access to knowledge for women. In other words, it helps women to overcome the lack of time, lack of trained professional to aid them and lack of resources. Another added advantage of the information technology is that it creates the contents of the course in the regional language.

Once the women have started learning, a phase of post-literacy and the urge to continue the education is triggered. Here the sustenance of the skills learnt by the neo-literates is taught and women engage themselves in their own educational programs acquiring extra-ordinary skills. They become avid learners and trigger a spontaneous chain reaction encouraging other women in the community to actively join them in this burgeoning "knowledge economy."

Knowledge economy is a term acknowledged by economists and they refer to increase in the knowledge and technology. Their current study shows that increase in literacy rate not only paves the way for a better stance for women in the society but also helps eradicate poverty. This is evident because there is a disturbingly linear relationship between poverty and illiteracy. And the figure of illiteracy is even more disturbing as the recent study by UNESCO in 2006 points that 771 million adults are illiterate and this accounts for 18% of the world population. Further narrowing down, 64% of the illiterate adults are women.

Empowerment of women succinctly put by Paz is as follows, "The ability to direct and control one's own life" (Paz, 1990). The vision of India or any other nation will only be complete when the women are said to be empowered compared to the current situation. In the process of empowering women, male counterparts should also recognize their gargantuan responsibility in making the world a better place for women to exercise their rights and lead a normal life. A harmony is born if and only if both men and women appreciate each other's participation in the social and political life of the community. And education is again emphasized to be instrumental in bringing about this harmony. In the words of Burma's democratic leader, Aung San Suu Kyi, "Education and empowerment of women throughout the world cannot fail to result in a more caring, tolerant, just and peaceful life for all."

References

http://www.census.gov/ipc/prod/wid-9801.pdf

http://www.unesco.org/education/pdf/283_102.pdf

http://www.unicef.org/education/files/TeachersIndia.pdf

http://www.cemca.org/cemca_womens_literacy.pdf

http://www.americanscience.org/journals/am-sci/am0611/50_3774am0611_426_434.pdf

11

Disparity in Tribal Education
An Exploratory Analysis

K. KRITHIGA AND R. ANNAPOORANI

INTRODUCTION

Education is an important social resource and a means of reducing inequality in society. Knowledge, skills, values and attitudes acquired through education helps one to achieve a desired quality of life. Therefore, education described as initiation into worthwhile activities or modes of thought and conduct.

According to Manmohan Singh (2006), "Education is an urgent priority, which needs to be attended to immediately." He stressed the need for huge investments to set-up more universities, professional colleges, nursing schools, etc. to meet the emerging domestic and international demand for various professional services. He also emphasized the need of a policy regime which facilitates investment in educational services. In the view of George (2007) education is crucial to development as it provides the individual with adequate skills for participating in various economic activities. During XI Five year plan the Government of India has allotted Rs. 56,450 lakhs for the development of education.

The importance of education is more pronounced for the tribals since they account for sizeable proportion of India's population -8.21 percent according to 2001 census. For the development of the tribal community education is most important element. It is a powerful instrument to change the values and attitude of the people and to create in them the urge of the necessary motivation to achieve social mobility and social ascendancy. According to Chakarvarty (2007) the overall development of tribals should include their empowerment in education. It is a pity that massive vacancies exist in tribal regions because of non-availability of educated tribals. However, the educational status of tribal population is poor as indicated by the literacy rate of 41.5 percent as compared to All India average of 65.4 percent. Hence, there is need for improving the literacy of tribals.

Realizing the importance of tribal education the Government had formulated many programmes to improve tribal education. Some of the measures are:

- Primary education continued through Sarva Shiksha Abhiyan with the participation of ST parents/ guardians in activities of school.
- Priority will be accorded to opening primary schools in tribal areas.
- Ashram schools/residential schools will be established on a large scale in tribal areas.
- Incentives schemes will be formulated for the STs, keeping in view their special needs and lifestyle.
- Mid-day meals acts as a support service to increase retention rates.

However, on an average in year 2001, difference between the literacy rate of general population and that of scheduled tribes has been around 15 percent. While at the national level, literacy among males was estimated as 75.9 percent and for females as 54.2 percent, the corresponding figures with regard to tribal males and females were found to be 59.2 percent and 34.8 percent.

In India research attempts (Ashuthosh Thakar (2001), Raghunath Rath (2006), Kukreti (2004), etc.) were made at analyzing the status of tribal education. But there had been little attempt concentrating on the analysis of disparity in tribal education. Hence the current study on "Disparity in tribal education—An exploratory analysis" is formulated with the expectation to fill up the research gap. The basic objectives of the study are:

- To find out the disparity in literacy rate, enrolment rate and composite educational index between tribal males and females, and
- To find out the disparity in literacy rate, enrolment rate and composite educational index between two tribal groups—Kurumbas and Todas.

METHODOLOGY

The study was related to Manjakombai and Avalanchi areas in Ooty block, Nilgiri District due to easy assessability. The required data related to general background, family background, enrolment, etc. are collected by administering the interview schedule from 65 households.

The study formulated the hypothesis that,

1. There is no disparity in literacy among tribal males and females, and
2. There is no disparity in tribal literacy among Kurumbas and Todas.

The study tried to construct composite educational index for the general and the scheduled tribes, following the approach of Nauriyal and Shahoo (2010). The composite educational index was calculated as follows.

Composite Educational Index (CEI) = (2 * LI + GI)/3

where LI (Literacy Index) =

$$\frac{\text{Actual literacy rate} - \text{Minimum literacy rate}}{\text{Maximum literacy rate} - \text{Minimum literacy rate}}$$

GI (GER Index) =

$$\frac{\text{Actual gross enrolment ratio} - \text{Minimum gross enrolment ratio rate}}{\text{Maximum gross enrolment ratio} - \text{Minimum gross enrolment ratio}}$$

where maximum value is 100 and minimum value is 0.

The disparity in literacy rate between males and females among selected population has been estimated using Sopher's (1974) disparity index. The index may be written as follows:

$$D = \log(X_2/X_1) + \log\ (Q-X_1)/Q-X_2$$

where X_1 and X_2 are per cent literate among the two groups of population and Q greater than 100. The index as proposed by Sopher lacks in certain desirable properties. Indicating this Kundu and Rao (1986) proposed Q greater than 200 and the current study follows the same. Lower value indicates lower disparity and higher values indicates higher disparity.

FINDINGS OF THE STUDY

(A) Disparity in Literacy Rate

Table 1 represents the male and female literacy rate for the selected tribal groups.

TABLE I

Disparity in Literacy Rate

Sl. No.	*Groups*	*Male Literacy Rate*	*Female Literacy Rate*	*Overall Literacy Rate*	*Disparity Among Male and Females*	*Disparity Among two tribal groups*
1.	Kurumbas	83.33	75.56	78.26	1.3381	1.1714
2.	Todas	87.5	98.04	92.93	1.2365	

The disparity in literacy rate between males and females were found to be higher among Kurumbas (1.3381) as compared to Todas (1.2365). The disparity in literacy rate of two groups was 1.1714.

(B) Disparity in Enrolment Rate

• The disparity in the enrolment of Kurumbas and Todas are given in Table 2.

TABLE 2

Disparity in Enrolment Rate

Sl. No.	*Groups*	*Male Enrolment Rate*	*Female Enrolment Rate*	*Overall Enrolment Rate*	*Disparity Among Male and Females*	*Disparity Among two groups*
1.	Kurumbas	91.40	48.10	54.76	5.1997	1.1217
2.	Todas	53.33	50.49	51.83	1.1189	

The disparity in enrolment rate between males and females were found to be higher among Kurumbas (5.1997) as compared to Todas (1.1189). The disparity in enrolment rate of two groups was 1.1217.

(C) Disparity in Composite Education Index

Using the two basic educational parameters—literacy rates and gross enrolment ratios the composite educational index was calculated and given in Table 3.

TABLE 3

Composite Education Index of Kurumbas and Todas

Sl. No.	*Groups*	*Male*	*Female*	*Overall*	*Disparity Among Male and Females*	*Disparity Among two groups*
1.	Kurumbas	0.66	0.60	0.77	1.1010	1.1855
2.	Todas	0.72	0.81	0.91	1.1267	

The disparity in composite education index between males and females were found to be higher among Todas (1.1267) as compared to Kurumbas (1.1010). The disparity in composite education index of two groups was 1.1855.

SUGGESTIONS

Based on the findings of the study, the followings suggestions were recommended to reduce the disparity in tribal education:

- To increase the enrolment and reduce dropout among the tribal students;
- Participation of work among children should be reduced;
- Creating awareness to the tribal families about the education facilities provided by Government; and
- Motivating all the parents to send the children to school and not to work.

REFERENCES

Asok Basu (2002), "Primary Education, Human Development and India's Disadvantaged Gropus', in Human Development and Economic Development, edited by Ruddar Datt, Deep and Deep Publications, New Delhi, pp. 355-57.

George, N.D. (2007), "Education: Challenge", *Yojana*, Vol. 51, No. 3, December, pp. 19-22.

Jakka Parthasarathy (2007), "Education and Development among the Tribes", Coonoor Printing, Coonoor, pp. 1-20.

Nageswara Rao and Rama Rao (2007), "State and Status of Tribals : Study of Munchingput Mandal", *Southern Economist*, Vol. 45, No. 1, March, pp. 31-34.

Parvinadu, D. (2001), "Literacy Trends and Variations in Tribal Sub-plan in Paravathipuram (Andhra Pradesh) in census 2001 and Human Development in India" edited by Ramachandrudu, G. and Prasada Rao, M., Serials Publications, New Delhi, pp. 251-53.

Ram Krishna Mandal (2008), "Role of Tribal Women in Socio-Economic Development", *Southern Economist*, Vol. 47, No. 8, August, pp. 9-14.

Sundra Murty, K., and Jagannadha Rao, K.V. (2001), "Primary Education of Tribals in a Backward Region in Andhra Pradesh—A Case Study of Vizianagaram District", in Census 2001 and Human Development in India, edited by Ramachandrudu, G. and Prasada Rao, M., Serials Publications, New Delhi, pp. 185-200.

12

Political Empowerment of Women

R. Srinivasan

INTRODUCTION

Empowerment refers to increasing the spiritual, political, social or economic strength of individuals and communities. It often involves the empowered developing confidence in the own capacities. Empowerment is then the process of obtaining these basic opportunities for marginalized people, either directly by those people, or through the help of non-marginalized others who share their own access to these opportunities. It also includes actively thwarting attempts to deny those opportunities. Empowerment and developing also includes encouraging and developing the skills for self-sufficiency, with a focus on eliminating the future need for charity or welfare in the individuals of the group. This process can be difficult to start and to implement effectively, but there are many examples of empowerment projects which have succeeded.

CAPABILITIES OF WOMEN EMPOWERMENT

- The ability to make decisions about personal collective circumstances.
- Ability to consider a range of options from which to choose.
- The ability to access informations and resources for decision-making.
- Ability to learn and access skills for improving personal.
- Ability to exercise assertiveness in collective decision-making.
- Having positive-thinking about the ability to make change.
- Involving the growth process and changes that is never ending and self-initiated.
- Ability to inform other's perceptions though exchange, education, and engagement.

TRENDS IN INDIA

The women representation in lower house of Parliament, the house of people, was not impressive in all the general elections. Over the Fifteen Lok Sabha elections the representations of women has witnessed a very slow improvement, despite the fact that women comprise almost 50 per cent of India's populations. As for Rajya Sabha from 1952 to 2002, 160 women have become members. However, the representation of women in Rajya Sabha at any given point of time has not beyond 30. In 1980, there were 29 women members out of a total of 242 members constituting 11.98 per cent of the House, which was the highest ever strength of women members in the House. At present, there are 25 women members in the Rajya Sabha.

Women's equality in power sharing and active participation in decision-making, including decision-making in political process at all levels will ensure the achievement of the goals of empowerment. Women-friendly personnel policies will encourage women to participate effectively in the developmental process. On 9th March 2010, the upper house of the Indian Parliament, the Rajya Sabha, passed the bill on the reservation of 33 per cent seats in the Lok Sabha, for India's women representatives. This has been hailed as a historic step towards a constitutional amendment that would significant representation of the women of India in the parliament. Currently, populations of almost 500 million Indian Women, it is represented by less than 60 elected representatives out of the 545 Lok Sabha seats. If the bill is implemented, the number of women representatives would increase three times to 181.

TABLE I

Empowerment of Women—Different Five Year Plans

Sl. No.	*Five Year Plans*	*Views on Women*
1.	First Plan (1951-56)	Sets-up the central social welfare board in 1953 to promote women welfare work through voluntary organizations, charitable trusts, etc.
2.	Second Plan (1956-61)	Supported the development of mahila mandals to work at the grassroots.
3.	Third, Fourth and Interim Plan (1961-74)	Had the provisions for women's education, pre-natal and child health services, supplementary feeding for children, nursing and expectant..
4.	Fifth Plan (1974-78)	A major shift in the approach towards women from welfare to development.
5.	Sixth Plan (1980-85)	Accepted women development as separate Economic Agenda. Took a multi-disciplinary approach with a three pronged thrust on health, education and employment.
6.	Seyenth Plan (1985-90)	Had the objective of bringing women into mainstream of National development.
7.	Eight Plan (1992-97)	Saw a paradigm shift from development to empowerment and benefits to women in the core sector of education, health and employment. Outlay for women rose from Rs. 4 crore in the First Plan to Rs. 2,000 crore in the Eight Plan.

8.	Ninth Plan (1997-02)	Had empowerment of women as its strategic objective. Accepted the concept of a woman's component plant to assure that at least 30% of funds/benefits from all development sector flow to women.
9.	Tenth Plan (2002-07)	Suggests specific strategies, policies and programs for the empowerment of women.
10.	Eleventh Plan (2007-11)	Special measures for gender empowerment and equity will be an essential component of the 11th plan. The plan will have a special focus on four aspects, Violence Against Women (VAW), economic development, political participation and women's health.

Source : "Women's Empowerment Dimensions and Directions: Social Welfare, March 2009.

TABLE 2

Women's Representation in the Parliament—General Elections

Year	*Total No. of Seats*	*No. of Women Members*	*Percentage to total*
1952	499	22	44
1957	500	27	54
1962	503	34	6.8
1967	523	31	5.9
1971	521	22	4.2
1977	544	19	3.5
1980	544	28	5.1
1984	517	44	8.1
1989	544	27	5.2
1991	544	39	7.2
1996	543	40	7.4
1998	543	43	7.9
1999	543	43	7.9
2004	543	49	8.8
2009	543	59	10.1

Source : Government of India.

Table 2 shows that the trend in General Elections. In the first general elections, held in the year 1952, out of 499 total seats there were 22 women members elected in the lower house of the parliament which was 4.4 per cent of the total. A record of 59 MPs have been elected to the 15th Parliament the highest ever since independence and 17 of them are aged less than 40 years. A majority of 23 women members, Uttar Pradesh has the maximum number of 13 women MPs representing the most populous state. It is followed by West Bengal with seven MPs. Fifteen per cent of 543 MPs in the present Parliament are the age group of 25-40 years. In all, 556 women contested the 2009 general elections, of which 59 were elected.

TABLE 3
Quota Type

Country	*Quota Type*	*Results in the last election*	*% of women in parliament*
Rewanda	Constitutional Quota for National Parliaments	45 of 80	56.3
Sweden	Political Party Quota for Electoral Candidates	165 of 349	47.3
South Africa	Constitutional or Legislative Quota	172 of 400	43.0
Argentina	Constitutional Quota for National Parliaments	107 of 257	41.6
Norway	Political Party Quota for Electoral Candidates	64 of 169	37.9
Netherlands	Political Party Quota for Electoral Candidates	55 of 150	36.74
Nepal	Constitutional Quota for National Parliaments	197 of 601	32.8
Germany	Constitutional Quota for National Parliaments	195 of 614	31.8
Afghanistan	Constitutional Quota for National Parliaments	68 of 249	27.3
Pakistan	Constitutional or Legislative Quota	73 of 342	21.3

Italy	Political Party Quota for Electoral Candidates	134 of 630	21.3
Canada	Political Party Quota for Electoral Candidates	64 of 308	20.8
China	Election Law Quota Regulation	604 of 2980	20.3
United Kingdom	Political Party Quota for Electoral Candidates	128 of 646	19.9
Bangladesh	Constitutional Quota for National Parliaments	64 of 3454	18.6
France	Political Party Quota for Electoral Candidates	107 of 577	18.5
India	Constitutional or Legislative Quota Proposed	59 of 543	10.9

The Table 3 shows that women get proper representation only with the help of quota. Here, it is praiseworthy to note that in some developing nations, like, Rewanda, Nepal, Afghanistan, Bangladesh, Pakistan proportion of women representing the parliament is almost equal to that of developed nations, like, Sweden, Italy, France, Canada, and UK. It is expected that where women are substantially represented in legislative bodies there is the likelihood of more gender-sensitive legislation. It will help to improve gender indicators, the survival of women (sex ratio at birth and missing women), education (literacy, school retention and higher school enrolment); nutrition and health (Malnutrition life expectancy and risk of maternal mortality); employment (work participation, wage gaps), security and voice (violence against women, political participation)

CONCLUSION

India is already ahead of many other countries in terms of women's participation in politics. India has a history of strong female politicians but still the percentage of women in legislatures and decision-making position always remained low. A record of 59 MPs have been elected to the 15th Parliament, the highest ever since independence and 17 of them are aged less than 40 years, a majority of 23 women members. Uttar Pradesh has the maximum number of 13 women MPs representing the most populous state. It is followed by West Bengal with seven MPs. Fifteen per cent of 543 MPs in the present Parliament are the age group of 25-40 years. In all, 556 women contested the 2009 general elections, of which 59 were elected. Currently, a population of almost 500 million Indian women is represented by less than 60 elected representations, out of the 545 Lok Sabha seats. If the bill is implemented, the number of women representations would increase three times to 181.

References

Deepti Agarwal, 2001, Empowerment of Rural Women in India, *Social Welfare*, 48 (4) pp. 3-4.

Gurumoorthi, T.P., 2000, Self help Groups Empowerment of Rural Women, *Kurukshetra*, 48 (5), pp. 37-41.

Jayesh Talati and Venkatakrishnan, V., 2001, Women's Empowerment in India in Jhabu District, M.P., *Social Welfare*, 47(11), 15-18.

13

Constitutional Rights for Empowerment of Indian Women

E. MURUGESAN

INTRODUCTION

"The women of India will not attain their full rights by the more generosity of men, they will have to fight and force their will on the men folk if they want to succeed".

— Jawaharlal Nehru

This Article attempts to analyze the Constitutional provisions that empower Indian women. It also analyses the enforceability of such Constitutional rights by using writs. Empowerment refers to conferment of powers on women. Rights are powers provided to protect their interests. Therefore, empowerment refers to conferment of power through rights and ability and enforceability of such rights by. women.

Prior to the Constitutional Law of India women were not treated equally, both in law as well as in practice. But the

Constitutional goals as found in the preamble clearly lay down that equality is to be secured. This right to equality finds its place in the fundamental rights from Arts. 14 to 18. However, Constitutional rights cannot exactly be considered on par with practical rights. Therefore, the social reality was women were not treated equally in the society. The Constitutional remedies as provided in Arts. 32 and 226 facilitate the affected women to approach the Constitutional courts to realize their Constitutional right of equality. However, for the speedy realization of equality of women both in law and in practice, the principle of protective discrimination enshrined in the constitution is being followed now. These constitutional provisions facilitate empowerment of women, which are analyzed below.

RIGHTS OF WOMEN UNDER THE CONSTITUTION OF INDIA

The Constitution of India guarantees equal rights to women and men. The preamble to the constitution, Parts III, IV, IV-A, IX and IX-A, have confer rights on women for their empowerment, particularly Parts IX and IX-A ensure 33% reservation for women in village panchayats and municipalities. The general provisions relate to the equal rights of women like right to vote and other political rights.

Women's rights under the Indian constitution are considered under three heads:

- Rights, which treat women equally with men.
- Rights, which are conferred on them additionally to realize their rights (Protective Discrimination/ Affirmative action).
- Rights which are given to women because of their specific biological differences from men.

In Constitution, certain rights are guaranteed for the upliftment of women since India has suppressed their rights for a long period. These rights guaranteed to women are on an equal footing with rights of men.

(A) The Preamble

The Preamble of the constitution encompasses, 'We the people of India' categorically recognizes equality of status and opportunity for all the citizens. Hence, the particular rights of equality have been incorporated to give equal rights to women and men in all status as well as in opportunities. On that basis, India has been enacting various laws for women empowerment.

(B) Fundamental Rights

Part-III of the Constitution provides fundamental political and basic human rights for all citizens in India. Articles 14, 15 and 16 of the Constitution ensures that women have equal rights with men—in equality, non-discrimination and non-discrimination in employment. These articles run as follows:

Art. 14	:	"The state shall not deny to any person equality before the law or the equal protection of the laws within the territory of India".
Art. 15	:	"Prohibition of discrimination on grounds of religion, race, caste, sex or place of birth".
Art. 15(3)	:	"Nothing in this article shall prevent the state from making by special provision for women and children".
Art. 16(1)	:	"There shall be equality of opportunity for all citizens in matters relating to employment or appointment to any office under the state".

Art. 15(3) of the Constitution provides that the state may make laws for the protection of women and children. The Constitution has been amended to provide 33% of seats reserved for women in Panchayat Raj institutions including municipal corporations. Similar amendments is in process to facilitate women to have 33% of seats reserved in the Legislative Assemblies and House of People.

Art. 17 of the Constitution provides for abolition of untouchability and prohibits it in any form, so the socially and economically backward classes of women may also participate actively in society. Adequate representation is given to local bodies, (i.e.), Panchayat Raj and Nagar Palika.

Art. 21of the constitution provides that no person shall be deprived of his life and personal liberty except according to procedure established by law. However, every person (Women and Men) has a natural right to life which is recognized under it. But their freedom cannot be curtailed without enactment of law. So half of the population in India that represent women are in miserable condition in many states and are not able to take part in public life.

These disadvantaged of women have to fight for their daily needs of life. They are exploited by the social evils like forcefully using women as prostitutes and bonded labours. Hence, Art. 23 of the Constitution provides that every person including a citizen has a right against exploitation. It is prohibited in any form, i.e. begging, slavery, etc.

The Parliament of India has enacted a law—Suppression of Immoral Traffic Act, 1956. The main object of this Act is to abolish prostitution and other forms of trafficking. Hence, the Constitution provides empowerment of women through legislative enactments both Central and State Governments.

(c) Directive Principles of State Policy

Part IV (Arts. 36 to 51) of the Directive Principles of State policy provides that the State may follow the principles contained in this part for fundamental governance of the state. Hence, the state governments in every states and union government must follow the principles enunciated in this part. But these provisions contain principles which are advisory in nature though certain principles are enforceable. It directs the goals of the governance of the state.

Art. 39(a) directs that the state shall ensure its policy towards securing all citizens, i.e. men and women to have equal rights to an adequate means of livelihood.

Art. 39(d) provides the state to secure equal pay for equal work for both men and women. The Parliament has enacted the Equal Remuneration Act, 1976 for enforcement of this direction.

Art. 39(e) of the Constitution directs the State to protect and maintain the workers' health condition and working environment and strength of workers for women and men. The Factories Act, 1976 emphasizes this principle.

Art. 42 of the Constitution provides that the state shall provide just and humane condition of work and maternity relief. Based on this principle, the parliament enacted the Maternity Benefit Act, 1961.

RESERVATION FOR WOMEN UNDER THE CONSTITUTION

The affirmative action is permitted in our Constitution apart from the equality of right conferred to women with men. After the 73rd and 74th Constitutional Amendments, Indian Women have been given an opportunity to participate in the political affairs at the grass-root level in the Panchayat Raj Institutions. It is a revolutionary measure where women have been empowered to take part in the political domain which was till then considered as men's affair in this traditional country. The constitutions Amendment Act provide for reservation of 33% seats for women in the election of village panchayats and Municipalities. Apart from these, recently the Women Reservation (Constitutional Amendment) Bill was passed by Lok Sabha. It provides for 33% reservation of seats in the House of People and State Legislative Assemblies of every state. It will empower the political participation of women in the decision-making process of the government. The National Commission for Women's Act, 1990 was passed by Parliament which provides for the constitution of National Commission for women to protect and promote their welfare.

ENFORCEMENT OF CONSTITUTIONAL RIGHTS OF WOMEN

Rights without having enforcement mechanism are ineffective. Hence in our Constitution, the supreme law of the land, which has Constitutional goals in the preamble and fundamental rights as its subjects, these rights and constitutional goals are to be achieved. That's why the

Constitution itself has enforcement of fundamental right within it as a fundamental right as it is recognized as 'Constitutional Remedies'.

Articles 32 and 226 of the Constitution provide for the enforcement of fundamental right through issuing five kinds of writs. These are *habeaus corpus, mandamus*, prohibition, *quo warranto* and *certiorari*. The Constitution contemplates provisions for empowerment of women by enlisting their rights in Part III as well as in other parts. It also provides enforcement mechanism by providing constitutional remedies under Arts. 32 and 226. Of course, the former itself is a fundamental right and latter is a mere Constitutional right. The Supreme Court by interpreting the Constitutional rights expands the powers of women and thereby women are better empowered. It is obvious from the landmark decision in *Vishaka* v. *State of Rajasthan* (1997) 6 SCC 241.

The Supreme Court in *Vikram Deo Singh Tomar* v. *State of Bihar*, AIR 1988 SC 1782 has directed Bihar Government to improve the care homes for women and children and ensure human dignity by providing at least minimum living condition in the care homes. In *Upendra Baxi* v. *State of U.P.* (1986) 4 SCC 106 the Supreme Court directed the State Government to provide living condition in protective homes at Agra.

The Supreme Court in *Abo Yusuf Abdul Azing* v. *State of Bombay*, AIR 1954 SC 321 held that the provision of Art. 15(3) of Constitution permit the state to take affirmative action to women and children for their empowerment.

However, the Supreme Court in the process of rendering gender justice to women went to an extent whereby it laid down detailed guidelines facilitating women employees working in offices, in industries and other places to work in a dignified manner and from being harassed by men whether employees or co-workers.

The law laid down in *Vishaka* v. *State of Rajasthan* (1997) 6 SCC 241 empowers women by enlisting the following rights which are against male employer or male co-worker.

- Preventing and protecting them from physical contact and advances.

- Preventing them from demanding or requesting for sexual favour.
- Preventing them from using sexually coloured remarks.
- Preventing them from showing pornography.
- Preventing them from exhibiting any other unwelcome physical, verbal or non-verbal conduct of sexual nature.

In this way, whenever the doors of the Supreme Court are knocked for protecting women and their rights, the Court issues direction for the same. Thus, women are empowered through the enforcement of Constitutional rights.

CONCLUSION

There is a sea-change between Indian women of 1950 and the Indian women of the present day. Before the introduction of the Constitution, equality of women was only a lip service. But today it has attained the stage of reality. The Constitution, legislative, executive and the judiciary go hand in hand and attempts to remove the differences faced by women with reference to gender-based inequality and discrimination. The Supreme Court of India has been a vociferous champion of women's right and from time to time delivers landmark judgment in rendering gender justice, so that women are today better empowered. But the process of empowerment of women is a long process and women have to travel a longer distance in realizing their equal powers on par with their counterparts through enforcement of their Constitutional rights.

References

Austin, Granville, *Working a Democratic Constitution* (New Delhi: Oxford University Press, 1999).

Basu, Durga Das, *Shorter Constitution of India* (Nagpur: Wadhwa & Co., 2001).

Basu, Durga Das, *Constitutional Remedies and Writs* (Calcutta: Kamal Law House, 1999).

Flavia Agnes, Sudhir Chandra and Monmayee Basu (eds.), *Women and Law in India* (New Delhi : Oxford University Press, 2004).

Jain, M.P., *Indian Constitutional Law* (Nagpur : Wadhwa Company, 2003).

Kapur, Promilla, *Empowering the Indian Women* (New Delhi: Publications Division (Govt. of India), 2001).

Rajkumar, C., Chockalingam, K. (eds.), *Human Rights Justice and Constitutional Empowerment* (New Delhi: Oxford University Press, 2007).

Saksena, K.P. (ed.), *Human Rights and the Constitutions* (New Delhi: Gyan Publishing House, 2003).

Santhanam, M.K., *50 Years of Indian Republic* (New Delhi: Publication Division (Government of India), 2000.

Seervai, H.M., *Constitutional Law of India* (Delhi: Universal Book Traders, 1997).

Shabbir Mohammed, *Quest for Human Rights* (New Delhi: Rawat Publications, 2005).

Roy, Rekha, *Women's Rights in India* (New Delhi: Akarsha Publishing House, 2006).

14

Decentralization and Political Empowerment of Scheduled Caste Women in Kerala

T. SUNDARA RAJ

INTRODUCTION

Decentralization processes can be indeed empowering women but only if empowerment is an explicit goal and well defined strategies adequate resources and commitment at top levels are in place. Panchayat Raj Institutions (PRIs) are the foundations of democratic decentralization in India as they seek to ensure planning and execution of development at local level. In Kerala, the democratic decentralization involves cross-sections of the people, including women in the process of decision-making and development. The study behind democratic decentralization lies in the mass participation in local socio-political and economic affairs affecting the local people particularly the Scheduled Caste Women and thus it helps them to attain socio-political and economic base. In this context, democratic decentralization forms an opportunity structure for Scheduled Caste (SC) women to come to the mainstream of the society. The supportive system of democratic decentralization is Gramasabhas, Self Help Groups (SHGs), Neighbourhood Groups (NHGs), etc. which plays major role for the empowerment of local population especially for SC women. But, in spite of this formal constitutional mechanism for ensuring participation and empowerment of all sections of the society, women's participation and empowerment are said to be not satisfactory. Among the SC women, the condition is more deplorable, owing to their lower placement in the socio-economic hierarchy.

Women constitute almost half the population of India. The movement for the empowerment of women has assumed great significance in the end of the 20th century. 2001 A.D was celebrated as the Women's Empowerment year. India has grown with strong tradition of democratic functioning, a vibrant public opinion and influential sections of society interested in the welfare of women. Women's empowerment movement is gathering strength gradually. This movement will make major contribution towards nation-building.

Politics is important for increased equality between the sexes. However, traditionally, political participation was considered to be the province of men. Women were not regarded as part of the political arena until recent times. Women's disinterests in politics, their family responsibilities, their economic dependency, their inferior status, their illiteracy are some of the important reasons offered for this phenomenon.

Gender equality is a prerequisite for the effective participation of women in politics. The role of Gender varies from one country to another. Almost everywhere in the global women are discriminated when compared with men in social, economic and political spheres of life whereas men are viewed as the principal decision-makers. Women often hold a subordinate position in negotiation about family matters, political activity and so on. The inferior positions of women in political structures affect the ability to challenge the subordination of women on all its manifestations.

Women's participation in politics is closely related to their marriage, family and employment. An important obstacle for their full participation in politics is the social attitudes that give importance to the domesticity of women. Another important deterrent factor is the prevailing political culture. The atmosphere of growing violence, character assassination and the ridiculous struggle for power also affects very badly the active participation of women in politics.

There can be no democracy and true people's participation in governance. The development without equal participation of women and men at different levels of decision-making are obvious in the society. The political participation of women may change the world by bringing new priorities and perspectives on the political process. If women are to be politically empowered, the immediate imperative is to resort different forms of affirmative action so that their voices are heard. If women are to be persons in their own right, they must be in control of their own bodies and suitably empowered.

METHODOLOGY

A prerequisite to empowerment necessitates stepping outside the home and participating in some form of collective undertaking. It can be successful in developing a sense of dependence and competence among the women. The creation of small important cohesive group members may identify closely. Because of face-to-face and voluntary nature of the association, many members gain valuable experience and confidence in both the leaderships and their tasks in the group. The activity should be designed so that its process and its goal attainment foster the development of a sense of self-esteem, competence and autonomy. Many work outside the home in urban areas to support their families. This kind of accessing income improves their authority in home.

The conditions of women living in the rural areas are worse when compared to those women in the urban area. In India, 70 percent of women live in rural areas, especially, SC women; a vast majority of women are leading a deplorable life. The SC women constitute the most depressed section of society in the Indian social structure. The Government of India has constitutionally reiterated its commitment to the development of Scheduled Caste. But, within the SC community itself, women have been placed in the lowest row of its hierarchal ladder. The present study analyses the political empowerment of the SC women after the implementation of democratic decentralization. On the basis of the objectives, the researcher has formulated a hypothesis that decentralization process may pave the way for the political and economic empowerment of SC women.

Thus, the SC women in Kerala formed the universe of the study. Since there are many divisions in Dalit community, it was decided to include in the population only from the Scheduled Caste women the sample areas selected for the study. The unit of the study is the Scheduled Caste women in Kerala participating in any of the developmental programmes of PRIs such as SHGs, Gramasabha and NHGs.

The field of the study was Palakkad and Thiruvananthapuram districts in Kerala. Samples of 300 SC women were selected for the purpose of the study. Multistage random sampling and purposive sampling were used for the study. Multistage sampling in 4 stages was used for the selection of wards.

PROFILE OF THE RESPONDENTS

The Scheduled Castes women constitute the downtrodden categories in our society. These women struggle a lot so that they do not lead their life in a good way. Their opportunities were often poor. These SC women live in thatched houses (huts) in congested manner. They work hard to earn and live. The SC women have to depend on their husband. Most of the husbands are drunkards and never give any money to their wives. These affected women play a dual role to feed their children, educate them and to provide them safety and security. These women never take care of their health and they are more eager to look after their kids and husbands' health.

The normal upbringing of a girl in the rural society is directed towards marriage as soon as she reaches maturity. This implies the early takeover of family responsibility. Women in the rural household were counted upon no less to contribute an additional helping hand both at home and at the land. Their formal education is not considered to be important.

Circumstances were that women had to toil all day long that she was not able to know what is happening in and around her. She leads a very prejudistic life. Not busy aware of anything in this world, she is not able to participate or avail any programmes that are implemented for her welfare. The interview was conducted with 300 respondents. Out of 300, 31% came under the age groups of 26-33; 27.3 per cent came under the age group of 34-41, 25.3 percent of the respondents belonged to the age group of 42 and above and the remaining 16.3 per cent of respondents belonged to the age category of 18-25.

These respondents were classified with reference to their attainment of education. 59.7% attained their education only up to primary level. 56 respondents (18.7%) were illiterate, 44 respondents had education up to pre-degree and 21 respondents (7%) were graduates. In this study, 271 respondents were married. Four per cent were unmarried, their husbands deserted nine respondents and eight respondents were divorced. This variable is not significant because 271 respondents were married. This happens because the SC women were married in their tender age itself. 130 (45%) respondents got married at the age of 18-21, 111 (38.5%) were married at the age of 22 and above and the remaining 47 women (16.3%) were married below 18 years.

The economic status of the SC women respondents were considered in the study. The respondents in the study were identified with the ration card, which they have. However, this process exploited the respondents. The ration card divides the people's economic status as Above Poverty Line (APL) and Below Poverty Line (BPL). 165 respondents (55%) were BPL and 131 respondents (43.7%) were APL. But many of the respondents were wrongly included in the APL category. The political parties known by different names exploited them. The remaining four respondents out of 300 did not even possess ration cards. This fact was further analysed with the significant independent variables as follows.

CONSTITUTIONAL MEASURES

The Constitution of India guarantees gender equality before law. Equal protection of law prohibits discrimination on the ground of sex according to Article 14. Article 23 and Article 42 have made provisions to provide for just and humane conditions of work along with maternity relief. Article 51A considers it as the constitutional duty of every citizen to renounce practices derogatory to the dignity of women. The 73rd Amendment passed by the Parliament in 1994 provides one-third reservation of seats for women at the local government level. It is a significant achievement in the empowerment of women. Around one million women have come as decision-makers at the Panchayat levels. The 81st Amendment regarding 33% reservations of seats for women in Parliament and Assemblies has been pending. It remains as a mirage in spite of the commitment affirmed by all political parties towards women's empowerment (Lekshmi, S. 2004).

The political empowerment of women is one of the most important aspects in the overall empowerment of women, because it gives women the capacity to influence the decision-making process. Women occupy a marginalized position in society because of several socio-economic constraints. This inhibited the effective participation of women in political processes and in the institutional structure of demography. Even after the five decades of the grant of political equality, statistics has revealed the fact. There is an acceptable visible manifestation of gender equality at the voter level. Gender visibility within the power structure causes for women concern. According to the document on Women's Development (1985), women's role in political structure has virtually remained unchanged, despite the rapid growth of informal political activity by them. In general, the women candidates have to cross two hurdles before they could aspire to enter the formal political structures: (a) they should be party electorate which is the 'gatekeeper' of power, and (b) they have to be voter-friendly. Besides, in the wide-ranging political participation, women's position has been severely limited due to the nexus of traditional status. Further, the political parties do not favour the nomination of women candidates, as they are not sure of their success. Although political parties do have a Women's Wing, a few women have access to the inner ring of the party. It is the core of the power structure. Majority of the women are illiterate, not politically conscious. Due to lack of information and political awareness, they make their choice based on suggestions from male members of the family. As a result, women were left on the periphery of political process.

However, with the Panchayat Raj Institutions getting constitutional status by the 73rd Amendment Act, it is hoped that the women will have better participation in the political process and decision-making capacity as the Act made the role mandatory and universal in India. Even today most of the women are uneducated. They have little or no property. They live in a tradition bound society. In such a case, the politicians can make them contest in elections for their own political gains. Another problem is that women, especially in rural areas, would not come forward to fight the elections. However, it is necessary that a breakthrough has to be made.

Gender, as a political ideology, views women as basically different from men psychologically, physiologically and often intellectually. Women's perception of life is like a wave and men's perception is that of ladder. Women stress more on attachment, affiliation, empathy and inter-dependence. Men emphasize on competition, independence, separation and formal rights.

Gender empowerment strategies under the circumstances require structural systematic change and basic attitudinal and value change. The real empowerment of women requires a thoroughgoing renewal of the political process on a democratic basis. Unless women are equipped with the necessary skill in political decision-making, their increased representation in the local bodies may not alter the existing set-up. It is necessary to sensitize the women in the women's perceptive, not in the narrow feminist sense. In the sense of honourable co-existence with men enable women to exercise their will and advance to their complete emancipation.

There is a need to extend greater affirmative action from the Panchayat level to the State and National level. The political consciousness should be raised. It should support the actions of women's organizations at the voter level to enhance self-potency and political efficacy. If these measures are followed, political participation of women will open up new vistas of development. Then it will automatically result in the real political empowerment of women in the society (Krishna, B., 2006).

Many sample respondents have highlighted the general difficulties in active participation. The factors that inhibit the participation in general are the backwardness of people, unwillingness to participate, absence of committed work, political interference, easy availability of funds, rigidity in programmes, etc. The obstacles to constructive participations are absence of organisation for the poor, limited access to technology, lack of local leadership, feudal agrarian structure, hierarchal social relationships, etc. Wolf, M. (1983) says that class composition of the society and conflict in the under-privileged group are against participation.

ATTITUDE TOWARDS POLITICAL ACTIVITIES

Empowerment of women in a process enables individuals and groups to realise their full identity and power in all shapes of their life. This process provides opportunities for greater access to knowledge, skills and resources. Women participate in the SHGs/NHGs/Gramasabha and that will definitely bring changes in their attitudes towards political activities. Their participation enables them interact PRIs sponsored programmes and such interaction certainly brings changes in their attitudes. The informants were asked about their level of attitudes towards the political activity before and after the participation in the development programmes through PRIs. Equally half of the respondents (50%) mentioned that their level of attitude remained the same. More than one-third of the respondents (34.3%) revealed that their level of attitude towards political activities increased to some extent. 8.7 per cent said that their level of attitude increased to greater extent. 5.7 per cent mentioned that their attitude decreased to some extent and remaining 1.3 per cent did the same. This factor was further analysed with the significant independent variables as follows.

TABLE I

Age and Attitude Towards Political Activities

Age	*Attitude towards political activities*					*Total*
	Increased to great extent (%)	*Increased to some extent (%)*	*Decreased to great extent (%)*	*Decreased to some extent (%)*	*Remained the same (%)*	
(1)	*(2)*	*(3)*	*(4)*	*(5)*	*(6)*	*(7)*
18-25	2 (4.1)	18 (36.7)	—	7 (14.3)	22 (44.9)	49
26-33	6 (6.5)	28 (30.1)	—	1 (1.1)	58 (62.4)	93
34-41	8 (9.8)	22 (26.8)	2 (2.4)	4 (4.9)	46 (56.1)	82
42 above	10 (13.2)	35 (46.1)	2 (2.6)	5 (6.6)	24 (31.6)	76
Total	26 (8.7)	103 (34.3)	4 (1.3)	17 (5.7)	150 (50)	300

** Significant at 1% level ($p<0.01$) $\chi 2 = 31.105$, df = 12, p-value = 0.002.

The highest percentage (62.4%) of women remains same without participating in political activities with respect to their age groups. Strong explanation for SC women's limited participation is related with the theory of women's backward consciousness. Another significant deterrent factor prevails in the political culture. Further, the atmosphere of growing violence, character assassination and unscrupulous struggles for power, have been a serious deterrent to SC women's participation in effective manner. Another important factor, which keeps women, away from active participation in politics, is its demanding nature. Age of the sample respondents acts as a bar in their political participation, because the male-dominated society never gives any security to the virginity of the SC women.

Education is one of the key that opens the door to women empowerment. Education not only widens mental horizons of the individual, but also helps a person to make use of rational and scientific approach to deal with life's situation. Education plays an important role in bringing about the changes in an individual like level of awareness, knowledge, perception, etc. When the level of education increases the level of individual's attitude may be increased. Devaki, J. (1996) found that usually the young women of 25-45 years of age, 20 per cent of the women had previous political experience. The pattern caste representation was the same as before the constitutional change. 60 per cent of the elected representatives whether men or women were from dominant caste.

ACCESS TO APPROACH POLITICAL LEADERS

Empowerment will increase individual's knowledge, competency, skills, resources and opportunities. They all enable more effective action and inter-personal relations. The women who are empowered become more human in the fullest sense of the world and such sense would enable them to get rid of all the hesitation, and fear to meet other persons, including political leaders. The respondents were asked about their level of meeting with political leaders before and after participation in the development programmes through PRIs. Nearly three-fifth of the respondents (56.7%) indicated that they met the political representatives for various purposes often. Nearly one-third of the respondents (30%) mentioned that they never met the political leaders and remaining 13 percent of the respondents revealed that they met the political leaders very often for various purposes. The above-mentioned factor was further analysed with the significant independent variables as follows.

The graduates (66.7%) very often met the political leaders to get things done, while the less educated very often fail to do so. Education gives them confidence to meet people, express their views and ideas, share their problems with the party members and take advantage of the policies and programs. The less educated are very much reluctant to meet the political leaders due to their low self-esteem. The sample informants' with their education in relation to meet their representatives comes descending from the illiterates.

The family type in which women happens to live is one of the fundamental aspects of women's status in society. The family is the key of social institution, which gives initiation to empowerment. Members of joint family may get more opportunity and time to meet the political leaders, since their household responsibilities are taken care of other members in the family also.

PARTICIPATION IN POLITICAL CAMPAIGNS

Empowerment of women is a holistic concept. It is a multi-dimensional in its approach and covers social, political and economic aspects of all these facts women's development. Whenever all these developments take place among the women, they become persons with dynamic personality and such personality certainly brings changes in the political attitudes. Subsequently, these changes definitely enable them to participate in the political campaigns. The vital purpose of the participatory process is the awakening of women Panchayat Members' dormant energies and unleashing of their creative powers. The process of conscientisation, or the emerging awareness of one's previously stifled creativities, should also be an objective in women's political participation. Conscientisation leads to self-organization as means of undertaking initiatives (Santhosh, N., 2003).

The respondents were asked about their participation in political campaigns. Nearly half of the respondents (46.71%) indicated that they participated in political campaigns often; more than one-third of the respondents (34.7%) mentioned that they never participated in the political campaigns and the remaining respondents (18.7%) revealed that they very often participated in political campaigns. This factor was further studied with the significant independent variables.

Social transformation through political campaigns in the political scenario was originally initiated by the PRIs. Participation of disadvantaged groups in local political campaigns is now considered a good development practice. Even though there are enormous structural constraints to the participation of women, education leads women in a proper channel to involve in local political campaigns. As the declining levels of participation in Gramasabhas indicate, the campaigns has moved beyond its mobilisation phone and now depends more on the commitment of active citizen, local politicians and local officials (Patrick, H., Harilal, K.N and Chaudhuri, S., 2007).

As literacy level increases, the participation in the political campaign also increases. When 61.9 per cent of the graduates participated in political campaigns and only 12.5 per cent of the illiterates did so. Women, particularly the SC women were confined within the four walls of their houses. NHGs, SHGs and Gramasabhas have played a major role to bring these women to the forefront. Education has also helped these women to change their outlook and participate in political campaigns what the senior generation never dreamt-off.

Most recent studies on the status of women tend to decry the low status of women measured among other factors by low figures in progress of education. Participation at the progressive change observed in the education level rural locality of SC women is within the space of generations.

WOMEN RESERVATION BILL

Reservation bill is a strategy, which aims at the welfare of the weaker section of the society like SCs, STs, OBCs, Minorities, Physically challenged and women. Even though there is a reservation quota for SCs, STs, OBCs, Minorities, physically challenged, there is no separate reservation for women. In each Parliament session, this issue was debated at various levels but no decision has so far been taken. Therefore, in the present study, the respondents were asked about their opinion on Women Reservation Bill. 51 per cent of the respondents mentioned that it was very good if it was introduced the same in India. 39 per cent of the respondents have no idea about such an issue and remaining 10 per cent of the respondents indicated that the Women Reservation Bill was not useful for women. This fact was further analysed with the significant independent variables.

TABLE 2
Descriptive Statistics of Political Empowerment by Age Group of Scheduled Caste Women

Age	*N*	*Mean*	*SD*
18-25	49	30.6939	8.27447
26-33	93	28.2796	8.56734
34-41	82	31.6585	9.77563
above 42	76	27.8947	8.13647

Table 2 clearly states that the political empowerment by age group of SC women are majority in the age group of 34-41 (Mean = 31.65, SD = 9.77), followed by the age group of 18-25 (Mean = 30.69, SD = 8.27). The lowest level of political empowerment of SC women was above 42 (Mean = 27.89, SD = 8.13).

For testing statistical significance of the mean differences, ANOVA was carried out. See ANOVA Table 3.

From the ANOVA table, the frequency ratio obtained is 3.411 which show that there is a statistically significant mean difference at 1% level. ($p<0.01$).

TABLE 3

Result of ANOVA by Age Group of Scheduled Caste Women and their Political Empowerment

Source of variation	*Sum of squares*	*df*	*Mean Squares*	*F*	*p-value*
Between Group	786.264	3	262.08	3.411**	.018
Within Group	22744.736	296	76.840		
Total	23531.000	299			

**Significant at 1% level.

CONCLUSION

Political empowerment of women is necessary as there can be no democracy, no true people's participation in governance and development without equal participation of women and men at different levels of decision-making. In this context, the PRI is acting as an effective opportunity structure for empowering the SC women politically. The attitude towards political activities remained as same for half of the respondents (50%) and for 34.3 per cent of them. It increased favourably to some extent. The cross-table analysis further showed that the variables such as age, education, occupation and monthly income had a statistically significant association with the dependant variable change in attitude towards political activities. Among the various categories of these variables, the positive attitude towards politics was found more among the elderly, educated, and employed and highly income categories.

The participation in various developmental programmes creates an opportunity to meet political leaders of various standings. More than half of the respondents (56.7%) often met political leaders for various purposes and a significant proportion of (30%) never met any political leader for any purpose. The cross-table analysis showed that the prevalence of meeting with political leaders was found to be higher among the graduates, nuclear family respondents. The respondents' level of participation in political campaigns is further analysed. About half of the respondents (46.7%) often participated in the political campaigns and 34.7 percent of them 'never'. The cross-tabular analysis further showed that the independent variables such as education, family type, occupation and income found to have statistically significant association.

In order to assess the level of political consciousness of the SC women respondents, they were asked about their opinion about women's reservation. About half of the respondents it is very good for women and further 39 percent of them had no idea about it. Further analysis showed that the variables such as age, education, occupation and income were found to have statically significant association with the opinion about women's reservation bill.

References

Lakshmi, Seetha V. (2004), Womens and Political Empowerment, Kerala Sociologist, *Journal of the Kerala Sociological Society*, Vol. XXXII, No. 1, June.

Wolf, M. (1983), Wolfe, Marshall, Participation, The View from Above, UNRISD Dialogue about Participation, No. 3, September, 1983.

Devaki, J. (1996), Panchayat Raj : Women Changing Governance September, Working Paper 368, Centre for Development Studies: Thiruvanathapuram.

(Santhosh, N. (2003), Santhosh Nandal, *Journal of International Women's Studies*, Vol. 5, Nov. 2003.

Patrick Heller, K.N. Harilal and Shubham Chaudhuri (2007), Building local Democracy, Evaluating the impact of Decentralization in Kerala, *India Journal of World Development*, Vol. 35, No. 4.

Parpart, L. Jane, Rai, M. Shirin and Staudt, Kathleen (2002), Rethinking Empowerment, Gender and Development in a Global/Local World, London : Routledge.

Panchayat Level Statistics (2006), Government of Kerala, Department of Economics and Statistics, Thiruvananthapuram.

Planning at the Grassroots Level—An Action Programme for the Eleventh Five Year Plan, Ministry of Panchayati Raj, Government of India, New Delhi.

Report of the Working Group on Empowerment of Women—for the 11th Plan, Ministry of Women and Child Development, Government of India, 2006.

15

Social Legislations and Women Empowerment

P. Ganesan and K. Suriyan

INTRODUCTION

Woman plays dynamic roles in the society as mother, wife, sister, daughter, teacher, public servant, political leader, etc. and contributes for national development. But women are not given due respect by men in all sphere of life in the society and their position is pathetic in nature. In the civilized and well structured society the women are considered as subservient to men through the patriarchal, patrilocal and patrilinial form of marriages which warrants that daughter has to depend upon her husband and mother upon her son in social and economic spheres and responsibilities for well-being. To accelerate overall growth and prosperity of the nation it is very important to create opportunities for socio-economic development of women in India as they constitute half of the population and play a vital role in development of the family and society. (Suguna, 2006) especially rural women constitute about 73 per cent of the total Indian women population.

Both Central and State Governments have been taking steps to empower women by making them to use their own rights and freedom to develop themselves in strict implementation/practice of constitutional rights. But in reality they are handicapped due to their illiteracy, ignorance, stigmatized avoidance in the form of culture, values, etc. The authors analyzed the reality prevalence in the contemporary society in respect of prevention, protection, and development of the women with the help of secondary sources of data, which are covered in the following chapter. Perhaps, education and employment of women is on the increase in the transitional modern society, irrespective of education, status and position most of the women are not in a position to get empowered fully due to various drawbacks. At this juncture they must know their rights and it can be related for their empowerment. Both right and empowerment are inter-related, the right is the legal aspect of empowerment and the empowerment is the social aspect of the right. Right can be practiced by an individual with the approval of the society and strict implementation by the government. Empowerment is achieved by an individual through demand, approval and grant. Right is associated with duties and enforcement. But the empowerment is not like right; it depends upon the individual's initiative, acceptance of the society and vigilance by the government institutions. Mere grant of provisions is not enough but proper utilization and enforcement of rights only can improve women empowerment, which subsequently improves women status and position and contributes for national development gender inequality in India stems from two important sources between men and women, i.e (i) earning capacity that make women utterly dependant upon men, (ii) cultural taboos and traditions that greatly restrict the autonomy of women. But women have some drawbacks such as : (i) organized sector, (ii) unorganized sector, and (iii) domestic activities.

ORGANIZED SECTORS

Though women are recognized and given equal employment opportunity and payment in this sector based on education and potentials, but they are not accepted as equal as by male boss or colleagues. When women work under male boss they have to ask some help under certain circumstances when they are aloof. It is very common among police personnel. In the case of women police they are facing so many problems in the office such as, ill-treatment, teasing, mental agony, denial of rights, molestation some kind of violence against women, sexual harassment, etc. Most of the affected women hesitate to knock the doors of the legal institutions considering the difficulty of getting support from the family, neighborhood and political institutions. In the process of enforcement of women rights there is no good precedents in our country. For example, young girl like Ruchica of Haryana, tennis player and her family faced many hardships when making war against tennis coach and former DGP of Police for sexual harassment and finally unable to face his tortures she committed suicide during the legal process of getting justice. The other reasons for non-readiness to avail and enforce women welfare legislations are familial responsibility, stress and mental agony, unawareness, fear of action by higher authority, complicated legal process, corruption, criminalization of administration, etc.

UNORGANIZED SECTORS

Most of the illiterate women both in rural as well as in urban areas involved in unorganized works. They do their works chosen by themselves and invest according to their conveniences. Perhaps, they are unprotected due to the prevailing social system. Their inability may be either socially or economically or biologically or both. On the other the awareness, caste dominance, social stigma that women are inferior to men, and other socio-economic and political factors.

Domestic

In the family where woman is supposed to enjoy freedom

sometimes family becomes a hell for her and faces so many troubles. Woman spends more time in the family with parents, brothers, sisters, in-laws, husband and other relatives. She is given stress, strain, verbal and physical or sexual abuse by her near kith and kin. Denial of equality, freedom, property rights, marital, abortion, and other rights are denied in the modern societies. Though constitutional and other legal provisions are available for a woman against her family members she is not dare to go for legal actions against her blood relations. She is accustomed to adjust all the problems in the family because of ignorance, economic dependence, obligation to maintain good relations, lack of capacity to fight, expensive and complicated legal process, distance residence, legal inadequacy and other socio-cultural reasons.

Protection

As far as protection is concerned that in the preamble of constitution of India speaks of securing all citizens in equality of status and opportunity, social justice and political participation. It is guaranteed that the state shall not make discrimination on the ground of sex.

CONSTITUTIONAL PROVISIONS

Indian constitution provides certain provisions for women empowerment. They are as follows: (i) Right to equality, i.e., equality of opportunity, equality before law, equal protection of law, no discrimination on ground of sex and no discrimination in public employment, (ii) Right to freedom, i.e., freedom of speech, expression, residence, occupation and mobility, (iii) Right against exploitation, i.e., against forced labour, (iv) Right to freedom of religion, i.e., professing, practicing and propagating religion freely, (v) Cultural rights i.e. Conserving one's own culture and seeking admission to educational institutions, and (vi) Right to constitutional remedy.

Social

(i) monogamous marriage and divorce, i.e., a Hindu woman can compel her husband not to marry again and she can get divorce on certain grounds when he is continuously giving problems to her,

(ii) right against child marriage (the Child Marriage Restraint Act, 1976) i.e., a woman minor girl can enforce her right not to give her in marriage against her will,

(iii) age at marriage, i.e a minor girl should not be give in marriage,

(iv) mate selection, i.e right to choose life partner,

(v) right against dowry (the Dowry Prohibition Act, 1987),

(vi) abortion rights up to 1970 any type of abortion was made as offence but now rape or failure of contraceptive devices, or certain other reasons a qualified doctor can make abortion within 12 weeks of pregnancy. However, she should not be compelled to abort her child on any other reason (the Medical Termination of Pregnancy Act, 1976),

(vii) right of remarriage,

(viii) right to custody of child,

(ix) national commission for women protection, i.e. any woman can approach the commission to enforce her legal right and this commission works for women empowerment, and

(x) right against teasing and ragging.

Economic

(i) Property Rights

(a) Equal share from husband's property.

(b) Equal share from father's property (The Hindu Succession Act, 1956).

(ii) Employment Rights and Social Security

(a) Maternity rights—labour legislations and social security laws such as Maternity Benefit Act 1961, the Factories Act, 1948, Employees State Insurance Act, 1948.

(b) equal wages, bonus and other labour protections.
(c) working conditions such as hours of working, no work between 10 am and 5 am, leave and rest and other so many legal rights are available for women in Indian society.

Political

(i) female enfranchisement—which was denied till 1917.
(ii) reservation of seats in elections, especially local self-government.

Realities: When freedom was obtained from British regime Indian society faced certain challenges like communal riots, partition of Pakistan, political instability, population growth, economic problems, etc. Mere enactments were not enough to empower the women in all aspects of their social life. All social institutions were facing barriers for planning and development. The development programs were not reached to the women due to various reasons. Orthodox and traditional bound beliefs and practices cannot be stuffed overnight (Ram Ahuja, 1997, p. 109)

Loopholes: However, constitutional rights and other legal rights are made for women we do not have sufficient legislations for environment, old age protection, human rights, etc. As far as property rights it is not similar among states. In almost all the welfare and development programs inadequacies, lack of awareness, corruption, and other drawbacks are common. Till now we have been rectifying the irregularities and loopholes in the implementation of welfare schemes. The procedures and technicalities of implementing the laws and welfare schemes are not fully clear both on the part of the implementing authorities and beneficiaries. Therefore, the true objectives of the government are not carried out, so that the expected level of development of women is not reached.

Necessities: Education and training of women is the predominant need. Economic and social empowerment can be achieved through education. Compulsory education is provided to the children from 6 to 14 years of age. But in certain states it is not fully implemented. At this stage it becomes necessary that beneficiaries should keep an eye on different programmes so that they are implemented in true spirit. Government should check that the benefits of the programs reach only to deserving beneficiaries. The issues concerning women should not be discussed separately without having direct link with the overall development while planning programs for their development, woman, rather, than family should remain the basic unit while formulating policies and programs for their development. If the basic education is given for women most of the women problems will be solved. Awareness of awareness available rights is needed for women, especially; the illiterate women should be educated by women organizations, NGOs, etc. through group activities and mass media.

DEVELOPMENT STRATEGIES AVAILABLE

Government Policies and planning: Government is helping women in every sphere of life in the society. The first step by the government to strengthen the national mechanism and focus on women's development was the setting of an exclusive department of women and child development under the ministry of human resources development in 1985 and designating the same as the national machinery for the advancement of women in India. Joint committee of parliament on empowerment of women has been set-up with the functions of examining measures for women's equality and considering the reports of national commission for women

The national policy for women development (2001) has been drafted after nation-wide consultations to enforce the status of women in all walks of life on par with men and to actualize the constitutional guarantee of equality without discrimination on ground of sex. The goal of the policy is to bring about the advancement, development, and empowerment of women, enjoyment of all human rights and fundamental duties, equal access to participation and decision-making, health care, equality, education, employment, elimination of all forms of discrimination against women, changing social attitude and building and strengthening partnership with civil society particularly women's organization. National Commission for Women is functioning for helping and improving the socio-economic conditions of women.

National Commission on self-employed women and women in informal sector (1988) examines the entire gamut of issues facing women in organized sector and makes a number recommendations for the betterment of women in the informal sector relating to employment, occupational hazards, legislative protection, training and skill development, entrepreneurship development, marketing and credit, etc. The other programs are Swarna Jayanthi Gram Swarozger Yojana; a holistic self-employment for women (1999), Jawahar Gram Samridhi Yojana, wage employment 30 per cent reserved for women, Indira Awas Yojana, National Social Assistance Programme, Central Rural Sanitation Programme, Accelerated Rural Water Supply Programme (Pankajam, 2005.)

Non-Governmental Organization: The self-help groups is an exclusive organization of women as direct stakeholders and also democratically organized and managed. Women have valuable stakes in the SHG which promoted (or) voluntarily organized in the community. Such common stake in the group significantly has an effect on their effective participation and also decision-making of their groups.

STRATEGIES TO OVERCOME

Four important aspects are to ensure to overcome the problems and empower women : (a) Inter-spouse consultation, which is necessary to know to what extent husband discuss household affairs, (b) Individual autonomy which represents women's self-reported freedom of physical movement outside the house in matters of spending money, (c) the authority which reports on actual decision-making power which is traditionally in the hands of male member of the family, and (d) changes in women's mobility and interaction. Economic empowerment is necessary for these four aspects of women's life. Economically woman is self-reliant or supportive to her family all other aspects of life she will be empowered. Education and creation of awareness is necessary then only woman is able to improve economic empowerment.

STRATEGIES NEEDED

Women are superstitious, suppressed and oppressed because of their limited skills. They should be trained, educated and organized so that they are empowered to be equal with men.

Social: Promotion of organizations among women, co-operatives, mahila mandals, SHGs, thrift groups poverty alleviation and eliminate drudgery in their day-to-day activities. Women should break the barriers of traditional house keeping, serving the family, non-availing of matrimonial and property rights. They should turn to participate in the main stream of national development through education, awareness, earning, political participation, etc..

Economic: They cease to be only consumers of economic goods and services to turn to producers. Thus, participate in social reproduction and associate as reproduction of labour for the next generation, (Devadoss, 1999). Women's participation in labour force also bring about change in awareness and attitude which may have long-term benefits such as, assess to health and education, reduction in birth rates, thrift and savings, etc. Self-employment of women should be improved by modifying the existing schemes and proper implementation.

Political or legal: A number of programs have been implemented for the betterment and upliftment of women. But they are not working satisfactorily and needs immediate attention of the Government. 33 per cent reservation in panchayat elections is not properly utilized. Most of the elected women are said to follow the foot of their husband or brother or father. This position should be changed. However, voting rights are given for all the women who attained 18 years of age. It is doubtful whether all of them exercise their rights. Even then they are voting it is questionable whether they vote according to their whims and fans. Awareness should be created to ensure that they exercise their voting voluntarily without fail. 33 per cent reservation should be properly implemented in elections. Government to set-up common activity group for their sustainable development as has been done in N.G.Os. Panchayats make appropriate plans and programs to enable them empower in all aspects of their life.

EMPOWERMENT

Empowerment is "the expansion in people's ability to make strategic life choices in a context where this ability was previously denied to them" (Kabeer, 2001). "Empowerment is a movement from power of elite to power of the people. It is a new way of seeing power" (John Joseph Puthenkalam, 2004). The process of women's empowerment is multi-dimensional. It enables women to realize their full potential and empower them in all spheres of life. Women's empowerment in fact, begins with the awareness about their rights and capabilities and understanding as to how the socio-economic and political forces affect them. Empowerment is defines as a redistribution of social power and control of resources in favour of women (Rangareddy, 2002, p. 198). Empowerment of women means enhancing awareness of individuals that can facilitate social development, politically active, and independent that enable to make their choices and appropriate decisions in matters at individual, family and community level.

Economic: If a woman is economically parasite, she can never claim an equal status with her counterpart man. The problem of poverty cannot be in a way tackled without providing opportunities to productive employment to women. Women are not allowed to participate in the decision-making process because they are economically not independent.

Educational: Nearly 53 per cent of Indian women are illiterate (2001, census). Education is important for women for women empowerment, but if education is increased other aspects of life will be improved. Government provides compulsory education to the children for 6 to 14 years of age. But previously women education was optional of the parents or male members of the family. Male children were preferred to send to school, especially for higher education. Girls were made to shoulder household works or field work. Traditional male dominant society has been changing now-a-days through women welfare legislations. Women literacy rate should be increased. Education empowerment can improve economic and political empowerment.

Political: Women's political participation has been considered as a symbol of women's empowerment. It is important to know the number of women in Parliament, Judiciary or Local Bodies. The women should come forward voluntarily to contest in election by availing 33 per cent reservation. It is criticized that the elected representatives in local bodies are not allowed to act freely by their male relatives. It is not real political empowerment. A woman should be able to perform her duties in administration. 33 per cent reservation is given on paper but not in practice. Women's stigmatized values is also a reason for this drawbacks. It should be changed to give real empowerment for women. Indian cultural traditions do not allow a girl to participate in politics with men. This kind of attitude should be changed.

CONCLUSION

The valuable legal rights for women empowerment are not availed and enforced by the women. The democratic political system has created a myth that women get equality, freedom, and justice. But all these are seen on paper only not in actual practice. Government has been taking steps to empower the women by providing all the required legal protection. Educational values and employment opportunities can make women to aware of their rights. "Better practice of women rights seem to women empowerment". Women's participation in income generating activities is believed to increase their status and decision-making power with empowerment. Women do not remain as objects of social chance but becomes agents of it.

SUGGESTIONS

The following suggestions are given to effective use of legal rights for women empowerment: (i) Integrated approach by government and NGOs to create awareness among the women, (ii) Value education and capacity building through training, (iii) Establishment of women commission in micro-levels and counter against government officers, who act against women's interest, and (iv) Women organizations and associations should be encouraged to set-up their branches in rural areas and report familial violence to legal institutions, and (v) Self-defense methods must be given in schools and colleges.

Despite Government and NGOs implement various schemes to create awareness among rural mass, women scarcely avail their legal rights. They have to consider even then they got education and awareness their socio-economic and cultural backgrounds before they demand for empowerment.

References

Suguna, B., (2006), *Empowering Rural India: Experiments and Experience.* Edit: Venkata Ravi, New Delhi: Krishna Publishers.

Ranga, Reddy A., *Women Development through Ecology is a New Paradigm,* Edit : Sunderraj, D., New Delhi: Serials Publications.

Rajammal, P. Devadoss (1999), *Empowerment of Women through Self-Help Groups: An Indian Experience in Empowering Women a Key to Third World Development,* Edit : Samanta, R.K., New Delhi, M.D. Publishers.

PART III

SOCIO-ECONOMIC EMPOWERMENT

16

Women Entrepreneurs
A Pathway to Women Empowerment

U.K. Teke and S.B. Sanap

INTRODUCTION TO WOMEN ENTREPRENEUR

"Women in Business" is considered a recent phenomenon in India. The fact that almost half the population of this large country comprises of females while businesses owned and operated by them constitute less than 5 percent, is a reflection on social, cultural as well as economic distortions in the decades of development. As education has spread and compulsions for earnings have grown, more and more women have started to go out of the homes and opt either for wage employment or self-employment/entrepreneurial carrier.

Women and men as equal members of the society have the right to the equality of opportunities and treatment. The right to support one and to contribute to the economic well being of one's family is as important for women as men. In fact, majority of women want and need to work and their income earning capacity is essential for their own survival and that of their families.

PROBLEMS FACED BY WOMEN ENTREPRENEUR AND SUGGESTIONS TO THEM

Life for a women entrepreneur is not a bed of roses. The individual women entrepreneur single-handedly faces a plethora of seemingly endless problems. In fact from the moment an entrepreneur conceives the idea to start her own unit she has to work hard against heavy odds. The problems of women entrepreneur whether is small, medium or large business are almost similar but their nature and scope vary.

In this section we deals with problems and constraints faced by women entrepreneur from the starting and managing their respective enterprises suggestions for overcoming these problems also discussed. This can help to new women entrepreneur who try to catch new business opportunity which problems before them and how can remove these problems.

The problems have been categorized into seven main heads as under :

(1) Socio personal problems
(2) Marketing problems
(3) Occupational Mobility problems
(4) Government assistance Problems
(5) Financial Problems
(6) Production Problems
(7) Personnel Problems

1. Socio-Personal Problems

Women especially in our country, face certain problems, which are different from their male counterparts, in the course starting and managing their own business. The management of domestic commitments and child care support are the two issues where women have to play a greater role.

This Socio-personal problem are under:

- Resistance from husband or other family members at the time of starting business.
- Women feel stress while discharging the dual duties of as entrepreneur and as house wife.
- Indifferent attitude of the society towards them because society has yet to accept women in their new role as entrepreneur.
- Non co-operation by their family members as one of the obstacles in successful running of business.
- Backbiting by other people. People jealous of successful women entrepreneur and always try to mentally upset.
- Male dominance, i.e. typical male ego of their husbands come in the way of their successful operation.
- The limited liberty given to women as a result they are not able to take their venture to the height.
- Lack of experience and self-confidence, odd hours of work, etc.

Suggested Solutions

- Overcoming of initial resistance from husband and family members the prospective women entrepreneurs are advised to maintain herself cool and keep on convincing them in a positive way regarding the usefulness of setting up enterprises.
- For effective discharge of dual duties of an entrepreneur and housewife a women entrepreneur can resort to better time management keep balance between two fronts setting up home-based business.
- To raise their standard in society they must work very hard and should prove that they are as par with men folks. Women must acquire more education and should become mentally strong.
- For getting co-operation from family members handle member with care and love. Avoid confronting her in laws and be better quietly keep on doing her job.

- The backbiting by other persons need to be tackled with smile, keeping silent will also prove effective weapon in this regard.
- To tide over the problem of male ego. maintain co-operative atmosphere and humility established in home or choose ambitions partner at the time of marriage.
- Problem of limited liberty can be tide over by soliciting co-operation from family members.

2. Marketing Problems

Marketing is another area which very often proves to be the graveyard of many small scale entrepreneurs. It has been seen that the small scale entrepreneurs, owing to their high achievement orientation, generally set higher goals in terms of marketing of their products/services, but latter on find them difficult to achieve because of heavy competition and many other factors as under :

- Cut throat competition in the market.
- Lack of information on changing markets.
- Indifferent attitude of customers.
- Non-proactive attitude of entrepreneur.
- Availability of spurious products.
- Lack of travelling mobility on account of purchase and sale.
- Problem in collection of payment.
- Inadequate publicity due to meagre financial resources.

Suggested Solutions

- As regards marketing of products it is suggested that the women entrepreneur must establish her credibility first in terms of quality and competitiveness of product.
- She should acquire relevant techniques and skills on winning the customer's loyalty. Personal contacts could also be established with people. For this, help of family members can be taken.

- There should be an effective check on spurious goods available in the market.
- The problem of travelling can be solved by taking the help of husband or other family members. E-commerce businesses will also help greatly in this regard.
- The problem of collection of payments can be solved by discounting the bills arising out of the transaction. For this utilize the scheme of SIDBI which directly discounts the bills.
- For cheaper publicity use local TV Cable Network, pamphlets, slides in cinema theatres, putting banners in public location, proper use of information technology.

3. Problem of Occupational Mobility

Occupational mobility, i.e. shifting from one product line to another is an area where women entrepreneurs are generally found to be more disadvantageous position than their male counterparts.

- Preference for stability/security orientation as the prime reason which inhibit women entrepreneurs from exhibiting occupational mobility.
- Multiple duties towards home.
- Lack of resources for turn to another area.
- Lack of 'Self-confidence' amongst women as the reason which prevents them from moving on to another lucrative products,
- Lack of fully grown up business mind.
- Fear of unknown, social pressure, less patience than man, lack of technical know-how, etc.

Suggested Solutions

- Personality development and acquiring more entrepreneurial skills can help in offsetting the problem of lack of occupational mobility.
- The women entrepreneurs are advised to shed their security-oriented frame of mind and be flexible

enough to shift to more lucrative business line as and when they find one such line.

- The latest area of E-commerce probably suits women the most, they should grab this opportunity to further expand their business also.

4. Problem of Availing Government Assistance

Getting assistance from support agencies has generally been found to be not trouble free. Women entrepreneurs were found to be facing the problem of pertaining to government assistance.

- Harassment in Government Department corruption being major reason behind it.
- Large amount of paper formalities in Government Organizations.
- Unnecessary Government interference in terms of a number of inspectors visiting their premises.
- Discrimination with women entrepreneurs.
- Ignorance about various procedures, laws and complicated bureaucratic set-up of Government Department.

Suggested Solutions

- As regards the harassment of women entrepreneurs in the Government Department it is suggested that guilty should be severally punished so that it acts as a deterrent for other also. Women entrepreneurs should avoid dealing with the lower staff and directly contact with officers and adopt more practical approach instead of idealistic approach by way of using soft corner.
- Women inspectors should be asked to inspect women enterprises.
- Women entrepreneurs must work doubly hard to make their presence felt.
- They should also acquire the relevent knowledge about various procedures and laws and skill to

effectively deal with officials of support agencies.

- Workshop and seminars also arranged for the official support agencies and the women entrepreneurs with a view to make their relationship more cordial.

5. Financial Problems

Typically entrepreneurs of small scale enterprises start well but after some time they down the line in their day-to-day operations and miss the route to success reason behind it is financial mismanagement. The financial Problems are as under :

- Reluctance by financial Institutions to extend credit to women entrepreneurs.
- Inability to provide collateral security and margin money of project cost due to no property on name of women.
- Due to tight repayment schedule women entrepreneurs find difficulty to adhere to heavy repayment instalments.
- Inability to understand nitty gritty of financial management due to general educational background.

Suggested Solutions

- For arranging adequate finance free from lengthy procedural difficulties the entrepreneurs can look for non-formal sources of finance like private financiers, relatives, friends and committees, but avoid private money lenders. Contact with banks those are targeted for disbursement loans to women entrepreneurs.
- Collateral security should be dispensed away within the case of women entrepreneurs because women have no property in their name. Margin money for projects to be implemented by women entrepreneurs should not more than ten percent. Subsidy also given to women entrepreneurs at the initial stage.
- It is also suggested that the women entrepreneurs must also convince their husband/family members to unhesitatingly pour in money in their enterprises.

- Women entrepreneurs therefore also need to undergo training in various aspects of financial management to understand its finer nuances.

6. Production Problems

Production in manufacturing enterprises involves co-ordination of a number of activities. While some of these activities are in the control of entrepreneur there are others over which she has little control. Improper co-ordination on unintended delay in execution of any activity is going to cause production problems.

- Inadequate availability of proper working area (shed/plot) for running their business.
- Inadequate technical support for machinery utilization.
- High cost of technology acquisition and inability of women entrepreneurs to keep pace with latest advances in technology.
- Frequent price rise of raw material which result in increasing cost of production and decreasing profitability.

Suggested Solution

- For proper working place women entrepreneurs suggested that plots/sheds should be used reserved for deserving women entrepreneurs or women should operate their business from their own house.
- Higher cost of technology acquisition can be offset to some extent if technology is provided to women entrepreneurs at subsidized charges by organizations like National Research Development Corporation, Research Development Laboratories, etc.
- Further it is suggested that the women entrepreneurs should keep themselves abreast with latest technology development in their field by regularly attending training programmes and reading relevent literature.

7. Personnel Problems

Efficient management of human resources is an important factor in determining the growth and prosperity of business enterprise. Number of problems faced by women entrepreneurs pertain to labour forces as under :

- Hesitation of male labour to work under lady boss.
- Retention of trained labours.
- Inability to change the negative attitude of labour force.
- Lack of experience and self-confidence to deal with male workers.

Suggested Solutions

- It is suggested that the women entrepreneurs should acquire relevant training in technology and details of their machinery so that the labour is neither able to befool them nor it becomes too indispensable for them.
- Effective incentive system should be formulated by the women entrepreneurs which may go a long way in improving the efficiency of the workers.
- For effective management, women entrepreneurs must get themselves trained in management skill.
- In order to buildup loyal, efficient and committed workforce women must pay adequate attention to hiring, training and employee development activities.

CONCLUSION

The women force of India will acquire a new dimension, if the entrepreneurial skill among the women is developed and channeled appropriately. When proper exposure and knowledge is imparted to them, Indian women will prove themselves to highly potential productive force. For strengthening the position of women in society give her proper education, proper business handling training and making the entrepreneurial environment. These solutions to problems can provide path for empowerment of women through entrepreneurship.

References

Women Entrepreneurs, Dr. S.K. Dhameja, Deep and Deep Publications Pvt. Ltd.

The New Global Order : Challenges and Opportunities to Entrepreneurship Edited by: Dr. Shaila Bootwala, Prof. Akbar Ali Sayyed, Prof. Amrut Shejwalkar, Published by Abeda Inamdar Senior College, Pune.

Entrepreneurship Development, Dr. Jasmer Singh Saini, Deep and Deep Publications Pvt. Ltd.

Grassroots Entrepreneurship, Glimpses of Self Help Groups Case Studies, N. Lalitha, Dominent Publications.

Business Entrepreneurship, By Dr. P.C. Pardeshi, Nirali Prakashan, Pune.

Women and Micro Credit, M. Laxmi Narasaiah, Saheli Publications.

Entrepreneurship Development, By E. Gorden and Natrajan, Himalaya Publications.

Women Empowerment Through Entrepreneurship

Profile, Barriers and Practical Recommendations

S. Arulkumar and C. Madhavi

INTRODUCTION

Early work on entrepreneurship (Schumpeter, 1934; Kirzner, 1973) implicitly assumed that most entrepreneurs would be men, perhaps because most business creation at that time was a male preserve. However, the situation has changed markedly, with women now owning more than 42 score points of the privately held firms in the India (WEO Report, 2010). The phenomenon of female entrepreneurship is also increasingly global, with a recent Global Entrepreneurship Monitor (GEM) study estimating that companies owned by women comprise between 25 percent and 33 percent of formal sector business around the world. These developments have led to the emergence of a large literature on female entrepreneurship, analysing for example personal attributes, access to finance and the role of social networks. While male and female entrepreneurs are similar in terms of motivation, age and education, significant differences have been identified. Of these, the most important for female entrepreneurs concern the sectors chosen for new firm creation (service and retail rather than manufacturing (Hirisch and Brush, 1984)); access to resources (some studies indicate less use of debt and greater difficulty in accumulating resources for start up (Verheul and Thurik, 2001)); and the use of less varied social networks, Brush, 2006).

The main aim of this paper is to examine women entrepreneurship development. This issue is currently very important since it is part of ongoing national efforts to alleviate poverty in developing countries in relation to the Millennium Development Goals (MDGs). Since entrepreneurship development is usually associated with some constrains and influence, this paper addresses three research questions. First, what is the importance and present growth of women entrepreneurship? Second, what are the demographic and economic factors influencing women's entrepreneurial behaviour? Third, what are the main barriers facing women to become entrepreneurs or existing women entrepreneurs to sustain or grow in the region?

METHODOLOGY

This study is based on a review of key literature and a descriptive analysis of secondary data, from government sources, International Labour Organization (ILO), World Economic Opportunity Report as well as Global Entrepreneurship Monitor and various reports and individual case studies from books, journals and e-journals on women entrepreneurs in Asian developing countries.

IMPORTANCE OF WOMEN ENTREPRENEURS

Women entrepreneurs encounters only one-third of all

entrepreneurs. And as half the population on this planet is women there is an unnatural gap between genders. There is thus potential to enhance the level of women entrepreneurs. Women entrepreneurs have a massive potential which are yet to be unleashed. Not only due to the gender gap, but also because women bring in diversity to the innovation process. Solutions to market inequalities are not solved just by male entrepreneurs with male thinking innovation. Now women also brings in solutions to market inequalities and their innovations may not be alike those of the man. Thus women entrepreneurship is to be seen as part of the diversity question.

One good example here relates to user driven innovation. Where consumer needs are the key driver for innovation. In order to produce user driven innovation the agent needs to adapt the need from the consumer. The results of that are bound to be different whereas the agents are a man or a woman and they can possibly lead to another kind of innovation. Women entrepreneurs are mainly employed in the service sector that is tourism, ICT, health, social services, etc. A common factor is the great potential of these sectors. Together with creative and new ways of thinking innovation, involving the consumer and the gender gap the potential in promoting women entrepreneurs are obvious. Women entrepreneurship receives a great deal of attention in developed countries. They conclude that among other changing mindsets, adapt policies to allow better family life and work balance by using specific instruments like tax regulation, allowances; leave provision, etc. will promote women entrepreneurship (Tulus Tambunan, 2009).

DEVELOPMENT OF WOMEN ENTREPRENEURSHIP

As in other parts of the world, women's entrepreneurship development in Asian developing countries has also a tremendous potential in empowering women and transforming society in the region. Yet in many countries, especially where the level of economic development, reflected by the level of income per capita and the degree of industrialization, is still low, this potential remains largely untapped. Sinhal (2005), for instance, observed that less than 10 percent of the entrepreneurs in South Asia, comprising Bangladesh, Bhutan, India, Maldives, Nepal, Pakistan and Sri Lanka, are women (Tulus Tambunan, 2009).

Existing literature from Asian developing countries suggest that there are three categories of women entrepreneurs, that is, "Chance", "forced" and "created" entrepreneurs. These different categories are based on how their businesses got started, or the main reasons or motivations behind starting their own businesses, Walkor (2001). Chance entrepreneurs are those who start a business without any clear goals or plans. Their businesses probably evolved from hobbies to economic enterprises over time. Forced entrepreneurs are those who were compelled by circumstances (e.g., death of a spouse, the family facing financial difficulties) to start a business, their primary motivation, hence, tend to be financial. Created entrepreneurs are those who are "located, motivated, encouraged and developed" through, for instance, entrepreneurship development programs. According to one study by Das (2007), the most common reasons given were either financial reason or to keep busy. He found that only about one-fifth of women were drawn to entrepreneurship by "pull" factors, for instance, the need for a challenge, the urge to try something on their own and to be independent and to show others that they are capable of doing well in business. It is often stated in the literature that the degree of women entrepreneurship development is closely related to the degree of gender equity, which in developing countries is generally lower than that in developed countries. Although, within the developing countries, the degree varies by country, depending on many factors, including level of economic development, reflected by the level of income per capita, and social, cultural and political factors. Gender equity has many dimensions and it is not easy to measure, due to the lack of accurate, gender discriminated social indicators in many countries, especially in the developing world.

DEMOGRAPHIC AND ECONOMIC FACTORS INFLUENCING WOMEN'S ENTREPRENEURIAL BEHAVIOUR

Research has shown that age, work status, education, income, social ties, and perceptions are all significant socio-economic factors in a person's decision to start a business. Global Entrepreneurship Monitor provides insight into the demographic, economic and perceptual characteristics of women entrepreneurs world-wide. While the relationships among these characteristics tend to be consistent around the globe, there are some differences among the developed and developing country groups.

Age

The findings from recent results reveal that patterns in entrepreneurial activity do not vary greatly from country to country with respect to age. Further, the pattern of age distribution of men and women entrepreneurs is similar and comparable regardless of country or stage of entrepreneurship. In the developing countries like India, women are most likely to be early stage entrepreneurs between the ages of 25 to 34, and to become established business owners between the ages of 35 to 44. In developed countries, the age window for women's entrepreneurial activity broadens, with early stage entrepreneurial activity most likely among women ages 25 to 44 and established business ownership most likely among women 35 to 54.

Work Status

Regardless of gender or country group, employment matters to entrepreneurial activity. The likelihood of being involved in entrepreneurial activity is three to four times higher for those who also are employed in a wage job (whether full or part time) compared to those who are not working, are retired, or are students. This suggests that working may provide access to resources, social capital, and ideas that may aid in establishing an entrepreneurial venture.

Education

While educational level typically influences individuals' opportunities for employment and thereby has the potential to indirectly impact women's entrepreneurial behaviour, the direct influence of education on women's entrepreneurial activity is complex and varies among countries. Surprisingly, in both developing and developed countries the level of educational attainment is not consistently higher for women who are established business owners than for women who are early stage entrepreneurs.

Household Income

A considerable challenge faced by all entrepreneurs globally is access to capital to start a business. Women and men in households with the highest incomes are more likely to be involved in early stage entrepreneurial activity. Considering the interactions of employment, income level, and education, some interesting results appear. For those with a household income in the lowest group, having a job makes a woman more than three times as likely to be involved in early stage entrepreneurship than if she is not employed. So it provides a valuable platform toward starting a business.

BARRIERS OF WOMEN ENTREPRENEURSHIP

1. Credit Barriers

The importance of access to credit is identified as a major barrier to entry into self-employment throughout the world. Women setting up micro-enterprises, SMEs, or formal large-scale businesses all encounter varying degrees of difficulty in obtaining capital, collateral, and fair lending terms. The banking sector has thus far shown little interest in small loans or micro-credits, given the relatively high handling costs, with the result that institutionalized banking practices remain, for the most part, rigidly opposed to micro-credit concepts because of inclined towards low risk ventures.

Women were more likely to observe that they were not given due respect by financial institutions; they did not think their account managers were easy to talk to; they reported that they were not made to feel comfortable by financial institutions; and they perceived that bank employees discriminated against women. Bankers' pessimistic view of women's creditworthiness fosters a reluctance to grant credits. This constitutes another obstacle to female entrepreneurship.

2. Technology, Education and Training

Creating educational tactics for improving technical skills

is fundamental for entrepreneurial growth. Technology, education, and training issues are tightly interwoven and can prevent women entrepreneurs from reaching their profitability potential. The training is the essential component for producing an able corps of entrepreneurs who not only survive but thrive and contribute to the local, and ultimately, the global economy.. Skill-based training, technical training, technology training, and delivery of management skills are necessary to strengthen not only entrepreneurs, but also associations. Technical Assistance, in other words, is especially valuable in developing and transitional economies where business and managerial skills are often completely lacking.

3. Double Shift and Double Burden

The combination of two jobs, one at work and one at home, is difficult for a woman in any country, but it is doubly taxing for a woman in a developing or transitional economy where poverty and lack of infrastructure can make the most basic tasks harder and more time-consuming. Researchers from public health department strongly believe "exhorted women to be both producers and reproducers. As a consequence, they [bear] the double load of full-time work and all domestic responsibilities." In many ways the "double shift, double burden" stems from patriarchal traditions that are still followed in the majority of the world's countries. Yet, change is happening as countries modernize and integrate with the global economy.

4. Business-oriented Risk

Production and marketing efficiency are important determinants of entrepreneurial success. Unfortunately, many entrepreneurs cannot ensure their production and marketing efficiency due to their poor managerial and technical skills. Some of the women entrepreneurs suffered from operational inefficiency in rural areas due to the raw-materials and traditional production process. Consequently, they created a problem in the marketing of goods.

5. Knowledge Barriers

One of the major problems of women entrepreneurs is

lack of business knowledge. They have little knowledge about accounting and keeping records. Lack of knowledge in keeping accounts, estimating cost and profit and determination of price adversely affect their operations. Most of the women entrepreneurs have lack of knowledge in their business. The lack of business knowledge is a barrier for expansion of business.

6. Lack of Awareness about the Financial Assistance

It refers to different rules of the Government that facilitates women entrepreneurship development. Regulation requires relatively clear demands, effective supervision and significant sanctions. Beyond this it also matters whether the mechanisms employed are mostly those of power involving obligation of authority where the coercive agent is viewed as a legitimate agent of control or whether they rely on the use of inducements. Woman entrepreneur may not be aware of all the assistance provided by the government.

RECOMMENDATIONS FOR PROMOTION OF WOMEN ENTREPRENEURSHIP

To promote women entrepreneurs, these are the areas where intervention is needed: (1) grassroots level as an individual entrepreneur, (2) operational level in cooperation with women's business associations, and (3) policy and institutional level to systematize governmental efforts. The suggestions below are based on best practices that have proven successful for female entrepreneurs and their business associations. It is classified into five broad categories.

1. Empathetic Actions of Government

The Government can influence both economic and non-economic field for the entrepreneurs through its actions. Government can provide a facilitative socio-economic setting for women entrepreneurs. Such encouraging setting minimizes the risk entrepreneurs are to encounter. Compassionate actions of the Government can therefore be considered as the most advantageous for entrepreneurial growth. Similarly, negative governmental actions, such as colonial disruption, act as inhibiting factors of entrepreneurial development. Commitment of the Government can flourish entrepreneurship development in any country.

Action Agenda

- Commitment of the Government can flourish women entrepreneurship development, but such commitment would require establishing some special entrepreneurship development policies and rules.
- The Government needs to be more proactive in monitoring credit operations of various NGOs through proper audit and control. Cheap credit should be ensured to promote women entrepreneurship.
- Compile local and national directories on women entrepreneurs at all levels (micro, small, medium-sized, and large), in all sectors, and include international trade activity and give importance when policies are formulated and complement their activities with basic information, training and education also carefully monitor their business operations run by their credit.
- Special attentions should be given to promote income-generating programs in rural areas. Programs need to be taken to train and literate the rural entrepreneurs and make them socially aware. Both electronic and print media can be used to create social awareness among rural population.

2. Technology, Education and Training

Provide management, marketing, business planning, technology, and technical assistance to women entrepreneurs. Training was a top concern for women business owners. The women running SMEs are quite frequently handicapped by lack of management training; further, he criticized higher education for not sufficiently emphasizing SMEs. With high-speed technology blurring an entrepreneur's market edge, technology skills and business ownership education must be made available and constantly updated.

Action Agenda

- Survey women entrepreneurs through existing associations to establish a baseline for technology, education, and training needs; then generate the supporting training structures and/or partnerships to expand businesses and overcome obstacles.
- Better educational facilities and schemes should be extended to women folk from for updating their current knowledge.
- Adequate training programme on professional competence, management and leadership skills to be provided to women community.
- Organize training-*cum*-production workshops for understand the production process and production management and to remove psychological causes like lack of self-confidence and fear of success

3. Access to Credit

A major impediment to starting and later expanding a business is finance. Access to credit for women can be improved by linking women's business associations' awareness campaigns and public policy platforms to government and institutional policies.

Action Agenda

- Identify, define, and explain the common problems women experience in obtaining credit. Research credit schemes that have worked in other countries that would be applicable to your community; assess transferability and adaptability. Organize, lobby, and campaign for funds that women's business associations can disburse to members.
- Bank loan policy should be linked with industrial policy of the country. There should be an allocation of fund in the loan portfolio of banks to supplement the Government development plan and industrial policy. Coordination is also required for proper

allocation and distribution of fund to rural entrepreneurs.

- State finance corporations and financing institutions should permit by statute to extend purely trade-related finance to women entrepreneurs.
- The financial institutions should provide more working capital assistance both for small scale venture and large scale ventures.
- Making provision of micro-credit system and enterprise credit system to the women entrepreneurs at local level.

4. Legal Issues

Prescribing necessary policies and institutional reforms to improve the business environment facing women entrepreneurs is tied into the regulatory and legal framework governing competition, investment, commercial transactions, contractual laws, labour regulations, taxes, property rights, and procurement procedures.

Action Agenda

- Turn the obstacles, challenges, and problems into legitimate policy papers. Advocate using public forums, media targeting, and direct lobby pressure upon legislators to change laws that are discriminatory toward women entrepreneurs.

5. Association Leadership

Business women's associations can disseminate information, explain change, and provide services to help members handle economic and political shifts effectively.

Action Agenda

- The need for marketing support for selling the output of rural entrepreneurs is vital factor; channel of distribution should be built up with Government assistance. Annual fair, events and exhibition of products can be arranged in regional, national and international levels.

- Natural disasters and the lack of training affect the expansion of business. In this situation, the women entrepreneurs should be provided with sufficient informal training to improve their skills to take care of their business. Bank officials may contact NGOs to conduct training for all Bank loaners.
- In order to avoid overlapping, banks should co-ordinate their activities with other NGOs that are also engaged in delivering micro-credit among rural poor. Coordinated efforts with bank type organizations may prevent switching over of the borrowers from one organization to another. It is also widely recognized that imposing sound credit supervision system may solve the problem of fund diversions and improper utilization of money.
- Host international trade training and offer participants a variety of conference sessions dealing with international trade.

CONCLUSION

It can be said that today we are in transition stage wherein women participation in the field of entrepreneurship is increasing at a considerable rate, efforts are being taken at the economy as well as global level to enhance women's involvement in the enterprise sector. This is mainly because of attitude change, diverted conservative mindset of society to modern one, daring and risk-taking abilities of women, support and cooperation by society members, changes and relaxations in government policies, granting some up-liftment schemes to women entrepreneurs, etc. Thus, what else is required for attaining better position with the above trend, emphasizing on educating women strata of population, spreading awareness and consciousness amongst women to outshine in the enterprise field, making them realize their strengths, and important position in the society and the great contribution they can make for their industry as well as the entire economy.

REFERENCES

Brush, C. (2006), "Women Entrepreneurs: A Research Overview", in Basu, A., M. Casson, Yeung, B., Wadesdon, (2006), N., *Oxford Handbook of Entrepreneurship*, Oxford: Oxford University Press, 2006.

Das, K. (2007), "SMEs in India: Issues and Possibilities in Times of Globalisation", in Hank Lim (ed.), "Asian SMEs and Globalization", *ERIA Research Project Report 2007*, No. 5, March, ERIA, Bangkok.

GEM (2010), Global Report 2009, *Niels Bosma, Jonathan Levie and Global Entrepreneurship Research Association (GERA)* from http://www.gemconsortium.org

Hirisch, R.D. and Brush, C.G. (1984), "The Woman Entrepreneur: Management Skills and Business Problems", *Journal of Small Business Management*, 22(1), 30-37.

ILO (2008), Global Employment Trends for Women, 2008, March, Geneva: International Labour Office.

Kirzner, I. (1973), *Competition and Entrepreneurship*, Chicago: University of Chicago.

Schumpeter, J. (1934), *The Theory of Economic Development* (Cambridge, MA: Harvard University Press).

Schwartz, E. (1976), Entrepreneurship: A New Female Frontier, *Journal of Contemporary Business*, 5, 47-76.

Sinha, A. (2003), Experience of SMEs in South and South-East Asia, Washington, D.C., SEDF and World Bank.

Sinhal, S. (2005), "Developing Women Entrepreneurs in South Asia: Issues, Initiatives and Experiences", ST/ESCAP/2401, Trade and Investment Division, Bangkok: UNESCAP.

Tulus Tambunan (2009), Women Entrepreneurship in Asian Developing Countries: Their Development and Main Constraints, *Journal of Development and Agricultural Economics*, Vol. 1(2), pp. 027-040.

Verheul, I., Thurik, R. (2001), "Start-up Capital: Does Gender Matter?" *Small Business Economics*, 16, 329-41.

18

Women Empowerment Through the Role Performance of SHG Leaders

K. Krishnakumar and P.M. Sugavnaswari

INTRODUCTION

Women play a predominant role in our country and there is an imperative need to bring them into the mainstream of economic, social and cultural development of the economy. There is also a need to facilitate the growth and progress of women and nature their talents and skills in every field of economic activity and even in the area of industry. Over the last few years, "people's participation" and "Empowerment" have become the buzzwords in rural development and local planning. In this content, self-help group (SHG) has emerged as the most successful strategy, in the process of participating development and empowerment of women. The rural women all the marginalized groups of our society. Due to socio-economic constraints in the rural areas, women's potential for development remained for from fully utilized and they have been pushed further back into the social hierarchical system. The self-help group (SHG) models women as responsible citizens of the country achieving social and economic status. In all stages of economic and social activities, involvement of women has given added significance to them. Women-led SHGs in many parts of the country have achieved success in bringing the women to the mainstream of decision-making. The self-help group (SHG) in our country has become a source of inspiration for women's welfare. *Now-a-days*, formation of SHG is a viable alternative to achieve the objectives of rural development and to set community participation in all rural development programmes. SHG is also a viable organized set up to disburse micro-credit to the rural women and encouraging them to enter into entrepreneurial activities.

"The status of women is a barometer of the democratism of any state, an indicator of how human rights are respected in it".

EMPOWERMENT APPROACH

The discourse prevailed in the 1990s was of empowerment approach. The Eight Five Year Plan (1992-97), stated that the strategy for women's empowerment would be to enable them to function as equal partners and participation in development and not merely as beneficiaries. The need for changing societal attitudes towards women had been a serious commitment of Ninth Five Years Plan (1997-02). It stated for the first time, categorically that for empowering women as agents of social change and development, a "National policy for empowerment of women" would be formulated. The year 2001 had been declared as "Women empowerment year".

EMPOWERMENT MEANING AND DEFINITION

"Empower" means making one powerful or equipping one with the power to face the challenges of life to overcome disabilities, handicaps and inequalities. So empowerment is an active multidimensional process, which should enable women to realize their identity and power in all spheres of life. Further empowerment would consist of providing greater access to knowledge and resources, more autonomy in decision-making, greater ability to plan their lives, more control over the circumstances, which influence their lives and freedom from custom, belief and practice.

Empowerment is a process of awareness and capacity building leading to greater participation to greater decision-making power and control and transformation action. Empowerment is a multidimensional process which should enable the individuals as a group of individuals to realize their full identity and powers in all spheres of life.

EMPOWERMENT OF WOMEN IN INDIA

Even after sixty-two years of Indian independence, women are still one of the most powerless and marginalized sections of Indian society. The 2001 Census shows that the sex ratio for India is 933, which is lowest in the world. Percentage of female literacy is 54.16 against male literacy of 75.85 percent. In India, women's representation in Parliament and in the State Assemblies has never beyond 8 and 10 percent respectively. Most of the working women remain outside the organized sector. A mere 2.3 percent women are administrators and managers, 20.5 percent professional and the technical workers all of whom collectively earn 25 percent of the shared income. (Siddhartha Dash, 2004) Indian constitution in its fundamental rights has provisions for equality, social justice and protection of women. These goals are yet to be realized. Still women continue to be discriminated, exploited and exposed to inequalities of various levels. So the concept of empowerment as a goal of development projects and programmes has been gaining wider acceptance. Women in India are still a neglected lot, despite the assurance given in the constitution and commitment towards women empowerment. They are poorest of the poor receiving little education, low medical attention, lower value for their work, etc. They are still subjected to frequent pregnancies resulting in pregnancy wastage and increasing risk of maternal mortality. In India it was assumed that trickle down effect of rapid economic growth will improve the quality of life of the downtrodden and weaker sections of the population. It was realized that unless exclusive women development programmes are initiated, women's development would not be possible.

The Constitution not only grants equality to women, but also empowers the state to adopt measures of positive discrimination in favour of women. The 73rd and 74th Amendments (1993) to the Constitution of India provided for reservation of seats (at least one-third) in the local bodies of Panchayats and Municipalities for women. Another Constitutional Amendment (84th Constitutional Amendment Act, 1998) reserving 33 percent seats in Parliament and State Legislatures is in the pipeline. To safeguard women's various constitutional rights the government has enacted women-specific and women-related legislation like the Equal Remuneration Act, (1976), the Hindu Marriage Act as amended in 1966, the Immoral Traffic (Prevention) Act, of 1956 as amended and renamed in 1986 and Dowry Prohibition Act, (1961), the Indecent Representation of Women (Prohibition) Act, of 1986 and the Commission of Sati (Prevention) Act, 1987, Maternity Benefits Act, (1961), Family Courts Act, (1984). The Medical Termination of Pregnancy Act, (1971), The National Commission for Women Act, (1990) has also been passed to protect the dignity of women of women and prevent their exploitation.

The twelve salient strategies spelt out focused on empowering women by making women economically independent and self-reliant. It was being hoped that the strategies would be realized through the National policy for empowerment of women. Remarkably Self Help Groups were considered to be one of the strategies to mark the beginning of major process of empowering women.

Committee on the empowerment of women was constituted on April 1997 to improve the status of women. It consisted of 30 members, 20 members of Lok Sabha, 10 members of Rajya Sabha of Indian parliament. The committee presented its first report on "Developmental schemes for rural women" to Lok Sabha on 21 April 1999. Planning Commission (1999-2000) had given specific emphasis on empowerment of women, besides the continuation of the important initiative programmes like *Rural Women's Development and Empowerment Project (RWDEP)* was introduced in the status of Uttar Pradesh, Madhya Pradesh, Bihar, Haryana, Karnataka and Gujarat for a period of five years. The overall objective of the project is to enable empowerment of women by establishing Self Help Groups which will improve the quality of their lives through greater access to and control over resources.

CONSTITUTIONAL PROVISIONS AND SPECIAL LAWS FOR WOMEN

1. Equality before law for women (Article 14).
2. The State not to discriminate against any citizen on ground only of religion, race, caste, sex, place of birth or any of them (Article 15(i)).
3. The State to make any special provision in favour of women and children (Article 15(3)).
4. Equality of opportunity in matters relating to employment or appointment to any office under the state (Article 16).
5. The State to direct its policy towards securing men and women equally, the right to an adequate means of livelihood (Article 39(a)); and equal pay for equal work for both men and women (Article 39(d)).
6. The State to make provision for securing just and humane conditions of work and for maternity relief (Article 42).
7. To promote harmony and the spirit of common brotherhood amongst all the people of India and to renounce practices derogatory to the dignity of women (Article 51(A)(e)).
8. Not less than one-third of the total number of offices of chairpersons in the panchayats at each level to be reserved for women (Article 243D(4)).
9. Reservation of offices of chairpersons in municipalities for the SC, ST and women in such manner as the legislature of a state may by law provide (Article 243T(4)).

ORIGIN AND CONCEPT OF SHG

The origin of SHGs is from the brainchild of Grameen Bank of Bangladesh, which was founded by Mohammed Yunus. SHGs were started and formed in 1975. In India NABARD is initiated in 1986-87. But the real effort was taken after 1991-92 from the linkage of SHGs with the banks. A SHG is a small economically homogeneous affinity group of the rural poor voluntarily coming together to save small amount regularly, which are deposited in a common fund to meet member's emergency needs and to provide collateral free loans decided by the group. (Abhaskumar Sha, 2000). SHG is a media for the development of saving habit among the women (S. Rajamohan, 2003). SHGs enhance the equality of status of women as participants, decision-makers and beneficiaries in the democratic, economic, social and cultural spheres of life (Ritu Jain, 2003). The basic principles of the SHGs are group approach, mutual trust, organization of small and manageable groups, group cohesiveness, sprit of thrift, demand-based lending, collateral tree, women-friendly loan, peer group pressure in repayment, skill training capacity building and empowerment (N. Lalitha).

In Tamilnadu the SHGs were started in 1989 at Dharmapuri District. At present 1.40 lakh groups are functioning with 23.83 lakh members. At present, many men also eager to form SHGs.

FUNCTIONS AND CHARACTERISTICS OF SHG

Self-help groups are mostly informal groups where members pool savings as a thrift deposit. The groups have common perception of need and improvise towards collective activity. Many such groups formed around specific production activities, promote savings among members and use the pooled resources to meet the various credit needs of members. Where funds generation is low in the initial phases due to low savings capacities, this is supplemented by external resources. Thus self-help groups have been able to provide primitive banking service to its members that are cost effective, flexible and without defaults, based on local requirements. Self-help groups have also evolved their own characteristics of functioning.

NEEDS AND OBJECTIVES OF SHG

In order to avoid credit system, formation of self-help groups for rural unemployed women would ensure the best satisfaction of the poor in a credit programme. The membership in a group activity gives him a feeling of co-operation and protection. The poverty alleviation is based on the formation of self-help groups at the grass-root level. This brings about the necessity for organizing them in a group by which they set the benefit of collective perception, collective decision-making and collective implementation of programme for common benefits. This organization holds the power and provides strength and acts as anti-dotes to the helplessness of the poor. The group savings of self-help groups serve a wide range of objective other than immediate investment.

- Improves discipline in group members in developing saving habit.
- Savings enhance self-confidence of the individual as it is a sign of group encouragement.
- Group savings of the poor can demonstrate the strength of unity of members.
- Savings can cover the individual's risk against normal business risk.

LINKAGE MECHANISM OF SHG

In this model groups are formed by agencies like NGOs, Government Agencies or other Community-based organizations. The groups are nurtured and trained by these agencies. The Bank opens savings accounts and then provides credit facility directly to Self Help Groups after observing their operators. While the bank provides loans to the groups directly to the Self Help Groups, the facilitating agencies continue their interactions with the Self Help Groups.

The NGOs act as both facilitator and micro-finance intermediaries (MFIs). The Krishi Vigyan Kendra and Training Institutions provide vocational training in order to income earning activities.

ROLE OF NGOS

The SHG system in India initiated by NGOs is used for financial intermediation both by commercial banks and by micro-finance institutions by April 2001. NGOs are serving in rural areas in social fields with their local familiarities are the prime movers for formation SHG groups and other credit innovations.

As per the recent information, there are 420 NGOs were involved in the SHG movement in Tamilnadu and their cooperation provided effective, commending the role played by NGOs in promoting the concept. They are :

- Motivate and organize the rural people into SHGs.
- Inculcate and promote thrift and savings leading to development of institutions and individuals.
- Educate and train the group members in maintenance of accounts, conducting meetings, managing funds, etc.
- Improve resource availability in initial stages by providing seed capital assistance.
- Act as facilitators to link rural poor with bank.
- Upgrade skills and technology of members for making the best use of resources.
- Act as a friend, philosopher and guide to the SHGs.

TRAINING PROGRAMMES FOR SHG

The district administration, with the help of developmental departments has prepared network programme to impart skill-oriented training programmes to build up the capacity of rural women in the district, so that, they come forward to state employment benefit programmes. These training programmes are conducted at regular intervals at training and technology development centre (T & TDC) at Mahila Programe in the district.

The training programme imparted to the group leaders and members includes subjects like,

1. Capacity building training.
2. Group dynamics training.
3. Leadership quality training.
4. Book keeping training.
5. General awareness training.
6. Exposure visit training.
7. Computer training.
8. Entrepreneurship training
9. HIV, AIDS awareness training

Who helps to form Self-Help Groups?

A reasonably educated and helpful local person has to initially help the poor people to form groups. He or She tells them about the benefits of thrift and the advantages of forming groups. This person is called an "Animator" or "Facilitator". Usually, any of the following persons can be a successful animator:

- Retired school teacher or retired government servant, who is well known locally.
- A health worker/a field officer/staff of a development agency or department of the state government.
- The field officer or a staff member of a commercial bank/regional rural or a field staff from the local co-operative bank or society can also help the poor in forming groups.

- A field level functionary of an NGO.
- An unemployed educated local person, having an inclination to help others.
- A member or participant in the Vikas Volunteer Vahini (VVV) programme of NABARD.
- Women animators can play more effective role in organizing women SHGs.

The animators cannot organize the groups all alone. He or she will need guidance, training, reading material, etc. Usually, one of the following agencies help:

I. A voluntary agency or Non-Governmental Organization (NGO).
II. The development department of the state Government.
III. The local branch of a bank.

What does the Animator do?

The animator talks to people in the village or at their homes. He or she explains the benefits of the thrift and group formation. No promise of bank loan is given to anyone. He or she helps the group members to hold meetings, keeping books, etc. The animator conducts two or three meetings every month. The group members save small amounts out of their earnings and contribute to a common fund. They lend to the members for meeting their emergent credit needs.

The loans are available for consumption and small production purposes. Rates of interest, period of loans and other terms are decided by the group. Such groups may be informal or registered and should not have a membership of more than 20 (the legal ceiling on a membership for informal groups). The credit is available virtually at the doorstep of the borrower, reducing the transaction cost.

ROLE OF ANIMATOR

- Convene and Conduct Women's group meeting at regular intervals.
- Create awareness of present social position, objectives

of the programme and motivate building up of team spirit and teamwork.

- Work for improvement of literacy and numeracy of the group members.
- Disseminate information to members about Government Development and Welfare schemes, especially in relation to health and family welfare, education, etc.
- Disseminate information received during training sessions to SHG members, e.g., relating to SHG management, general hygiene environment consciousness, women and the law.
- Facilitate group to identify appropriate income generating activities for members, co-ordinate with banks for getting loans and ensure prompt repayment.
- Training the members in the procedures of bank transactions.
- Motivate members towards collective thinking and action.
- Working for improvement of socio-economic development of members.
- Ensure regular group savings by members.
- Prompt up dating and proper maintenance of minute book and all other account books. Animator must not handle cash.
- Observing all rules and procedures for passing resolution for grant of loans.
- Assist group in getting bank loan, asset creation and motivation for repayment.
- Motivating all members to speak out and ensure participation of all in every meeting.
- Make regular house visits and motivate absentees to attend meetings regularly.
- Attend training organized by NGO/PIU, brief, discuss and decide on implementation of the learning with all SHG Members.
- Attend BLCC, CLF and other review meetings.
- Motivating the members to act with unity and

integrity by ensuring transparent operations of transactions in the SHGs.

- Allocate responsibilities to every member in order to develop the abilities of each member, like sending members to banks or taking them along for important meetings by rotation.
- Ensure that SHGs become self-reliant and sustainable over 2 or 3 years.

ROLE OF REPRESENTATIVES

- Convening the group meetings at regular intervals.
- Assist the animator in the achievement of programme objectives.
- Operate bank account jointly as authorized by group.
- Disseminate information received during training sessions to SHG members, e.g. Relating to SHG management general hygiene environment consciousness, women and the law, etc.
- Assist group in getting bank loan, asset creation and motivation for repayment.
- Handling cash and all related banking activities.
- Help problem-solving within the group.
- Try to mobilize local resources for benefit of the group/village.
- Management and effective use of Group savings and Loan funds.
- Provide (assist) training of group members to improve their business skills, management of their activities and understanding of credit and banking procedures.
- Carry out decisions of the group.
- Represent the group in other forums like BLCC, CLF, review meetings.

ROLE OF SHG MEMBERS

- Promptly attend SHG meetings.
- Fully participate in SHG meetings and voice opinion clearly and freely.

- Share responsibility of SHG collectively like going to banks by rotation.
- Prompt repayment of SHG loans.
- Participate in village and social action programs.
- To ensure unity and mutual trust between all members and adopt the principle of "give and take".
- Ask questions/doubts openly and ensure that the SHG functions transparently.
- Ensure prompt annual re-election of a least representatives and also animators.
- Study and document the statistics relating to poor women in cluster area. Identify the poorest and inaccessible habitations promptly attend training programs and ensure implementation of good practices.
- Share problems, experience, feelings and ideas with all members of the SHG.

SUGGESTIONS

- ➢ Rural women's traits relating to various entrepreneurs to be enhanced.
- ➢ Compulsory education to be given.
- ➢ Gainful employment opportunity to be created.
- ➢ Formation of SHGs in all viable areas with strong support of government.
- ➢ Banks how to intend their credit facilities to women folk with real spirit and involvement.
- ➢ Rotation of representatives has to be made compulsory so that it will lead to women's empowerment.
- ➢ Training in non-traditional activities has to be given.
- ➢ The VOs (voluntary organization) and government should take necessary steps for marketing the goods produced by the SHGs.
- ➢ Development of entrepreneurial abilities of women by organizing special types of training.
- ➢ Encouraging women to take up part-time jobs while being in the house itself to earn additional income to support the family.

- Central and state governments to place more emphasis in untouched areas in the service sector to involve women.

CONCLUSION

The Self Help Groups are taking the lead and playing an important and pivotal role in social transformation, welfare activities and infrastructure building and they have served the cause of women empowerment, social solidarity and socio-economic betterment of the poor.

This conceptual study reveals that majority of the SHG leaders performed the seven roles, it is concluded that the SHGs played a vital role in bringing leadership which is very much essential for development of the rural women. Members previously never known to leadership qualities have become animators and members confined within their house, hither to have become rural entrepreneurs and business women as a result of these the lifestyle of the member's personality of the members have changed drastically. It also concludes that many members never exposed to politics now, wish to become political leaders. This is what the freedom fighters of our nation and father our nation dreamt for SHG has helped to realize their dreams. In Toto the SHG made a positive impact in the life of members socially, politically, economically and culturally.

References

Dr. A. Abdul Raheem and H. Yasmeen Sultana, "Empowerment of Women through Self Help Group: An Overview", *Kisan World*, March 2007.

Dr. A. Selvaraj, "Empowerment of Women", *Kisan World*, July 2007.

Dr. (Mrs.) Marama Dinto, "Development through Empowerment of Women in India", *Kurukshetra*, August 1995.

V.M.S. Perumal, "SHGs: Empowering Women at the Grass Roots", *Social Welfare*, July 2005.

Dr. H.D. Dwarakanath, "Rural Credit and Women Self Help Groups", *Kurukshetra*, Nov. 2002.

A. Sakunthalai, K. Ramakrishnan and S. Mahendran, "Socio-economic Empowerment of Women", *Kisan World*, July 2006.

SHGs : A Tool for Empowering Women

A Case Study in Dharmapuri

R. Rathidevi

INTRODUCTION

The role and status of men and women are governed by traditions and cultural practices. The social evils like, illiteracy, poverty, violence against women and girls and low health status continue to be persisting areas of concern for women. As a result women continue to have a lower status in the society. In India, at the end of Ninth Five Year Plan 26.1% of the population was living below the poverty line. In the rural areas 27.1% of the population was living under poverty. The overall unemployment rate is estimated to 7.32%. The female unemployment rate is 8.5%. The rate of growth of women unemployment in the rural areas is 9.8%. This is because of the growth rate of new and productive employment. The government has introduced various schemes to reduce poverty and to promote the gainful employment. But the more attractive schemes with less effort (finance) in "Self Help Group". It is a too to remove poverty and improve the rural development (Sabyasachi Das, 2003).

NEED FOR EMPOWERMENT OF WOMEN

I. By empowerment, women would be able to develop self-esteem, confidence, realize their potential and enhance their collective bargaining power.

II. Awareness building about women's status, discrimination, rights and opportunities is a vital step towards gender equality.

III. Capacity building and skill development, especially the ability to plan, make decisions, organize, manage and carry out activities to deal with people and institutions in the world around them.

IV. Participation and greater control and decision-making in the affairs of home, community and in the society.

V. Action to bring about greater equality between men and women

Thus empowerment is a process of awareness and capacity building, leading to greater participation, greater decision-making power and control of the transformative action. The empowerment of women covers both individual and collective transformation. It strengthens their innate ability through acquiring knowledge, power and experience. (Dr. T. Ramachandran and A. Seilan, 2005).

ORIGIN AND CONCEPT OF SHGs

The origin of SHGs is from the brainchild of Grameen Bank of Bangladesh, which was founded by Mohammed Yunus. SHGs were started and formed in 1975. In India NABARD is initiated in 1986-87. But the real effort was taken after 1991-92 from the linkage of SHGs with the banks. A SHG is a small economically homogeneous affinity group of the rural poor voluntarily coming together to save small amount regularly, which are deposited in a common fund to meet member's emergency needs and to provide collateral free loans decided by the group. (Abhaskumar Jha, 2000). They have been recognized as useful tool to help the poor and as an alternative mechanism to meet the urgent credit needs of poor through thrift (V.M. Rao, 2002) SHG is a media for the development of saving habit among the women (S. Rajamohan, 2003). SHGs enhance the equality of status of women as participants, decision-makers and beneficiaries in the democratic, economic, social and cultural spheres of life. (Ritu Jain, 2003). The basic principles of the SHGs are group approach, mutual trust, organization of small and manageable groups, group cohesiveness, sprit of thrift, demand-based lending, collateral free, women-friendly loan, peer group pressure in repayment, skill training capacity building and empowerment (N. Lalitha).

In Tamil Nadu the SHGs were started in 1989 at Dharmapuri District. The SHGs were formed in this district with the assistance of International Fund for Agricultural Development (IFAD). Later the scheme was extended to the erstwhile Salem and South Arcot districts in the year 1991-92 and further extended to Madurai and Ramanathapuram in the year 1992-93. Following the success of the IFAD project, Mahalir Thittam project was launched with State Government funding from 1997-98 and was progressively introduced in all districts of the State. Today the SHG movement is a very vibrant movement spread across all districts of the State with nearly 59,00,000 women as members. As on 31.3.2008, there are 3,65,709 SHGs with a total savings of Rs. 1737.81 crores.

WORKING OF SHGs

SHGs are working in democratic manner. The upper limit of members in a group is restricted to 20. Among them a member is selected as an 'animator' and two members are selected as the representatives. The animator is selected for the period of two years. The group members meet every week. They discuss about the group savings, rotation of sangha funds, bank loan, repayment of loan, social and community action programmes.

Functions of SHGs

- Create a common fund by the members through their regular savings.
- Flexible working system and pool the resources in a democratic way.
- Periodical meeting. The decision-making through group meeting.
- The loan amount is small and reasonable. So that easy to repay in time.
- The rate of interest is affordable, varying group to group and loan to loan. However, it is little higher than the banks but lower than the money lenders.

From the previous studies related to SHGs, it is clearly understood that the SHGs are tool to promote rural savings and gainful employment. Through this the rural poverty is reduced considerably. Therefore, women members are economically independent and their contribution to household income is also increased. The present study is also focusing the economic improvement of women after them joining SHGs.

Objectives

The overall objective of the present study is to analysis the economic empowerment of women through SHGs in the north districts of Tamil Nadu. However more specifically:

1. To study the income, expenditure and savings of the members after joining SHGs.
2. To assess the impact of Self Help Groups in empowering women in sample district.
3. To suggest measures in order to strengthen the Self Help Group in the process of women empowerment.

Methodology

The present study was undertaken in Dharmapuri District, which is one of the most backward districts in Tamilnadu. Of the eight blocks in Dharmapuri District, Three blocks were selected and from each of these blocks fifteen villages were selected. From each village Ten SHGs were selected and from each SHG one member was selected as respondent. Thus 150 respondents were selected for the present study.

Simple random sampling method was used for the section of blocks, villages, SHGs and respondents. For this study both primary and secondary data were used. Primary data were collected using well-prepared interview schedule. Secondary data were collected from various journals, records of District Rural Davelopment Agency (DRDA), Dharmapuri, NABARD annual reports, periodicals, etc., This is purely a descriptive study. Therefore, no complicated models and tools were used; only percentage and average were used for the analysis.

SOURCES OF INFORMATION ABOUT SELF HELP GROUPS

Voluntary Organizations play an important role in mobilizing the rural poor women to form Self Help Group. The VO's field workers visit the villages and explain the advantages of forming Self Help Groups. Table 1 shows the source of information about the Self Help Groups.

TABLE I

Sources of Information about Self Help Groups

Sources	*No. of Respondents*	*Percentage*
Friends	39	26
Mahalir Thittam	24	16
Neighbours	45	30
NGOs	42	28
Total	150	100

Source : Primary Data.

The Table 1 shows that 26 percent of the respondents have come to know about the Self Help Groups through their friends, 16 percent of them have come to know through Mahalir Thittam (Mathi women's group), 30 percent of them have come to know through their neighbours and another 28 percent of them have come to know about the Self Help Group through the VOs.

TYPE OF SAVINGS ADOPTED

Savings is an important element in the SHG. In certain groups savings are collected from the members weakly, whereas in certain groups savings are collected monthly. The type of savings adopted by the SHGs are analyzed in the following table.

TABLE 2
Type of Savings Adopted

Type of Savings	*No. of Respondents*	*Percentage*
Weekly	84	56
Fortnightly	36	24
Monthly	30	20
Total	150	100

Source : Primary Data.

Table 2 reveals that 56 percent of the Self Help Groups have weekly savings, 24 percent of SHGs have fortnightly savings and the remaining 20 percent of the SHGs have monthly savings.

AGE GROUP OF MEMBERS OF SHGs

The Age and socio-economic activities are inter-related. The young and middle age group people can actively participate in the socio-economic activities, which is true in the activities of SHGs in the study area. In the three blocks of this district of Tamil Nadu, 20-30 and 30-40 age groups are actively participated in the SHGs activities (Table 3). The aged people

(40-50) are also in the SHGs, their role is also important for SHGs. They can only control and solve the problems arise in the groups.

TABLE 3

Age Group of Members of SHGs

Age Group	*No. of Respondents*	*Percentage*
Less than 20	15	10.00
20-30	30	20.00
30-40	43	28.67
40-50	38	28.67
Above 50	24	16.00
Total	150	100.00

Source : Primary Data.

REASONS FOR JOINING SHGs

The major aim of the SHGs is to promote savings and to credit for the productive and consumption purposes. This is true because many people in the study area joins the SHGs for getting loan and promote their personal savings, in addition to get social status (Table 4). In the study area many people (43.33%) joins the SHGs for getting financial assistance, 26.67%

TABLE 4

Reasons for Joining SHGs

Reasons	*No. of Respondents*	*Percentage*
For getting loan	65	43.33
For promoting savings	40	26.67
For social status	32	21.33
For other reasons	13	8.67
Total	150	100.00

Source : Primary Data.

of the respondents joins for improving savings in the SHGs, 21.33% of the respondents joins for the social status, because SHGs give the identify to the members. For social, cultural and political improvement (other reasons 8.67%) some members join in the SHGs.

INCOME LEVEL OF THE MEMBERS

Income is the major determinant of the standard of living of the people. The SHGs member income has been increased after joining the SHGs. Hence women members of the groups are independent to meet their personal expenditure, and they contribute more to their household income. Many housewives (24%) did not earn anything before joining SHGs, but after a member of the SHGs, they are also earning reasonably. This increases the willingness to participate in the SHGs' activities (Table 5). Many women members independently involve in the

TABLE 5
Monthly Income of the Members before and After Joining SHGs

Sl. No.	*Monthly Income (Rs.)*	*Before Joining SHGs*		*After Joining SHGs*	
		No. of Respon-dents	*Percentage*	*No. of Respon-dents*	*Percentage*
1.	Less than 1000	16	10.67	5	3.33
2.	1000-2000	30	20.00	32	21.33
3.	2000-3000	44	29.33	50	33.33
4.	3000-4000	9	6.00	30	20.00
5.	4000-5000	10	6.67	22	14.67
6.	Above 5000	5	3.33	7	4.67
7.	Non-earning members	36	24.00	4	2.67
	Total	150	100.00	150	100.00

Source : Primary Data.

economic activities individually and with other group members after joining SHGs. Therefore, they are now economically independent and contribute to increase their household income.

EXPENDITURE OF THE SHG MEMBERS' FAMILY

The family expenditure has been increased due to positive change in the SHGs members' income. The incremental income not only enhances the expenditure of the family but also promote the savings of the family after they join in the SHGs. Here the objective of the SHGs is fulfilled. This is an achievement of the women SHGs in the study area (Tables 6 and 7). Usually working women are being respected by the household members and the society. Nowadays women in the SHGs are also respected by the others, because they are independent in earning the income and they are contributing to household income, expenditure and savings. Therefore, the above discussion clearly states that after joining in the SHGs, the members' well-being has been increased.

TABLE 6

Monthly Family Expenditure of the Members before and after Joining SHGs

Sl. No.	*Monthly Income (Rs.)*	*Before Joining SHGs*		*After Joining SHGs*	
		No. of Respon-dents	*Percentage*	*No. of Respon-dents*	*Percentage*
1.	Less than 1000	45	30.00	25	16.67
2.	1000-2000	61	40.67	39	26.00
3.	2000-3000	32	21.33	48	32.00
4.	3000-4000	7	4.67	27	18.00
5.	Above 4000	5	3.33	11	7.33
	Total	150	100.00	150	100.00

Source : Primary Data.

TABLE 7

Monthly Family Savings of the Members Before and After Joining SHGs

Sl. No.	Monthly Income (Rs.)	Before Joining SHGs		After Joining SHGs	
		No. of Respon-dents	Percentage	No. of Respon-dents	Percentage
1.	Below 100	54	36.00	18	12.00
2.	100-300	33	22.00	29	9.33
3.	300-500	26	17.33	55	36.67
4.	500-700	18	12.00	27	18.00
5.	700-900	10	6.67	12	8.00
6.	900-1100	7	4.67	6	4.00
7.	Above 1100	2	1.33	3	2.00
	Total	150	100.00	150	100.00

Source : Primary Data.

RURAL CREDIT AND SHGs

One of the reasons for joining SHGs is to avails credit (V.M. Rao, 2002), which is true in the present study area. The second objective of the present is to know the rural credit by SHGs. This part is discussed the rural credit and SHGs in study area. The credit organizations like nationalized banks, Co-operative Societies and so on, follow many formalities to provide credit to the rural people. At the same time village money lenders charge very high rate of interest. In this situation SHGs are the boon to the rural people, because instead of approaching banks as individual, SHGs members can easily approach the banks and other institutions to get loan. The SHGs get loan from credit institutions then, they refinance (share) to the members in the SHGs. The SHGs charge reasonable interest. In the study area the prevailing interest rate is 1% to 2%. All the members are responsible to repay the loan to the banks. Therefore, members are repaid the loan in time (Table 10). Moreover, banks instruct the members to save minimum Rs. 200 per month. So re-payment is very easy to SHGs. The loans can be used by individual group members for their personal needs, sometime the group may invest in any economic activities. Nowadays many SHGs are starting small business, cottage industries, food processing units, etc. The SHGs in the study area grant the loan to their member for various purposes. The maximum loan amount per member is decided by the general body meeting (Table 8). Almost all the members in the study area are availing loan facilities in their SHGs (Table 9).

TABLE 8
Types of Loans in the SHGs

Sl. No.	*Types of the Loan*	*Maximum amount (Rs.)*
1.	Business Loan	20,000 to 25,000
2.	Marriage Loan	Upto 20,000
3.	Repay the old Loan	10,000 to 15,000
4.	Medical Loan	10,000 to 15,000
5.	House repairing Loan	Upto 5,000
6.	Cattle Loan	5,000 to 7,500

Note : The rate of interest is 1% to 2%. It varies group to group.
Source : Primary Data.

TABLE 9
Amount of Loan Availed by the Members through SHGs

Sl. No.	*Availed Loan Amount (Rs.)*	*No. of Respondents*	*Percentage*
1.	Less than 5,000	17	11.33
2.	5,000 to 10,000	33	22.00
3.	10,000 to 15,000	28	18.67
4.	15,000 to 20,000	47	31.33
5.	Above 20,000	25	16.67
	Total	150	100.00

Source : Primary Data.

TABLE 10
Repayment of Loan by SHGs' Members

Sl.No.	Particulars	No. of Respondents	Percentage
1.	Repayment in time	105	70.00
2.	Repayment in advance	32	21.33
3.	Repayment not in time	13	8.67
	Total	150	100.00

Source : Primary Data.

INCOME GENERATING ACTIVITIES (IGA) UNDERTAKEN BY THE SELF HELP GROUPS

Once the SHGs have got loan, the next stage is to choose the Income generating activities undertaken by the Self Help Groups are explained in Table 11.

TABLE 11
Income Generating Activities Undertaken by the Self Help Groups

Sl. No.	Type of Activity	No. of SHGs	Percentage
1.	Mat-making	12	8.00
2.	Food processing	38	25.33
3.	Canteen	15	10.00
4.	Textile business	12	8.00
5.	Cottage industries	21	14.00
6.	Handloom	18	12.00
7.	Milch animals	30	20.00
8.	Others	4	2.67
	Total	150	100.00

Source : Primary Data.

Table 11 shows that 8% of the Self Help Groups are involved in mat-making activity, 25.33% of the Self Help

Groups are in Food processing activity, 10% of the Self Help Groups in the activity of running Canteen, 8% of the Self Help Groups doing Textile business, 14% of the Self Help Groups are in the activity of Cottage industries, 12% of the Self Help Groups in Handloom activity, 20% of the Self Help Groups are rearing Milch animals and 2.67% of the Self Help Groups are doing other activities.

REASON FOR CHOOSING A PARTICULAR INCOME GENERATING ACTIVITY

The Self Help Group choose the income generating activity which is most appropriate for them based on certain factors such as the local resources available, the skill they are having, demand for the product and easy marketability. The (Table 12) clearly explains the reason for choosing a particular income generating activity by the SHGs.

TABLE 12

Reason for Choosing a Particular Income Generating Activity by the SHGs

Sl. No.	*Reasons*	*No. of SHGs*	*Percentage*
1.	Already having the Skill	33	22.00
2.	Demand for this product	15	10.00
3.	Cheap Capital	28	18.67
4.	Easy Marketability	12	8.00
5.	Unemployment	51	34.00
6.	Other Reasons	11	7.33
	Total	150	100.00

Source : Primary Data.

The above table shows that 22% of the SHGs have chosen this activity because the members already had the skill, 10% have chosen because of the demand for the product, 18.67% have chosen because of cheap capital, 8% have chosen because of easy marketability, 34% have undertake this activity because of the problem of Unemployment and the remaining 7.33% have chosen this activity because of their traditional and cultural aspect.

MONTHLY INCOME PER MEMBER FROM INCOME GENERATING ACTIVITY

The profit obtained from the income generating activity is being shared by the Self Help Group members involved in income generating activity. Based on the bank loan and the activities undertaken the profit become varies. The monthly income per member from income generating activity is explained in Table 13.

TABLE 13
Monthly Income Per Member from Income Generating Activity

Monthly Income	*No. of SHGs*	*Percentage*
Below-300	17	11.33
300-600	43	28.67
600-900	55	36.67
900-1200	24	16.00
Above 1200	11	7.33
Total	150	100.00

Source : Primary Data.

Table 13 shows that 11.33% of the respondents have got a monthly income of below Rs. 300 from the income generating activity, 28.67% of them have got a monthly income of Rs. 300-Rs. 600, 36.67% of them got a income of Rs. 600-Rs. 900 monthly, most of them have got this amount of income and only 7.33% got a monthly income of above Rs. 1200.

BENEFITS OF SELF HELP GROUPS

Membership in Self Help Group has given certain benefits

to its members. Self Help Group members' opinion about benefits received by them is analyzed in the Table 14.

TABLE 14
Benefits Received by the Self Help Group Members

Benefits of SHGs	*Opinion*			*Total*
	Agree	*No opinion*	*Disagree*	
Increase savings habit among poor	142 (94.67)	8 (5.33)	—	150 (100.00)
Avoid external lending (borrowed from outsiders with high rate of interest)	110 (73.33)	15 (10.00)	25 (16.67)	150 (100.00)
Start new business	92 (61.33)	45 (30.00)	13 (8.67)	150 (100.00)
Access to various promotional assistance	93 (62.00)	35 (23.33)	22 (14.67)	150 (100.00)

Source : Primary Data.
Figures in brackets denote percentage.

Table 14 shows that 94.62% of respondents are of the opinion that they have increased their savings habit, 73.33% of them said that they have protected from external lenders with high rate of interest, 61.33% said that they have started new income generating activities and 62% of them agreed that the SHG has given its members access to various promotional assistance.

EMPOWERMENT THROUGH SELF HELP GROUP

The Self Help Group programme mainly focuses attention on empowerment of rural women and making them financially, socially and politically capable. Table 15 analyses the empowerment of Self Help Group women in the Study area.

Table 15 reveals the opinion of the respondents regarding empowerment where 94.67% of the respondents agree that they are able to contribute towards the family income, 42.00% of them agree that they have got skill upgradation, 58% of the respondents agree that they now understand the banking

TABLE 15

Empowerment through Self Help Group

Benefits of SHGs	*Opinion*			*Total*
	Agree	*No opinion*	*Disagree*	
Able to contribute towards the family income	142 (94.67)	8 (5.33)	— (100.00)	150
Skill upgradation	63 (42.00)	31 (20.67)	56 (37.33)	150 (100.00)
Understand the banking operations	87 (58.00)	29 (19.33)	34 (22.67)	150 (100.00)
Standard of living has improved	52 (34.67)	48 (32.00)	50 (33.33)	150 (100.00)
Better leadership and communication skills	83 (55.33)	33 (22.00)	34 (22.67)	150 (100.00)
Awareness in health education	91 (60.67)	17 (11.33)	42 (28.00)	150 (100.00)
Decision-making of women in community village and in household	72 (48.00)	39 (26.00)	39 (26.00)	150 (100.00)

Source : Primary Data.
Figures in brackets denote percentage.

operations, 34.67% are of the opinion that their standard of living has improved, 55.33% of the respondents said that they have got better leadership and communication skills, 60.67% of the respondents are now aware of their health educaton and 48% of the members agree that they have now made decisions in community village and in household.

SUGGESTIONS

Based on the above findings the following suggestions are made:

1. Attendance of members in group meetings has to be made compulsory.
2. Rate of interest can be reduced and number of instalments for repayment can be increased. It will

useful to members for repaying the loan amount in time.

3. Rotation of Animator and representatives has to be made compulsory so that it will lead to women's empowerment.
4. More training has to be given.
5. The NGOs and Government should take necessary steps for marketing the goods produced by the SHGs.

CONCLUSION

The study was undertaken the women empowerment through SHGs in Dharmapuri District of Tamilnadu. It is found that the income of the women has been increased after joining the SHGs. So that the monthly household expenditure also has been raised considerable level. But the savings is increasing at slow rate, because the incremental expenditure is higher. Mostly they are spending for present consumption. The members should change it. The good practice of the women SHGs in the study area is repayment of the loan in time. Nearly 70% of the debtor paid their monthly due within the time, even some members (21.33%) paid their due in advance. A few members do not pay in time but this is not affecting the further credit of SHGs. Since the repayment of loan is regular and within the time, we may conclude that the economic activities of SHGs are quite success. The SHGs playing an important and pivotal role in social transformation, welfare activities and infrastructure building and they have served the cause of women empowerment, social solidarity and socio-economic betterment of the poor.

References

Krishana, Vijaya R. and Das, Amarnath R. (2003), "Self Help Groups"— A Study in A.P. District, *HRD Times*, May.

Rasure, K.A. (2003), "Women's Empowerment Through SHGs", *Journal of Fact for you*, November.

Rose, K. (1992), Where Women are Leaders : The SEWA Movement in India, New Delhi: Vistar Publications (A Division of Sage Publications, India).

Siddiqui, Saif (2003), "Rural Entrepreneurship and Poverty Alleviation Programmes", *Yojana*, December.

Manimekalai, N. and G. Rajeswari (2002), "Grassroots Entrepreneurship through Self Help Groups (SHGs)", *SEDMI Journal*, Vol. 29 p. 2.

Naranaswamy, N.S. Manivel and B. Bhaskar (2003), "Networking SHGs and Cooperatives—An Analysis of Strengths and Weaknesses", *Journal of Rural Development*. Vol. 22, p. 3.

Simanowitz, A. (2000), "Targeting the Poor—Comparing Visual and Participatory Methods", *Small Enterprise Development*, Vol. 11, p. 1.

Ariz Ahmed, M. (1999), "Women Empowerment: Self Help Groups:, *Kurukshetra*, April, 47, 7: 19, 20 and 49.

Chatterjee, Sankar (2003), "Networking SGSY, Banks and SHGs: Initiatives in Uttar Pradesh", *Kurukshetra*, February, 51, 4: 27-29.

Damayanthi, U.T. (1999), "Development of Women and Children in Rural Areas—An Impact Study", *The Asian Economic Review*, August, 41, 2:349-357.

Dodkey, M.D. (1999), "SHGs and Micro Credit, Sustaining Rural Women", *Social Welfare*, March, 45.12: 19-20.

Gopalakrishnan, B.K. (1998), "SHGs and Social Defence", *Social Welfare*, January, 44. 10: 30-34.

Kokila, K. (2001), "Credit Groups for Women Workers, *Social Welfare*, May, 48.2: 23-25.

Lalitha, N. (1998), "Microfinance: Rural NGOs and Banks Networking", *Social Welfare*, October, 45.7:13-17.

Lalitha, N. and B.S. Nagarajan (2002), "Self Help Groups in Rural Development", New Delhi: Dominant Publishers and Distributors.

Mangathai, R.A. (2001), " Together We Stand (Success Story)", *Kurukshetra*, November, 50: 30-31.

Nair, Tara S. (1998), "Meeting the Credit Needs of the Micro Enterprise Sector: Issues in Focus", *The Indian Journal of Labour Economics*, July-Setember, 41.3: 531-38.

Narashimhan, Sakuntala, (1999), "Empowering Women: An Alternative Strategy for Rural India", New Delhi: Sage Publications India Pvt. Ltd.

Abhaskumar, Jha (2004), "Lending to the Poor: Designs for Credit", *EPW*, Vol. XXXV, No. 8 and 9.

Jeyanthi, Gayari, R. (2002), "SHGs in Kanyakumari District", M.Phil., Dissertation submitted to Alagappa University, Karaikudi, T.N.

Jeyaraman, R. *et al.*, (2004), "Role of Self Help Groups in Fisher Women Development", *Peninsular Economist*, Vol. XII, No. 2, pp. 197-200.

Lalitha, N., "Women Thrift and Credit Groups, Breaking the Barriers at the Grass Roots", *Peninsular Economist*, Vol. XII, No. 2, pp. 188-95.

Manimekalai, N. *et. al.*, "Grass-root Women Entreprenurship through SHGs", *Peninsular Economist*, Vol. XII, No. 2, pp. 181-87.

Rajamohan, S. (2003), "Activities of Self Help Groups in Virudhunagar District—A Study, *TNJC*, pp. 25-29.

Rao, V.M. (2003), Women Self Help Groups, Profiles from Andhra Pradesh and Karnataka", *Kurukshetra*, Vol. 50, No. 6, pp. 26-32.

Ritu Jain, (2003), "Socio-Economics Impact Through Self Help Groups", *Yojana*, Vol. 47, No. 7, pp. 11-12.

Sabyasachi Das, (2003), "Self Help Groups and Micro Credit Synbergic Integration", *Kurukshetra*, Vol. 51, No. 10, pp. 25-28.

Bandhyopadhyay, D., B.N. Yughandhar and Amitava Mukherjee (2000), "Convergencce of Programmes by Empowering SHGs and PRIs", *Economic and Political Weekly*, June 29.

20

Empowerment of Women Entrepreneur in Rural India

M. KETHARAJ

INTRODUCTION

The development of any nation primarily depends upon its industrial development which makes rich contribution to the growth of a nation. The economic role played by women cannot be isolated from the framework of development. Women remain significantly poor and are far less legally protected. The choices available to women in developing countries are even starker, and they are often forced to contribute their limited time in extremely poorly paid business.

'Women Entrepreneur' is becoming a global phenomenon today. All over the world, women are playing a vital role in the business community. In India, however women have made a comparatively late entry into the business scenario mainly due to the orthodox and traditional socio-cultural environment.

Though they are enjoying a special status in the society, women entrepreneurs face various problems in the process of establishing, developing and running their enterprises in the 21st century. Women entrepreneurs may be defined as the women or a group of women who initiate, organise and operate a business enterprise. Women are expected to innovate, imitate or adopt an economic activity to be called *Women Entrepreneurs*. In this paper an attempt has been made to analyse the *functions, special traits, problems and suggestions* to the upliftment of women entrepreneurs.

MEANING

A women entrepreneur as an "enterprise owned and administered by women entrepreneurs having a minimum financial interest of 51 percent of the share capital and giving at least 50 percent of the employment generated in the enterprise to women".

FUNCTIONS OF WOMEN ENTREPRENEURS

A women entrepreneur has five functions: There are:

1. Explore the prospects of starting new enterprises.
2. Undertaking of risks and the handling of economic and non-economic uncertainities.
3. Introduction of new innovations or imitation of successful ones in existence.
4. Co-ordination, administration and control.
5. Supervision and providing leadership in all aspects of the business.

TRAITS OF WOMEN ENTREPRENEURS

Normally the women entrepreneurs who prefer to start an enterprise should have the following traits:

1. Accept challenges
2. Adventurous

3. Ambitious
4. Conscientious
5. Full of drive
6. Educated
7. Enthusiastic
8. Hard working
9. Keen to learn and imbibe
10. Patient
11. Intelligent
12. Motivated
13. Skilful
14. Studious
15. Optimistic

Though women entrepreneurs in rural areas are having the above said qualities to a certain extent, they are facing some problems. The greatest deterrent to women entrepreneurs is that they are women.

PROBLEMS OF WOMEN ENTREPRENEURS

The main problems faced by the women entrepreneurs in recent days are:

1. Financial constraints
2. Over dependence on intermediaries
3. Scarcity of Raw materials
4. Intense competition
5. High cost of production
6. Low mobility
7. Family ties
8. Social attitudes
9. Lack of education
10. Absence of ambition for achievement

The above problems and stumbling blocks, which are most commonly mentioned by women entrepreneurs or prospective women entrepreneurs, are elaborately discussed under:

Access to Material Resources/Capital

- Credit/Financial services
- Land/Property/Assets
- Collateral/Security for accessing credit
- *Technologies*: know-how plus Machinery, Tools, Equipment etc.
- *Raw-materials*: regularity of supply, quality, infrastructural links, etc.

Access to Market and Market Information

Marketing strategies/Feasibility of a product in the market/trade-links/Competing effectively.

Access to Variety of Technical and Skills Training

Technical/Vocational/Managerial/Organizational, financial, personnel, production process, Self-confidence building, negotiation skills, assertiveness.

Access to Business Related Services

Business counselling and follow-up services after training or counselling.

Access to Information in all Aspects

Marketing, Credit facilities and financial services, technology, training and education.

Legal Issues

- Discriminating laws, e.g., Property Rights, Inheritance Laws which deprive women of capital (or) collateral/securities.
- Police harassment on grounds of certain regulations exist (e.g. License requirements); restrictions to operate in certain areas (e.g., residential *versus* commercial areas)

Gender Issues

- Mixed with socio-cultural factors, the concern of the

women's place and their role within the family and society; the perception of family and society's expectation on women, etc. and she is the care-taker of the family, and not the bread-winner. Her primary role is in the family sphere, and not in the public sphere. Even if the reality is often different, these social norms and expectations, limit women's options; they limit women's mobility and acceptability in the business world; they determine the approach of bankers/credit institutions to women; they determine the support or approval by family members; they affect the self-esteem and self-confidence; they influence the nature and quality of work experience which women "are allowed to" acquire; and the educational level and level of professional experience also have the influence on women entrepreneurs.

OVERCOME THE PROBLEMS TO EMPOWERMENT OF WOMEN

The above problems of women entrepreneurs can be solved by adoption of the following ways and means:

- As far as development of women entrepreneurship is concerned there is no dearth of entrepreneurial talent among women, what is needed is to develop a clear entrepreneurial attitude.
  Natural talents, aptitudes, capabilities can be multiplied through training programmes to develop self-confidence, self-esteem, assertiveness, courage and risk.
- Emergence of women entrepreneurship in a society depends to a great extent on the economic, social, religious, cultural and psychological factors prevailing in the society.
  Development of women entrepreneurship needs proper environment and for their healthy and sound entrepreneurial climate are to be created.

- Training programmes should be designed in such manners that women entrepreneurs can benefit out of their strengths and overcome their weaknesses.
- Training programmes should provide special assistance for selection of procedure/service so that women entrepreneur can be in a position to perceive and respond to various profitable opportunities.
- A good management ground is needed to women entrepreneurs for their better performance in their enterprises.
- There is an urgent need to educate women for taking up entrepreneurship and for stressing benefits of entrepreneurship. This awareness can be achieved through conferences, seminar, special training programmes, refresher courses, awareness camps and other related activities.
- Success stories of women entrepreneurs from varied backgrounds should be published through textbook of schools, and colleges and possible media should be used to project these role models effectively.
- Efforts are needed to remove the inferiority complex and to make women more confident about themselves.
- Efforts should be made to locate entrepreneurial potentialities amongst housewives and opportunities should be provided to them.
- Governmental and other non-governmental organisations should make efforts to provide facilities in the form of child care institutions like crèches, nurseries and child-care facilities to solve the problems of childcare.
- Illiteracy has been major barrier for women entrepreneurship development. Education develops the personality. Educated individuals can take independent decisions. Through education, knowledge and proper exposure, potentialities of women can be increased. For developing entrepreneurial talent and preventing the possibility of industrial failure, the financial and other agencies

should conduct training programmes before sanctioning and disbursing business assistance.

- Illiterate women should be trained modern techniques and latest trends in activities like sewing, dairy, bakery, spinning, weaving, leather products, screen-printing, etc. So that productive utilisation of their time and capacities can take place. Moreover, there is a tremendous scope for agro-based industries like animal husbandry, poultry, dairy, food processing, sericulture, agriculture, horticulture, etc.
- Women generally do not have their own money to invest. Further, they do not have courage and risk-bearing capacity, which is needed for successful entrepreneurship. In such cases, women with similar interests and similar economic background can form groups so as to share risk, knowledge and investment.
- Women should be encouraged to form Co-operative societies exclusively for women. It is the responsibility of the Co-operative sector of the State Government to provide all the necessary help and guidance. Then only with the help of Co-operative endeavour, women entrepreneurship will flourish.
- At district level, a separate organisation can be formed so as to took into all aspects of women entrepreneurship development. This organisation can help women entrepreneurs in fulfilling their requirements of financial assistance, marketing aid, obtaining subsidies, concessions, technical know-how, raw material assistance, conduct of market surveys to assess feasibility, counseling, follow-up guidance, etc.

CONCLUSION

For stimulating entrepreneurship among women in rural area an significant efforts have to be made by a number of departments of Central and State Governments in terms of offering incentives/benefits. Even the industrial policies, five-year plans emphasize the promotion of women entrepreneurship.

A variety of programmes have been undertaken by a multitude of organisations with the intention of stimulating women entrepreneurship. When such kind of support is extended, certainly there will be spurt in the number of rural women entrepreneurs to future economic prosperity of our rural-based nation.

21

Economic Empowerment of Tribal Women Through Entrepreneurship

R. ANNAPOORANI AND G. GNANARUBI

INTRODUCTION

Women entrepreneurs are key players in any developing country particularly in terms of their contribution to economic development. As such, entrepreneurship development among women is regarded as a tool to economic empowerment of women. A woman as an entrepreneur is economically more powerful because ownership not only confers control over assets but also gives her the freedom to take decisions. This will also uplift her social status significantly.

The United Nations Development Programme report titled Human Development Report, 1995, stated that 'women are essential agencies of political and economic changes. Investing in women capabilities and empowering them to examine their choices is not only valuable in itself' but is also the surest way to contribute to economic growth and overall development. The World Bank Report and the Fourth World conference on women declared that women are central to the success of poverty alleviation efforts. Hence the importance of women empowerment and their full participation is the basis of equality in all spheres of society.

In India tribal women occupy a significant place and the tribal women population was estimated as 4.6 million in 2001. In spite of many constitutional safeguards and economic protections, the position of women in tribal areas is in its lowest ebb. As a way of improving economic status of the family, tribal women are engaged in entrepreneurial activity. In India tribal women are taking up both traditional activities like handloom, knitting and embroidery, jam, jelly and pickle-making and also non-traditional activities like computer training, tours and travels, catering services, entertainment, fast foods, beauty parlour, etc. In this context a research study on *Economic empowerment of tribal women through entrepreneurship,* was undertaken. The *objectives* of the study were:

- (i) To study the socio-economic profile of tribal women entrepreneurs;
- (ii) To find out the factors motivating tribal women entrepreneurship; and
- (iii) To study financial performance of the entrepreneurial activities of tribal women.

METHODOLOGY

The study was related to hundred tribal women entrepreneurs in Theppakadu area in Gudalur taluk and in Kallichal area in Pandalur taluk of Nilgiris district of Tamilnadu. The required data were collected by conducting an interview to the respondents

TOOLS APPLIED

(i) Chi-square Analysis

The study applied chi-square test to find out the

association between education, type of entrepreneurial activity and profit earned.

(ii) Discriminant Analysis

The current study applied Discriminant analysis to find out the significant factors causing difference in the profit earned by tribal women entrepreneurs. In order to understand the effect of the selected variables on profit, the respondents were classified into two groups : (i) the respondents earning the profit less than the average profit termed as-group I, and (ii) the respondents earning profit more than the average profit-group II.

Using Discriminant analysis, an attempt was made to find out the variables, which significantly discriminated the profit earned by tribal women entrepreneurs. The variables chosen for the analysis were age of the respondent (X_1), number of years of schooling (X_2), number of labourers employed (X_3), amount of capital invested (X_4), year of establishment (X_5), size of family (X_6), marital status (X_7) and type of family (X_8).

When group I was compared with group II on the basis of measurement of several variables, a discriminant co-efficient function, which can discriminate between the two groups significantly was derived. To test whether there exists a significant difference between the two groups; the following 'F' tests were used.

$$F = \frac{N_1 + N_2 - (P - 1)}{P} \quad \frac{N_1 + N_2}{(N_1 + N_2)(N_1 + N_{2-2})} \times D^2$$

where, N_1 = Number of cases in group I

N_2 = Number of cases in group II

V_1 = P × (the number of variables included)

V_2 = $N_1 + N_2 - (P - 1)$ and

D^2 = Mahalanobis D-square statistic

In order to find out the relative importance of variables that discriminate between the two groups, the relative share of different variables had been calculated.

The relative share of each variable was calculated from DP^2 which can be expressed as

$$DP^2 = \lambda_1 d_1 + \lambda_2 d_2 + \lambda_3 d_3 + \lambda_4 d_4 \ldots\ldots\ldots + \lambda_p d_p$$

λ_1 is the co-efficient of first variable in the discriminant function separating the two groups and d_1 is the difference in the mean value of the two groups for the first variable. In DP^2, λ_i, d_i gave the contribution of ith variable to the total distance. The percentage of each variable to the total distance has been calculated to bring out the relatively more important variables in discriminating the two groups.

FINDINGS OF THE STUDY

A. General Information of the Respondents and Motivational Factors for Entrepreneurship

Majority of selected women (45 percent) were in the age group of 25-40. And only 11 percent of the elderly women take up entrepreneurial activities. One-fourth of the respondents were illiterate, and majority of the respondents (25 percent) have completed 8th standard. It is disheartening to note that only one respondent had finished the collegiate education. Majority of the selected respondents were belonging to nuclear family. This implies that in the absence that of elderly family members, women entrepreneurs have to take up dual responsibilities of looking after the family and the entrepreneurial units.

Table 1 represents the reasons for women entrepreneurship as stated by the respondents.

Women have been motivated to take up entrepreneurial activities through friends or by family members or through organizations. Table 2 represents the motivational factors for tribal women entrepreneurship.

B. Analysis about the Entrepreneurial Activities done by Tribal Women

Table 3 represents the list of entrepreneurial activities done by selected tribal women.

TABLE 1
Reasons to Take up the Entrepreneurship

Sl. No.	Reasons	Frequency
1.	To earn money	37
2.	For education of the children	21
3.	To meet future needs	27
4.	For family welfare	15
	Total	100

TABLE 2
Motivational Factors for Tribal Women Entrepreneurship

Sl. No.	Motivational factors	Frequency
1.	Self-motivation	21
2.	Friends	12
3.	Family members	15
4.	Relatives	11
5.	Organisation	
	(a) Niligiris Adivasi Welfare Association (NAWA)	14
	(b) Udagamandal Social Service Society (USSS)	10
	(c) Rural Development Organisation (RDO)	9
	(d) Centre for Tribal Rural Development (CTRD)	8

According to Table 3 tribal women were prepared to take up entrepreneurial activities like basket-making, embroidery, telephone booth, etc. Majority of them (28 percent) were involved in embroidery work.

Source of Finance

Women entrepreneurs were mobilizing fund from various sources own contribution, contribution from relatives, borrowing from bank and institutional support.

Table 4 helps to explain the source of finance for the selected women entrepreneurs.

TABLE 3
Entrepreneurial Activities done by Tribal Women

Sl. No.	*Entrepreneurial activities*	*Frequency*
1.	Basket-making	9
2.	Tailoring	10
3.	Coir production	5
4.	Sale of fruits and vegetables	5
5.	Embroidery	28
6.	Preparation and sale of Medicines	5
7.	Mat-weaving	3
8.	Provisional stores	8
9.	Eucalyptus oil selling	8
10.	Winter oil selling	11
11.	Telephone Booth	8

TABLE 4
Source of Finance for the Selected Women Entrepreneurs

Source	*Below Rs. 10000*	*Rs. 10000- Rs. 50000*	*Rs. 50000- Rs. 1 lakh*	*Above Rs. 1 lakh*
Own Fund	9	7	—	—
Bank	4	16	15	6
Institution Support	9	16	10	2
Relatives	4	2	—	—

According to Table 4 the average amount of contribution from bank was greater (Rs. 61585.37).

C. Financial Performance of the Entrepreneurial Units

Financial performance of the enterprises run by the tribal women is analysed in terms of profit earned.

It is evident that Telephone Booth activity was found to more profitable since women entrepreneurs doing this activity

Sl. No.	Activities	Below Rs. 5,000	Rs. 5,000- Rs. 10,000	Rs. 10,000- Rs. 15,000	Average
1.	Basket-making	5	4	—	4722
2.	Tailoring	3	4	3	7500
3.	Coir production	5	—	—	2500
4.	Sale of fruits and vegetables	2	3	—	5500
5.	Embroidery	10	11	7	6964
6.	Preparation and sale of medicines	—	3	—	7500
7.	Mat-weaving	3	—	—	2500
8.	Provisional stores	—	3	5	10625
9.	Eucalyptus oil selling	—	5	3	9375
10.	Winter green oil selling	—	3	—	7500
11.	Telephone booth	—	—	2	12500

are able to obtain more profit. The average profit earned from this activity was estimated to be Rs. 12500.

Identification of the Determinants of the Profit Earned by Selected Tribal Women

With the help of discriminant analysis the current study tried to find out the variables, which significantly discriminated the significant factors influencing the profit earned by tribal women. The variables chosen the analysis were, age (X_1), years of schooling (X_2), number of labourers employed (X_3), amount of capital invested (X_4), year of establishment (X_5), size of family (X_6), martial status (X_7) and type of family (X_8). Table 6 shows Wilk's lambda, its equivalent univariate F-test and significant level of the variables that vary hypothetical to discriminate between the two groups under investigation

The current study applied chi-square analysis to find out the association between the type of activity and profit earned. It found that there was no association between type of activity and profit earned since the calculated chi-square value (1.47) was less than $\chi^2_{0.05} = 3.54$.

TABLE 6

Wilk's Lambda and Relative Discriminating Power of the Selected Variables

Variable	*Wilk's lambda*	*Significance*	*Group I*	*Group II*	*Relative discriminating power*	*Contribution of the variable to discriminating power (in percent)*
(1)	(2)	(3)	(4)	(5)	(6)	(7)
X_1	1.0	.019	44.0755	43.8085	0.42	3.006
X_2	.624	59.117	1.3396	1.9362	.450	32.21
X_3	.995	.456	2.5472	2.6596	.296	21.19
X_4	.464	113.115	7037.74	11808.51	.337	24.12
X_5	.998	.188	1998.02	1998.28	.065	4.65
X_6	.980	1.982	3.5094	3.1915	.103	7.37
X_7	1.0	.038	1.0943	1.1064	.038	2.72
X_8	.993	.665	1.7547	1.6809	.066	4.72

Contribution to the Family

The current study found that all the respondents were spending the entire profit for the sake of family. Hence there was full contribution to family income by the selected tribal women.

Amount of Savings

Since savings is the source of fund, the current study tried to find out the mode and amount of savings. The study noted that of the total respondents 90 percent were saving through bank, post office, chits and the average amount of savings was estimated as Rs. 2980.

D. Problems Faced by Women Entrepreneurs

Women entrepreneurs are facing many problems relating to finance, raw-material, labour, etc. Limited finance is the major constraint of the tribal women entrepreneurs. Since many of the tribal families are living below poverty line, the women entrepreneurs cannot mobilise the required finance. The second important constraint faced by selected tribal women entrepreneurs is irregular supply of raw materials. For the women to be effectively involved, shortage of raw material poses a difficulty. Further the respondents felt that they did not receive recognition and appreciation from the family members.

Measures Recommended

1. There is need for developing self-confidence in tribal women by having an interaction with the successful women entrepreneurs;
2. Literacy level of tribal women should be enhanced;
3. All women entrepreneurs should join and form cooperative societies to run their enterprises effectively;
4. Tribal women should be made aware of various credit facilities, financial incentives and subsidies; and
5. Non-Governmental Organisations who have a direct control and influence on tribal people should play a

vital role in shaping and guiding them in running entrepreneurial activities.

References

Books

Govinda, Chandra Panda (2006), "Development of Tribal Women through Self-help Group", in "Rural Development of India", ed. by Narsimha Rao, Serials Publication, New Delhi, pp. 80-84.

Lalitha, N. (2007), "Grassroots Entrepreneurship-glimpses of Self Help Groups Case—Sasikamar, K. (2000), "Women Entrepreneurship", Vikas Publishing House Pvt. Ltd., New Delhi, pp. 141-47.

Setty, E.D. (2004), "Clinical Approach to Promotion of Entrepreneurship among Women", Anmol Publications Pvt. Ltd., New Delhi, pp. 18-36, 161-99.

Journals

Anuradha Mathu and Nilam Shukla (2005), "Women Entrepreneurship in India—Some Concerns", *Social Change*, Vol. 52, No. 6, pp. 8-10.

Arundhati Chattopadhya (2005), "Women and Entrepreneurship", *Yojana*, Vol. 49, pp. 27-33.

Inbalakshmi, M. (2004), "Development of Women Entrepreneurs", *Kisan World*, Vol. 31, No. 6, pp. 35-36.

Kamar, Jahan K. and R. Veerasekaran (2000), "Women Entrepreneurs in Urban Informal Sector", *Rural India*, Vol. 63, No. 10, pp. 199-201.

Rajanarayanan (2004), "Support Systems for the Success of Women Entrepreneurs", *Kisan World*, Vol. 31, No. 12, pp. 17-18.

Sardana, C.K. (2002), "Capacity Building for Entrepreneurship", *Laghu Udyog Samachar*, Vol. XXVI, Nos. 6-8, pp. 34-35.

Satya Sundaram I. (2004), "Encouraging Women's Entrepreneurship", *Social Welfare*, Vol. 50, No. 12, pp. 13-15.

Sunil Goyal (2004), "Women Entrepreneurship and Empowerment", *Social Welfare*, Vol. 50, No. 12, pp. 19-21.

Employment Generation Through SHGs in Dharmapuri District, Tamilnadu

T. SUBRAMANIAN AND C. PARAMASIVAN

INTRODUCTION

Women become a powerful and unavoidable part of the social and economic set-up of our country. Now in India women contribution to the industrial sectors is rapidly growing with multidimensional basis and Government encourage the women become and independent and self-sustainable person in the society, which will be only alternative for the fast and sustainable growth of the nation. Women entrepreneurs are completion for the future generation and it can't be avoided in the field of the socio-economic development of the nation.

Women empowerment through Self Help Groups constitutes an emerging and fast growing trend towards socio-economic development of the nation. Self Help Groups are one of the innovative and need-based schemes to accelerate the women entrepreneurship, women's Self-employment and women empowerment. This concept was successfully implemented in Bangladesh and in India it become the wide tools improve the social and economic development. Government also provides financial and non-financial assistance to promote the Self Help Groups for women empowerments; Banks and financial institutions also realized the impact of the Self Help Groups, hence they are channeling their funds for women and rural development through Self Help Groups.

OBJECTIVES OF THE STUDY

The primary objective of the research study is to examine the role of Self Help Groups towards the employment generation in Pappirettipatti Taluk of Dharmapuri district, Tamilnadu.

RESEARCH METHODOLOGY

The present research study is descriptive in nature and used both primary and secondary data. Primary data collected through interview with Self Help Groups and periodical observations. The secondary data collected through official Reports, Records and Published materials, etc. Some of the statistical tools were used to analyse and interpret the data.

PROFILE OF PAPPIREDDIPATTI

As of 2001 India Pappireddipatti had a population of 8591. Males constitute 51 per cent of the population and females 49 per cent. Pappireddipatti has an average literacy rate of 66 per cent, higher than the national average of 59.5 per cent: male literacy is 74 per cent, and female literacy is 57 per cent. In Pappireddipatti, 11 per cent of the population is under 6 years of age. Pappireddipatti is a small town (Taluk in Dharmapuri District) almost surrounded by 4 hills in four directions. The temperature varies from 21-35 degree Celsius.The literacy rate increasing in very fast manner. It has many skilled professional engineers and technically sound people.

WOMEN ENTREPRENEURSHIP AND EMPLOYMENT

Employment generation is one of the most important parts of any kind of Socio-economic development of the nation, which helps to solve many problems such as poverty, illiteracy, terrorisms and untouchables. Self Help Groups provides wide range of employment opportunities to rural women and they can empower in all the fields.

TABLE I

Women Entrepreneurship and Employment Generation

Sl. No.	Block Name	Women Entrepreneur	Employment
1.	Adikarapatty	289	789
2.	Balasamudaram	204	457
3.	Bommidi	373	1,055
4.	Buddireddipatti	250	759
5.	Venkatasamudram	207	491
	Total	1,323	3,551

Source : Primary data.

Table 1 presented that the employment generation through women Entrepreneurs in the study area. Pappirettipatti Taluk consists of 144 villages with 1323 small women entrepreneur and they are provides employment opportunity to 3551 women during the year 2007-08. Employment opportunities to 3551 women are the great achievement of the women entrepreneurs and it leads to improve the standard of living of the women. Correlation between the women entrepreneurs and employment is significant (0.972) at the 0.01 level (2-tailed).

EARNING CAPACITY OF WOMEN ENTREPRENEURS

Earning capacity depends upon the person to person and

it consists of some of the factors such as age, sex, education, skill and attitude. Women earning capacity based on the physical nature and their educational background. But now in India, women attitude towards employment has been changed and they are ready to involve in hard working activities. It leads to improve the earning capacity of the women.

TABLE 2
Earning Capacity of Women Entrepreneurs

Sl. No.	*Block*	*Women Entrepreneurs*	*Earnings (Rs. In Lakhs)*
1.	Adikarapatty	289	57.28
2.	Balasamudaram	204	41.32
3.	Bommidi	373	96.25
4.	Buddireddipatti	250	39.32
5.	Venkatasamudram	207	29.38
	Total	1,323	263.55

Source : Primary data.

Table 2 reveals that the earnings capacity of the women entrepreneurs in Pappirettipatti Taluk. There are 1323 women entrepreneurs earned Rs. 528.05 lakhs in the year 2008. It is a remarkable achievement of the women entrepreneurs. Correlation is significant (0.960) at the 0.01 level (2-tailed) between the women entrepreneurs and their earnings.

ECONOMIC DEVELOPMENT

Economic development is a concept, which provides information regarding the economic position of the country. Economic development can be measures with the help of various factors such as population, income, standard of living, punching power and money supply.

Table 3 shows that the economic development through self help group in Pappireddipatti Taluk during the study period. There are 1323 Women entrepreneurs are activity involved in various activities through SHGs in Pappireddipatti

TABLE 3
Economic Development through SHG

Sl. No.	*Economic Development*	*Impact*
1.	No. of Women Entrepreneurs	1323
2.	Employment generation	3551
3.	Savings of SHG	Rs. 13,523,385
4.	Earnings of SHG	Rs. 52,804,500
5.	Awareness about empowerment	80%
6.	Educational Support	50%

Source : Primary data.

Taluk. It is the greatest achievement of the Self Help Groups and the supporting agencies.

There are 3551 persons got employment opportunities with the help of the Self Help Groups remarkable savings and earnings were also recorded. 80 per cent of the women got social and economical awareness and 50 per cent of the women got educational facilities through Self Help Groups.

Table 4 shows that the activities of SHGs in Pappireddipatti Taluk. Majority of the SHGs involved in self-

TABLE 4
Business Activities of Self Help Groups

Sl. No.	*Business Activities Involved*	*No. of SHGs*	*Percentage*
1.	Self-Business	27	34.18
2.	Bricks Work	1	12.75
3.	Milch Animals	18	22.78
4.	Vegetable Stall	4	5.06
5.	Small Business	11	13.92
6.	Agriculture	5	6.33
7.	Petty Shop	3	3.80
8.	Flower Trading	1	1.27
9.	Sheep Shape ring	9	11.39
	Total	79	100

Source : Primary data.

business (34.18%), 22.78 per cent of SHGs involved in milch animals activities and 13.92 per cent in small business activities. Sheep Shape ring (11.39%), agriculture (6.33%), Petty Shop (3.80%), Vegetable Stall (5.06%), Flower Trading (1.27%) and Bricks work are also some of the activities involved by the SHGs in Pappirettipatti taluk.

FINDINGS

Women become a powerful and unavoidable part of social and economic set-up of our country. Women entrepreneurship through SHGs constitutes an emerging and fast growing trend towards socio-economic development, employment generation and women empowerment. There are 3551 women were got the employment opportunities through the SHGs.

The earning capacity of the Women entrepreneurs is Rs. 52 core from 1232 Women entrepreneurs. Women entrepreneurs also provide assistance to economic development of the Pappireddipatti taluk through, employment generation (355 persons), savings (Rs. 13 core) and Earnings (Rs. 52 core). There are 79 SHGs involving some of the business activities such as Self-business, Bricks Works, Milch Animals, Vegetable Stall, Flower trading, Petty shop, Sheep Shape ring, etc.

CONCLUSION

SHGs play a key role in the field of socio-economic development of the nation particularly in rural area. Modern SHGs involve almost all the business activities, promotion of SHGs leads to provides more employment opportunities to women in rural area Pappireddipatti is one of the most backward taluk in Dharmapuri district, which obtains the satisfactory level of employment opportunities, income generation and savings through SHG.

REFERENCES

Asohkan, R., Ponnarasu, S., Kalavathi, M.S., Inter-District Variations in the Performance of Self-Help Groups in Tamilnadu, *Cooperative Perspective*, Vol. 40, No. 2, July-September 2005.

Job, K.T., "Women Entrepreneurship Development—An Alternative for Gender Empowerment", *Women Entrepreneurship*, Sasikumar, K., Vikas Publishing House Private Limited, 1998, p. 89.

Khanka, S.S., Entrepreneurial Development, S. Chand and Company Ltd., New Delhi 1998.

Mustiray, Begum, Women Entrepreneurship in India : Challenges and Strategies, *University News*, 44(15), April 10-16, 2006.

Nanaware, H.S., and Mahadik, T.J., Impact of SHGs in Malshiras Tehsil in Solapur District of Maharashtra, *Indian Journal of Economics*, Mumbai, 2006.

Singh, K., Women Entrepreneurship, Ashish Publishing House, New Delhi, 1998.

23

Economic Empowerment of Migrant Women in Brick Manufacturing Units in Coimbatore

K. ARULSELVAM

Economic growth is a means to human well-being and to the expansion of human freedom. It is not an end in itself, with intrinsic value. The ends are realizing human rights and advancing human development. (*Human Development Report, 2000*)

Human resources have a two prolonged relationship with economic development. As a resource, people are available as factors of production to work in combination with other factors. As consumers, the goal of economic development is to maximize realization of their desires and aspirations. Fuller and better utilization of human resources is a means of achieving development in any country. Human resources especially women power that is women's share in development is considered as one of the most important factors. *(Dhingra and Garg, 2005)* Women are an integral part of society, and hence round development and harmonious growth of a nation would be possible only when women are given their desired place and position in the society.

Empowerment of women being one of the primary objectives of the Ninth Plan (1997-2002), every effort was made to create an enabling environment where women can freely exercise their rights both within and outside home as equal partners along with men.

Women as an independent target group, account for 495.74 million and represent 48.3 percent of the country's population as per 2001 census. Empowering women as a process demands a life-cycle approach. Therefore, every stage of their life counts as a priority in the planning process. Depending upon the developmental needs, at every stage, female population has been categorized into distinct sub-groups. They include:

- Girl children in the age group 0-14 years who account for 171.50 million (34.6 percent).
- Adolescent girls in the age group 15-19 years who account for 52.14 million (10.5 percent) are very sensitive from the view point of planning because of preparatory stage for their future, productive and reproductive role, in the society and family.
- Women in the reproductive age group that is 15-44 years which account for 233.72 million (41.7 percent) needs special care and attention.
- Women in the economically active age group 15-59 years who account for 289.40 million (58.4 percent) have different demand like those of education/ training, employment, income generation and participation in the developmental, process, decision-making, etc.
- The elderly women in the age group 60+ years numbering 34.897 million (7.0 percent) have limited needs and they need health, financial and emotional support.

Empowerment is a holistic concept. It is multi-dimensional in its approach and involves a basic realization and awareness of one's power and potentialities, capabilities and competencies and of one's right and opportunities for development in important spheres. Such dimensions of development or empowerment may be categorized as legal, political, economic and social.

The strategy of empowering women involves the following:

- Social Empowerment
- Economic Empowerment
- Gender Justice

SOCIAL EMPOWERMENT

Creating an enabling environment through various affirmative developmental policies and programmes for development of women, besides providing them easy and equal access to all the basic minimum services so as to enable them to realize their full potentials.

ECONOMIC EMPOWERMENT

To ensure provisions of training, employment and income generation activities with both 'forward' and 'backward' linkages with the ultimate objectives of making all potential women economically independent and self-reliant.

GENDER JUSTICE

To eliminate all forms of gender discrimination and thus allow women to enjoy all rights and fundamental freedom on par with men in all spheres, viz., political, economic, social, civil, cultural, etc.

As the ultimate goal or objective of empowering women is to make them economically independent and self-reliant, economic empowerment occupies an important position and utmost significance for a lasting and sustainable development of a society.

So, the current paper focuses on only economic empowerment of women and the sequence of the paper is as follows:

I. Present status of women in terms of select gender development indicators.
II. Employment situation and work participation.
III. Problems encountered by women in informal sector.
IV. Critical areas of concern and initiatives needed.

I. Present Status of Women

This section gives an account of achievements in the select indicators of demography, literacy and education, work and employment.

TABLE I

Population by Sex and Decennial Growth Rate

Census	*Male*		*Female*		*Total*	
	Population	*DGR*	*Population*	*DGR*	*Population*	*DGR*
1981	353.4	24.41	330.0	24.93	683.4	24.66
1991	439.2	24.30	407.1	23.37	846.3	23.86
2001	531.3	20.03	495.7	21.79	1027.0	21.34

Source : Census Figures 1981, 1991, 2001 : Registrar-General and Census Commissioner, GOI, New Delhi.

There has been a slight increase in the female population of the country; from 407.1 million in 1991 to 495.7 million in 2001, yet the demographic imbalances between women and men continue to exist till date.

The sex ratio which represents the survival scene of women, registered a very marginal improvement from 927 in 1991 to 93 in 2001 as evident in Table 2.

The mean age of marriage for females has also increased from 18.3 years in 1981 to 19.5 years in 1997, this is due to Child Marriage Restraint Act of 1976, education and employment of women/girls also played a very important role in raising the age of marriage. Literacy levels bear the important relationship to women's occupational behaviour. The

TABLE 2
Sex Ratio (1981-2001)

Census	Sex Ratio
1981	937
1991	927
2001	933

Note : Sex Ratio: Females per 1000 males.
Source : Census of India 2001, 1991 and 1981.

more education a woman status attains, the higher her occupational prestige and more time she spends in labour market.

II. Employment Situation and Work Participation

Details on women work participation in India are reported in Table 3.

TABLE 3
Work Participation Rate in India (1981-2001)

Year	Category	Persons	Male	Female
1981	Total	36.7	52.6	19.7
	Rural	38.8	53.8	23.1
	Urban	30.0	49.1	8.3
1991	Total	37.7	51.6	22.7
	Rural	40.2	52.5	27.2
	Urban	30.4	49.0	9.7
2001	Total	39.2	51.9	25.7
	Rural	42.0	52.4	31.0
	Urban	32.2	50.9	11.6

Source : Census of India, 1991, Series-1, (India) Paper 3 of 1991. Provisional Population Tables : Workers and their Distribution.

Main findings of the census figures are as follows:

- In general, the total work participation rate (WPR) had shown an increasing trend from 1981 onwards.

WPR was 36.7 percent in 1981; it improved to 37.7 percent in 1991 and further improved to 39.2 percent in 2001.

- Increase in work participation rate is more perceptible in rural than in urban areas. Work participation rate in rural areas was 42.0 percent in 2001 as against 40.2 percent in 1991 and that in urban area was 32.2 percent in 2001 as against 30.4 percent in 1991.
- In the case of males, WPR in rural areas was 52.4 percent in 2001 which was also the level attained in 1991; however, there is a slight improvement in WPR in urban areas in the WPR rising to 50.9 percent in 2001 as against 49.0 percent in 1991.
- The work participation rate for females in rural areas has increased from 27.2 percent in 1991 to 31.0 percent in 2001 an increase by 3.8 percent, but in the case of urban areas, WPR increased from 9.7 percent in 1991 to 11.6 percent in 2001, an increase by merely 1.7 percent.
- From the census data, the conclusion emerges that rural women are more burdened; not only they participate in larger numbers in economic activity, they have to return home from that activity to undertake domestic work like cooking, cleaning, tending of cattle and child bearing and child rearing.

TABLE 4

Women in the Organised Sector (Figures in Million)

Year	*Men*	*Women*	*Total*
1981	20.1	2.8 (12.2)	22.9
1991	23.0	3.8 (14.1)	26.7
2001	23.28	4.83 (17.2)	28.11

Figures within parenthesis indicate percentage to total.

The informal sector in the Indian economy grew out of bounds because the employment in the formal sector did not expand significantly inspite of the several five year plans. Employment in organized sector requires minimum education qualification and skill.

People who could not get employment in the organized sector landed up in the informal sector and they were open to all types of risks of uncertainty in income earnings, and suffered from insecurity of employment.

Informal sector which refers to employment which is completely outside the place of institutional protection like regulated working conditions and trade unionism. This sector accounts for 69 percent of non-agricultural employment in India in 1990-2000 *(Financial Express, 2003)*. The literature indicates that one of the distinct features of the informal sector is predominance of migrant population in different activities in rural/urban areas. Such an informal sector is the residual sector of employment for the low skilled, untrained women with little bargaining power. Households frequently choose to allocate labour to various self-employment activities, wage labour within or near the village or to migration *(Taylor et. al., 2004)*. Women get absorbed in large numbers as construction worker, self-employed persons and causal labour in urban areas in informal sector.

III. Problem Faced by Women in Informal Sector

The building and construction industry is the second largest industry and absorbs of the bulk of the Indian labour force in the unorganized sector. This industry is characterized by aspect like instability, short duration, wide range of skill, management of complex information, exploitation of workers, etc. *(Anand, 1998)*.

The construction industry is a highly labour intensive activity absorbing a large number of skilled and unskilled human power. The building and construction industry cover a wide spectrum of activities ranging from construction for habitation, institutions for commercial and industry purpose to construction of large developmental structures like dams, tunnels, towers and so on. It also supports the other closely linked ancillary industries like brick kilns, tile factories, stone quarrying, etc.

Coimbatore, one of the districts of Tamilnadu due to its growing urbanization and commercialization hosts a large migrant population in its different activities especially in construction industry. Brick-making units are heavily concentrated in one of the blocks in Coimbatore viz., Perianaickenpalayam (Kanuvai, Thadagam and Verrapandipudur). In these units around 5000 migrant workers are employed as seasonal workers who had migrated from the districts of Madurai, Theni, Trichy, Salem, Dharmapuri, Kanyakumari and Dindigul, etc.

Nature and Conditions of Work for Women in Brick Units

Women workers constitute around 50 percent of the total work force in a typical brick unit. They normally move into these units with their men or families. They are involved in different stages brick-making. The first stage involves the preparation of clay out of two different types of soil, which is used for cutting of bricks. In making clay, both men and women are involved, whereas in cutting of bricks. Only men work as it involves some kind of skill. These cut bricks are transferred to brick sheds with women assisting mostly kept in shades to dry for one week. The raw bricks will be shifted to chamber/kiln for heating purpose. The arranging of raw brick in chamber is really hazardous to health as workers are constantly exposed to dust and heat. After one week's time, the finished bricks will be ready for sale. In loading of bricks in the lorries from the chamber, women participate in large number.

Women working in industry work for about 8 to 9 hours per day on an average (the working time, starts from 7.30 onwards). They are paid in the range of Rs. 40-50 per day as piece rate, (brick shifting, and brick lifting). As women are to work continuously, they become very tried and monotony makes them less productive.

On the basis of gender, there is problem of wage discrimination mainly because of unawareness and lack of bargaining power to struggle for higher wages in brick industry. Women in brick industry are exposed to lot of health hazards like back pain and hip pain especially when they are associated with brick loading. They are provided with basis amenities in the work place like free sheds to reside, drinking water, meeting out medical expenses by the owners of brick chamber in the case of serious injuries at the work spot. Only in recent times, brick owners have started giving some incentives in the form of free clothes during festive seasons.

Issues of Concern

(a) Public Distribution Services

Fair price shops are basically meant for people falling below the poverty line. Brick workers form a large population earning less than subsistence level. None of the worker can avail the facility of a ration card due to the following reasons:

- There is no provision for issuing of temporary ration card to the worker, as they are not able to prove their identity as a migrant labour.
- Some of the migrant workers have ration cards at the places of their origin which had been either handed over to their relatives or mortgaged for some reason or other. Lot of time is wasted in locating the nearby grocery shops and managing the food items within the restrictive budget.

(b) Educational Facilities

The children of the brick industry workers especially at the pre-school age are just left scattered in and around the brick sheds. These children are indirectly forced to remain out of educational arena sealing their future as unskilled workers.

(c) Banking Facilities

The 'habit of saving' is totally absent among the brick workers. The condition of hand to mouth situation and the burden of repayment of old debts; they have no special saving schemes or loan facilities meant for them as these mobile workers are constrained to prove their identity.

(d) Health Conditions

Since the brick workers are to work continuously with no break, they are exposed to a lot of health problems like hip pain, shoulder pain and sometimes chest pain too. Their food consumption pattern consists mostly of cereals and no adequate nutritious meal is consumed. Along with this, their monotony at work spot also makes them less productive.

IV. Critical Areas of Concern and Initiatives Needed

In the global restructuring of economies, creating opportunities for women will be a prudent policy, for enhancing economic growth. Priority issues for planning human resources to further increase women's participation in workforce both quantitatively and qualitatively include the following:

- The present pattern of education deserves close scrutiny; introduction of practical, technical as an option in the educational system is urgently needed.
- There is need to indentify women in informal sector activities and they are not recognized in official statistics. Women must be identified according to the type of work performed, place of residence, age, social status and similar characteristics.
- Labour legislation, safety and health regulation and employment benefits do not normally apply to the informal sector. This should be considered while designing and planning various programmes.
- The constitutional commitment of "Equal Pay for Equal Work" to be strictly ensured among all workers.
- Special attention needs to be given to improve their working conditions as most of the women work under unhygienic and precarious condition.
- Better childcare facilities, maternity benefits, protection from occupational hazards need to be emphasized.
- Training programmes at the places of destination for migrant workers as they are displaced from their traditional sector need to the organized.
- Creating awareness about the on going governmental programmes on poverty alleviation and income generation need to be strengthened.

- Increasing access to credit facilities for women through banking network system, which help them, promoting entrepreneurial activities.
- Organizing more and more of Self-Help Groups both in rural and urban areas is urgently called for.
- A crucial policy issue for governments all over the world is how to provide adequate social protection for the labour force engaged in unorganized sector activities. So, designing effective social protection measures for these workers, which would serve as guarantee against poverty and at the same time provide adequate employment opportunities need to be given top priority.

CONCLUSION

These efforts will definitely enhance potentialities and capabilities of women to make them economically independent that will in turn lead to empowerment of women. Social groups, voluntary organizations and non-governmental organizations have active role in making these efforts fruitfull.

REFERENCES

Anand Vaijayanta, V. (1998), "Advocating for the Rights of Construction Workers, Nirman Experiences", *Indian Journal of Social Work*, Vol. 59, No. 3, pp. 847-63.

Dhingra, I.C. and Garg, V.K. (2005), "Economic Development And Planning in India", Sultan Chand and Sons, New Delhi, p. 105.

Human Development Report (2000), Oxford University Press, New York, pp. 19-29.

Taylor Edward, J., Rozelle Scott and Brauw Alan de, (2004), "Migration and Incomes in Source Communities: A New Economics of Migration Perspective from China", *Economic Development and Cultural Change*, October 2003, Vol. 52, No. 1.

Tenth Five Year Plan (2002-07), Planning Commission, Government of India, New Delhi, Vol. 2, pp. 217-50.

24

Empowerment of Rural Women Self Help Groups in Northern Tamilnadu

P. PALANIVEL, S. SIVAKUMAR
AND D. SURESHKUMAR

1. INTRODUCTION

Poverty and unemployment are the major problems of any under developed countries, to which India is no exception. In India, at the end of Ninth Five Year Plan 26.1% of the population was living below poverty line. In the rural area 27.1% of the population was living under poverty. The overall unemployment rate is estimated to 7.32%. The female unemployment rate is 8.5%. The rate of growth of women unemployment in the rural area is 9.8%. This is because of the low growth rate of new and productive employment. In the end of IX Plan the rate of growth of implemented various schemes to reduce poverty and to promote the gainful employment. But the more attractive scheme with less effort (finance) is "Self Help Group". It is a too to remove poverty and improve the rural development (Sabyasachi Das, 2003).

1. Origin and Concept of SHGs

The origin of SHGs is from the brainchild of Grameen Bank of Bangladesh, which was founded by Mohammed Yunus. SHGs were started and formed in 1975. In India NABARD is initiated in 1986-87. But the real effort was taken after 1991-92 from the linkage of SHGs with the banks. A SHG is a small economically homogeneous affinity group of the rural poor voluntarily coming together to save small amount regularly, which are deposited in a common fund to meet member's emergency needs and to provide collateral free loans decided by the group. (Abhaskumar Jha, 2000). They have been recognized as useful tool to help the poor and as an alternative mechanism to meet the urgent credit needs of poor through thrift (V.M. Rao, 2002) SHG is a media for the development of saving habit among the women (S. Rajamohan, 2003). SHGs enhance the equality of status of women as participants, decision-makers and beneficiaries in the democratic, economic, social and cultural spheres of life. (Ritu Jain, 2003). The basic principles of the SHGs are group approach, mutual trust, organization of small and manageable groups, group cohesiveness, sprit of thrift, demand-based lending, collateral free, women-friendly loan, peer group pressure in repayment, skill training capacity building and empowerment (N. Lalitha).

In Tamil Nadu the SHGs were started in 1989 at Dharmapuri District. At present 1.40 lakh groups are function with 23.83 lakh members. At present, many men also eager to form a SHG.

2. Working of Self Help Groups

A small homogeneous group of poor women consisting of 12 to 20 members voluntarily formed to promote savings and mutually agreeing to contribute a common fund to be lent to its members as per the group's decision is called as "Self Help Group" (SHG). The members have to be in the age group of 18-60 years.

The unique feature of the SHG is its ability to inculcate among its members sound habits of thrift, savings and banking. Due to this quality SHGs have been recognized as useful vehicles to help the poor in accessing financial resources, which were hitherto not available to them and has helped them break away from the clutches of exploitative moneylenders.

Regular savings, periodic meetings, compulsory attendance, and systematic training are the salient features of the SHG concept. Normally, each SHG member saves around Rs. 100 per month. Each group selects one animator and two representatives from among themselves. The animator is responsible for providing leadership to the group and to maintain the various registers. The representatives assist the animator and maintain the bank accounts of the group.

The SHGs excellent track record of repayment of loans is the cornerstone for the success of the SHG movement in the state. The percentage of repayment of loans by SHGs is as high as 98%. The SHG members use their collective wisdom and peer pressure to ensure proper end use of credit.

3. Functions of SHGs

- Create a common fund by the members through their regular savings.
- Flexible working system and pool the resources in a democratic way.
- Periodical meeting. The decision-making through group meeting.
- The loan amount is small and reasonable. So that easy to repay in time.
- The rate of interest is affordable, varying group to group and loan to loan. However, it is little higher than the banks but lower than the money lenders.

From the previous studies related to SHGs, it is clearly understood that the SHGs are tool to promote rural savings and gainful employment. Through this the rural poverty is reduced considerably. Therefore, women members are economically independent and their contribution to household income is also increased. The present study is also focusing the economic improvement of women after they joining SHGs.

4. Impact of Mahalir Thittam

Mahalir Thittam has systematically cultivated the SHG movement and strengthened their capacity through various training programmes which has resulted in perceptible change in the social status of women in general and rural women in particular. The SHG movement has brought about the following:

- Increased self-confidence and communication skills among SHG women.
- Greater awareness and participation of poor women in various welfare schemes of the Government.
- SHG women undertake multifarious economic activities leading to economic empowerment.
- Women have united together breaking the social barriers of caste, creed and religion.
- Participation in Gram Sabha and Panchayati Raj activities.
- More than 6800 women SHG members elected to Local Bodies in 2006.
- Easy access to credit and improved credit worthiness of women SHGs.
- The problem of "kandhu vatti" (usurious interest) system has been solved.
- Formation of youth groups encouraged by success of women SHGs.

5. Objectives of the Study

The overall objective of the present study is to analysis the economic empowerment of women through SHGs in the north districts of Tamil Nadu. However more specifically:

1. To study the income, expenditure and savings of the members after joining SHGs.
2. To know the role of SHGs in providing rural credit.

2. RESEARCH METHODOLOGY

1. Selection of Area

The present study has covered the three villages from north districts of Tamil Nadu viz., Thondamuthur Village of Coimbatore District, Kavindapadi Village of Erode District, and Ammapettai Village of Salem District. These three villages were selected for this study, because of the SHGs in these villages are functioning very successful manner. The Ammapettai village of Salem district is pioneer in starting make SHGs. Therefore, these villages were selected for the present study.

2. Data Collection and Tools Used

This study is compiled with the help of the primary data covered only one year period (2007-08). The primary data were collected with the help of specially prepared interview schedule. The schedule included the questions related to the general information about the SHG members, income, expenditure, savings and loan schemes available to SHGs' members. Totally 150 respondents were selected from 20 SHGs (450 total members) of three districts simple random sampling method. The sample size was 1/3 of the total members in the SHGs. This is purely a descriptive study. Therefore, no complicated models and tools were used, only percentage and average were used for the analysis.

3. ANALYSIS AND INTERPRETATION

The present study is related to the economic empowerment of women in the north Tamil Nadu. For this study three villages were selected from three districts.

This section deals the economic improvement of women through SHGs. In the study area totally twenty SHGs are functioning with 450 members (Table 1). From the 450 members 150 respondents were selected for the study.

Age Group of Members of SHGs

Age and socio-economic activities are inter-related. The young and middle age group people can actively participate in the socio-economic activities, which is true in the activities of

TABLE 1
Membership in SHGs

Sl. No.	Name of the Village	No. of SHGs	Total Members
1.	Thondamuthur (Coimbatore District)	6	147
2.	Kavindapadi (Erode District)	8	156
3.	Ammapettai (Salem District)	6	147
	Total	20	450

Source : Primary Data.

SHGs in the study area. In the three south districts of Tamil Nadu, 20-30 and 30-40 age groups are actively participated in the SHGs activities (Table 2). The aged people (40-50) are also in the SHGs, their role is also important for SHGs. They can only control and solve the problems arise in the groups.

TABLE 2
Age Group of Members of SHGs

Sl. No.	Age Group	No. of respondents	Percentage
1.	Less than 20	7	4.66
2.	20-30	34	22.67
3.	30-40	36	24.00
4.	40-50	40	26.66
5.	50-60	20	13.33
6.	Above 60	13	8.67
	Total	150	100.00

Source : Primary Data.

Reasons for Joining SHGs

The major aim of the SHGs is to promote savings and to credit for the productive and consumption purposes. This is true because many people in the study area joins the SHGs for getting loan and promote their personal savings, in addition to get social status (Table 3.3). In the study area many people (43.28%) joins the SHGs for getting financial assistance, 32.84% of the respondents joins the SHGs for the social status, because SHGs give the identify to the members. 14.92% of the respondents join for improving their savings. For social, cultural and political improvement (other reasons 8.96%) some members join in the SHGs.

TABLE 3

Reasons for Joining SHGs

Sl. No.	Reasons	No. of Respondents	Percentage
1.	For getting loan	64.93	43.29
2.	For promoting savings	22.39	14.93
3.	For social status	49.25	32.83
4.	For other reasons	13.43	8.95
	Total	150	100.00

Source : Primary Data.

Income Level of the Members

Income is the major determinant of the standard of living of the people. The SHGs member income has been increased after joining the SHGs. Hence women members of the groups are independent to meet their personal expenditure, and they contribute more to their household income. Many housewives (22.39%) did not earn anything before joining SHGs, but after a member of the SHGs, they are also earning reasonably. This increases the willingness to participate in the SHGs' activities (Table 4). Many women members independently involve in the economic activities individually and with other group members after joining SHGs. Therefore, they are now economically independent and contribute to increase their household income.

Expenditure of the SHG Members' Family

The family expenditure has been increased due to positive change in the SHG members' income. The incremental income not only enhance the expenditure of the family but also

TABLE 4
Monthly Incomes of the Members Before and After Joining SHGs

Sl. No.	Monthly Income (Rs.)	Before Joining SHGs		After Joining SHGs	
		No. of Respondents	Percentage	No. of Respondents	Percentage
1.	Less than 1000	18	12	6	4
2.	1000-2000	28	18.67	29	19.33
3.	2000-3000	47	31.35	50	33.33
4.	3000-4000	4	2.66	16	10.67
5.	4000-5000	11	7.33	37	24.68
6.	5000-6000	6	4	7	4.66
7.	Above 6000	2	1.33	3	2
8.	Non-earning members	34	22.66	2	1.33
	Total	150	100.00	150	100.00

Source : Primary Data.

promote the savings of the family after they join in the SHGs. Here the objective of the SHGs is fulfilled. This is a achievement of the women SHGs in the study area (Tables 5 and 6). Usually working women are being respected by the household members and the society. Nowadays the women in the SHGs are also respected by the others, because they are independent in earning the income and they are contributing to household income, expenditure and savings. Therefore, the above discussion clearly states that after joining in the SHGs, the members' well-being has been increased.

Rural Credit and SHGs

One of the reasons for joining SHGs is to avails credit (V.M. Rao, 2002), which is true in the present study area. The second objective of the present is to know the rural credit by SHGs. This part is discussed the rural credit and SHGs in study

TABLE 5

Monthly Family Expenditure of the Members before and After Joining SHGs

Sl. No.	Monthly Income (Rs.)	Before Joining SHGs		After Joining SHGs	
		No. of Respon-dents	Percen-tage	No. of Respon-dents	Percen-tage
1.	Less than 1000	50	33.33	24	16
2.	1000-2000	63	42	39	26
3.	2000-3000	28	18.67	49	32.67
4.	3000-4000	6	4	28	18.66
5.	Above 4000	3	2	10	6.67
	Total	150	100.00	150	100.00

Source : Primary Data.

TABLE 6

Monthly Family Expenditure of the Members Before and After Joining SHGs

Sl. No.	Monthly Income (Rs.)	Before Joining SHGs		After Joining SHGs	
		No. of Respon-dents	Percen-tage	No. of Respon-dents	Percen-tage
1.	Below 100	38	25.33	17	11.33
2.	100-200	34	22	26	17.33
3.	200-300	35	23.33	35	22.33
4.	300-400	17	11.33	21	14
5.	400-500	18	12	25	16.67
6.	500-600	3	2	20	13.33
7.	600-700	4	2.67	4	2.66
8.	Above 700	2	1.33	2	1.33
	Total	150	100.00	150	100.00

Source : Primary Data.

area. The credit organizations like nationalized banks, Co-operative Societies and so on, follow many formalities to provide credit to the rural people. At some time village money lenders change very high rate of interest. In this situation SHGs are the boon to the rural people, because instead of approaching banks individual, SHGs can easily approach the banks and other institutions to get loan. The SHGs get loan from credit institutions then, they refinance (share) to the members in the SHGs. The SHGs charge reasonable interest. In the study area the prevailing interest rate is 1% to 4%. All the members are responsible to repay the loan to the banks. Therefore, members are repaid the loan in time. (Table 9). Moreover, banks instruct the members to save minimum Rs. 200 per month. So re-payment is very easy to SHGs. The loans can be used by individual group members for their personal needs, sometime the group may invest on any economic activities. Now-a-days many SHGs are starting small business, cottage industries, food processing units, etc. The SHGs in the study area grant the loan to their member for various purposes. The maximum loan amount per members is decided by the general body meeting (Table 7). Almost all the members in the study area are availing the loan facilities in their SHGs (Table 8).

TABLE 7

Types of Loans in the SHGs

Sl. No.	*Types of the Loan*	*Maximum amount (Rs.)*
1.	Business Loan	20,000 to 25,000
2.	Marriage Loan	Upto 20,000
3.	Repay the old Loan	10,000 to 15,000
4.	Medical Loan	10,000 to 15,000
5.	House repairing Loan	Upto 5,000
6.	Cattle Loan	5,000 to 7,500

Note : The rate of interest is 1% to 4%. It varies group to group.
Source : Primary Data.

TABLE 8

Amount of Loan Availed by the Members Through SHGs

Sl. No.	*Availed Loan Amount (Rs.)*	*No. of Respondents*	*Percentage*
1.	Less than 5,000	25	16.67
2.	5,000 to 10,000	31	20.66
3.	10,000 to 15,000	33	22.00
4.	15,000 to 20,000	40	26.67
5.	Above 20,000	21	14.00
	Total	150	100.00

Source : Primary Data.

TABLE 9

Repayment of Loan by SHGs' Members

Sl. No.	*Particulars*	*No. of Respondents*	*Percentage*
1.	Repayment in time	97	64.67
2.	Repayment in advance	28	18.67
3.	Repayment not in time	25	16.66
	Total	150	100.00

Source : Primary Data.

CONCLUSION

The study was undertaken the women empowerment through SHGs in the north Tamil Nadu. It is found that the income of the women has been increased after joining the SHGs. So that the monthly household expenditure also has been raised considerable level. But the savings is increasing at slow rate, because the incremental expenditure is higher. Mostly they are spending for present consumption. The members should change it. The good practice of the women SHGs in the study area is repayment of the loan in time. Nearly 64.67% of the debtor paid their monthly due within the time, even some members (18.67%) paid their due in advance. A few members do not pay in time but this is not affecting the further credit of SHGs. Since the repayment of loan is regular and within the time, we may conclude that the economic activities of SHGs are quite success. In this way SHGs in north Tamil Nadu are very successful to develop women empowerment and rural areas.

References

Krishana, Vijaya R. and Das, Amarnath, R. (2003), "Self Help Groups"—A Study in A.P. District, *HRD Times*, May.

Rose, K. (1992), Where Women are Leaders : The SEWA Movement in India, New Delhi: Vistar Publications (A Division of Sage Publications India).

Siddiqui, Saif (2003), "Rural Entrepreneurship and Poverty Alleviation Programmes", *Yojana*, December.

Manimekalai, N. and G. Rajeswari (2002), "Grassroots Entrepreneurship through Self Help Groups (SHGs)", *SEDMI Journal*, Vol. 29, p. 2.

Naraynaswamy, N.S. Manivel and B. Bhaskar (2003), "Networking SHGs and Cooperatives—An Analysis of Strengths and Weaknesses", *Journal of Rural Development*, Vol. 22, p. 3.

Ariz Ahmed, M. (1999), "Women Empowerment: Self Help Groups", *Kurukshetra*, April, 47, 7: 19, 20 and 49.

Lalitha, N. and B.S. Nagarajan (2002), "Self Help Groups in Rural Development", New Delhi: Dominant Publishers and Distributors.

Narashimban, Sakunatala, (1999), "Empowering Women: An Alternative Strategy for Rural India", New Delhi: Sage Publications India Pvt. Ltd.

Abhaskumar, Jha (2004), "Lending to the Poor: Designs for Credit", *EPW*, Vol. XXXV, Nos. 8 and 9.

Sureshkumar, D., (2007), "SHGs and Microcredit in Coimbatore District", M.Phil., Dissertation submitted to Bharathiar University, Coimbatore, Tamil Nadu.

Rao, V.M. (2003), "Women Self Help Groups, Profiles from Andhra Pradesh and Karnataka", *Kurukshetra*, Vol. 50, No. 6, pp. 26-32.

Ritu Jain, (2003), "Socio-Economics Impact Through Self Help Groups", *Yojana*, Vol. 47, No. 7, pp. 11-12.

Sabyasachi Das, (2003), "Self Help Groups and Microcredit Synbergic Integration", *Kurushetra*, Vol. 51, No. 10, pp. 25-28.

Bandhyopadhyay, D., B.N. Yughandhar and Amitava Mukherjee (2000), "Convergencce of Programmes by Empowering SHGs and PRIs", *Economic and Political Weekly*, June 29.

25

Women Empowerment Through Microfinance

M. CHANDRASEKARAN

INTRODUCTION

Women constitute more than half of the country's population. Women constitute about 66% of the agricultural work force. Around 48% self-employed farmers are women and 64% of the informal sector work force depending on agriculture in women. Since the 1990's women have been identified as key agents of sustainable development and women's equality and empowerment are seen as central to a more holistic approach towards establishing new patterns and processes of development that are sustainable. Since the 1980's the Government of India has shown increasing concern for women's issues through a variety of legislation promoting the education and political participation of women (Collier, 1998). International organizations like the World Bank and United

Nations have focused on women's issues especially the empowerment of poor women in rural areas.

Women are suffering from diverse socio-cultural and economic discrimination and disadvantages. Even today the mindset and the look of the society is same towards women what it was long ago. They have been discriminated, suppressed, oppressed, exploited and deprived of their rights and opportunities. They have lower status and low paid occupations, lower economic positions so they are less conscious and lack self-confidence. Hence, it is imperative and worth life to focus our attention on these efforts put up to tackle the issues of women in society by analyzing, critically reviewing and assessing the present situation to ascertain empirically the impact and implications of these academic and policy initiatives.

There is a necessity to empower the women in our nation. Though there are lot of ways to empower them. It is appropriate to empower them economically. This paper is made an attempt to describe the importance and ways to empower the women economically.

OBJECTIVES

The following are the important objectives will be studied to fulfil the requirement of the study:

1. *To know the problems in women empowerment* : It describes the important challenges in the women empowerment.
2. *To document the need for women empowerment* : It gives you the necessity for the empowered women for the development of nation.
3. *To study the role of microfinance in women empowerment* : It analyze the important role of microfinance in women empowerment.
4. *To study women empowerment in Tamil Nadu* : It gives an overview of women empowerment programs in Tamil Nadu state.

MICROFINANCE

The term microfinance is of recent origin and is commonly used in addressing issues related to poverty alleviation, financial support to micro entrepreneurs, gender development etc. There is, however, no statutory definition of microfinance.

The taskforce on supportitative policy and Regulatory Framework for Microfinance has defined microfinance as "Provision of thrift, credit and other financial services and products of very small amounts to the poor in rural, semi-urban or urban areas for enabling them to raise their income levels and improve living standards".

The term "Micro" literally means "small". But the task force has not defined any amount. However, as per Micro Credit Special Cell of the Reserve Bank of India, the borrowal amounts upto the limit of Rs. 25,000 could be considered as microcredit products and this amount could be gradually increased up to Rs. 40,000 over a period of time which roughly equals to $ 500—a standard for South Asia as per international perceptions.

The term microfinance, sometimes is used interchangeably with the term micro credit. However, while microcredit refers to purveyance of loans in small quantities, the term microfinance has a broader meaning covering in its ambit other financial services like saving, insurance, etc. as well.

The "Microfinance" is banking through groups. The essential features of the approach are to provide financial services through the groups of individuals, formed either in joint liability or co-obligation mode.

WOMEN EMPOWERMENT

Empowerment implies expansion of assets and capabilities of people to influence control and hold accountable institution that affects their lives. Empowerment is the process of enabling or authorizing an individual to think, behave, take action and control work in an autonomous way. It is the state of feelings of self-empowered to take control of one's own destiny.

Empowerment can be viewed as a means of creating a social environment in which one can take decisions and make choice either individually or collectively for social transformation. Empowerment occurs within sociological, psychological, economic, spheres and at various levels, such as individual, group and community and challenges our assumptions about *status quo*, asymmetrical power relationship and social dynamics. Empowering women puts the spotlight on education and employment which are an essential element to sustainable development.

Empowerment as a process of awareness and conscientization, of capacity building leading to greater participation, effective decision-making power and control leading to transformative action. This involves ability to get what one wants and to influence others on our concerns. With reference to women the power relation that has to be involved includes their lives at multiple levels, family, community, market and the state. Importantly it involves at the psychological level women's ability to assert themselves and this is constructed by the 'gender roles' assigned to her specially in a cultural which resists change like India.

Women Empowerment is the ability of women to exercise full control over one's actions. In the past, women were treated as mere house-makers. The government has passed many laws so as to empower the women. These rules have empowered them socially, economically, legally and politically. Not only the government but various non-governmental organisations have done a lot so as to improve the status of woman in our society.

According to Namtip Aksornkool "It is a process in which women gain control over their own lives by knowing and claiming their rights at all levels of society at the international, local, and household levels. Self-empowerment means that women gain autonomy, are able to set their own agenda and are fully involved in the economic, political and social decision-making process."

In recent years many steps have been taken so as to increase the participation of women in the political system. The Women's reservation policy bill is however a very sad story as it is repeatedly being scuttled in parliament. Further, there is the Panchayati Raj system, where women have been given representation as a sign of political empowerment. There are many elected women representatives at the village council level. However, their power is restricted, as the men wield all authority. Their decisions are often over-ruled by the government machinery.

COMPONENTS IN WOMEN EMPOWERMENT

Cognitive Component

It refers that, women understand of their conditions of subordination and the causes of such conditions at both micro and macrolevels of society. It involves acquiring new knowledge to create a different understanding of gender relations as well as destroying old beliefs.

Psychological Component

On the other hand, it would include the development of feelings that women can act upon to improve their condition. This means formation of the belief that they can succeed in change efforts.

Economic Component

It requires that women can be able to engage in a productive activity that will allow them some degree of autonomy, no matter how small and hard to obtain at the beginning. Education is considered one of the most important means to empower women with the knowledge, skills and self-confidence necessary to participate fully in development processes.

Political Component

It would encompass the ability to organize and mobilize for change. Consequently, an empowerment process must involve not only individual awareness but collective awareness and collective action.

Social Component

It is a process to change the distribution of power in interpersonal relations among different people, cultures, activities of the society. In past awareness regarding the society is unknown to the women but present scenario reveals completely different pictures and knows they are equally participating in all activities of the society.

Legal Component

Protection is needed for the women in terms of health, harassments, superstitions, cultural barriers etc., and child marriages which are the basic barriers for the girls development. But now there are no such traditions to be in practice. Make them aware of the civil rights, Exercising the legal rights whenever necessary, Preparing and canvassing the documents regarding the legal freedom for women.

NEED FOR WOMEN EMPOWERMENT

The World Bank reports that societies that discriminate on the basis of gender have greater poverty, slower economic growth, weaker governance, and a lower standard of living.

While many microfinance institutions seek to empower women as an implicit or explicit goal, others believe they cannot afford to focus on empowerment because it is incompatible with financial sustainability or because it detracts from the core business of providing financial services.

It is worth looking at several institutions that are both focused on empowerment and are financially self-sufficient, such as Working Women's Forum (WWF) in India, which organizes women to achieve better wages and working conditions; ADOPEM in the Dominican Republic, which provides business training and training on democratic processes and civil society; and OMB in the Philippines, whose commitment to holistic transformation includes leadership training, personal development, and business training.

In India, Women have been the vulnerable section of society and constitute a sizeable segment of the poverty-struck population. Women face gender specific barriers to access education, health, employment, etc. Since women's empowerment is the key to socio-economic development of the community; bringing women into the mainstream of national development has been a major concern of government. The ministry of rural development has special components for women in its programmes. Funds are earmarked as "Women's component" to ensure flow of adequate resources for the same. Besides Swarnajayanti Grameen Swarozgar Yojana (SGSY), Ministry of Rural Development is implementing other schemes having women's component. They are the Indira Awas Yojana (IAJ), National Social Assistance Programme (NSAP), Restructured Rural Sanitation Programme, Accelerated Rural Water Supply Programme (ARWSP), the (erstwhile) Integrated Rural Development Programme (IRDP), the (erstwhile) Development of Women and Children in Rural Areas (DWCRA) and the Jawahar Rozgar Yojana (JRY).

PROBLEMS IN WOMEN EMPOWERMENT

Understanding that empowerment is a complex issue with varying interpretations in different societal, national and cultural contexts. There are some constraints for women empowerment are listed :

Heavy work load of women;
Isolation of women from each other;.
Illiteracy;
Traditional views that limit women's participation;
No funds;
Internal strife/militarization/wars;
Disagreements/conflicts among women's groups;
Structural adjustment policies;
Discriminatory policy environment; and
Negative and sensational coverage of media.

ROLE OF MICROFINANCE IN WOMEN EMPOWERMENT

Micro credit is about much more than access to money. It is about women gaining control over the means to make a living. It is about women lifting themselves out of poverty and vulnerability. It is about women achieving economic and political empowerment within their homes, their villages, their countries'.

Microfinance is now a proven strategy for reaching poor women. The Microcredit Summit Campaign reports that 14.2

million of the world's poorest women now have access to financial services—accounting for nearly 74% of the 19.3 million poorest served by microfinance.

Microfinance is emerging as a powerful instrument for poverty alleviation in the new economy. Microfinance refers to a collection of banking practices built around providing small loans (typically without collateral) and accepting tiny deposits. In India, microfinance scene is dominated by Self Help Groups (SHGs)—Bank Linkage Programme, aimed at providing a cost-effective mechanism for providing financial services to the "unreached poor".

Microfinance for the poor and women has received extensive recognition as a strategy for poverty reduction and for women's economic empowerment. There are good reasons to target women. Gender equality turns out to be good for everybody. The World Bank reports that societies that discriminate on the basis of gender have greater poverty, slower economic growth, weaker governance, and a lower standard of living. Women are poorer and more disadvantaged than men. Again, every microfinance institution has stories of women who not only are better-off economically as a result of access to financial services, but who are empowered as well. Simply getting cash into the hands of women (by way of working capital) can lead to increased self-esteem, control and empowerment by helping them achieve greater economic independence and security, which in turns gives them the chance to contribute financially to their households and communities.

Women clients have also experienced improved status and gender relations in the home. Women's financial contributions helped them earn greater respect from their husbands and children, negotiate husband's help with housework, and avoid family quarrels over money.

Microfinance for the poor and women has received extensive recognition as a strategy for poverty reduction and for economic empowerment. Increasingly in the last five years, there is questioning of whether micro credit is most effective approach to economic empowerment of poorest and, among them, women in particular. Development practitioners in India and developing countries often argue that the exaggerated focus on microfinance as a solution for the poor has led to neglect by the state and public institutions in addressing employment and livelihood needs of the poor.

MICROFINANCE INSTRUMENT FOR WOMEN'S EMPOWERMENT

Before 1990's, credit schemes for rural women were almost negligible. The concept of women's credit was born on the insistence by women oriented studies that highlighted the discrimination and struggle of women in having the access of credit. However, there is a perceptible gap in financing genuine credit needs of the poor especially women in the rural sector.

Microfinance is emerging as a powerful instrument for poverty alleviation in the new economy. In India, microfinance scene is dominated by Self Help Groups (SHGs)—Bank Linkage Programme, aimed at providing a cost effective mechanism for providing financial services to the "unreached poor". Based on the philosophy of peer pressure and group savings as collateral substitute, the SHG programme has been successful in not only in meeting peculiar needs of the rural poor, but also in strengthening collective self-help capacities of the poor at the local level, leading to their empowerment.

The Karnataka Women's Corporation has plans to set-up a resource centre, which apart from acting as a data bank, will also provide counselling and prepare research and evaluation studies. Group financing is being extended through banks operating with NABARD refinance, under the IRDP and the training and production centre programme implemented mainly through Mahila Samajas of the Karnataka Women's Development Corporation.

A widely utilised scheme was the Small Industries Development Bank of India's (SIDBI)'s Mahila Udyam Nidhi which covers projects up to Rs. 10 lakh and provides 15 percent margin money and a service charge of 1 percent (the promoters' contribution is only 10 percent).

Credit for empowerment is about organizing people, particularly around credit and building capacities to manage money. The focus is on getting the poor to mobilize their own funds, building their capacities and empowering them to leverage external credit. Perception women is that learning to manage money and rotate funds builds women's capacities and confidence to intervene in local governance beyond the limited goals of ensuring access to credit. Further, it combines the goals of financial sustainability with that of creating community owned institutions.

There are certain misconception about the poor people that they need loan at subsidized rate of interest on soft terms, they lack education, skill, capacity to save, credit worthiness and therefore are not bankable. Nevertheless, the experience of several SHGs reveals that rural poor are actually efficient managers of credit and finance. Availability of timely and adequate credit is essential for them to undertake any economic activity rather than credit subsidy.

The Government measures have attempted to help the poor by implementing different poverty alleviation programmes but with little success. Since most of them are target based involving lengthy procedures for loan disbursement, high transaction costs, and lack of supervision and monitoring. Since the credit requirements of the rural poor cannot be adopted on project lending app roach as it is in the case of organized sector, there emerged the need for an informal credit supply through SHGs. The rural poor with the assistance from NGOs have demonstrated their potential for self-help to secure economic and financial strength. Various case studies show that there is a positive correlation between credit availability and women's empowerment.

WOMEN EMPOWERMENT IN TAMIL NADU

The Tamil Nadu Women's Development Project (TNWDP) has considerable achievements. It has almost reached the quantitative targets of loans disbursed and has over-achieved by 40%, the number of groups to be formed specified in the Appraisal Report. Its strongest positive points are the following:

(i) Women's groups have been formed and group members have been helped to develop the habit of systematic savings.

(ii) It has made it possible for unregistered self-help women's groups to open savings bank accounts, an important achievement in itself.

(iii) When the Non-Governmental Organisations (NGOs) involved in the project, and the bank's branches allowed groups to rotate their savings as small, flexible, internal loans for a minimum of one year, group members were able to develop a "repayment culture".

(iv) The recovery rate of bank loans is excellent due to the extensive support system developed by the project. This has demonstrated that banks can give loans to women's self-help groups and enjoy high repayment rates. As a result of this positive experience, the Indian Bank is now in the process of experimenting with a scheme that will further decrease transaction costs through investment group lending.

(v) Despite initial difficulties, good coordination has been established between the Government, the Tamil Nadu Women's Development Corporation and officers from line departments, the Bank and the NGOs.

(vi) There is evidence of considerable social impact of the project on women, especially in well functioning, homogeneous groups of very poor women, in which women report a greater degree of self-confidence, greater mobility, and greater ease to visit banks and to converse with different officials visiting the village, compared to what was the case before group formation.

CONCLUSION

Numerous traditional and informal system of credit that were already in existence before microfinance came into vogue. Viability of microfinance needs to be understood from a dimension that is far broader—in looking at its long-term aspects too very little attention has been given to empowerment questions or ways in which both empowerment and sustainability aims may be accommodated. Failure to take into account impact on income also has potentially adverse implications for both repayment and outreach, and hence also for financial sustainability. An effort is made here to present some of these aspects to complete the picture.

While many microfinance institutions seek to empower women as an implicit or explicit goal, others believe they cannot afford to focus on empowerment because it is incompatible with financial sustainability or because it detracts from the core business of providing financial services.

Microfinance can contribute to solving the problems of inadequate housing and urban services as an integral part of poverty alleviation programmes. The challenge lies in finding the level of flexibility in the credit instrument that could make it match the multiple credit requirements of the low income borrower without imposing unbearably high cost of monitoring its end use upon the lenders. A promising solution is to provide multipurpose lone or composite credit for income generation, housing improvement and consumption support. Consumption loan is found to be especially important during the gestation period between commencing a new economic activity and deriving positive income. Careful research on demand for financing and savings behaviour of the potential borrowers and their participation in determining the mix of multi-purpose loans are essential in making the concept work.

There are also some negative impacts and limitations to empowerment. A number of studies show an increase in women's workloads. As they expand their businesses and participate in microfinance meeting. Some women have reported ill-health and exhaustion. However, the majority of women who experienced increased workloads were happy to make that choice and felt that the benefits out-weighed the costs of participation.

There is also the issue of loans pass-through, in which women receive a loan and hand it over to their husbands or another male in the household.

Besides the above, there are other limitations including limits to the level and kinds of change in women's social status, decision-making power limited to making small purchases or other smaller decisions, clients' husbands withdrawing their support from the household, and women hiding their savings or even their businesses from their husbands.

Credit is important for development but cannot by itself enable very poor women to overcome their poverty. Making credit available to women does not automatically mean they have control over its use and over any income they might generate from micro enterprises. In situations of chronic poverty it is more important to provide saving services than to offer credit. A useful indicator of the tangible impact of micro-credit schemes is the number of additional proposals and demands presented by local villagers to public authorities.

26

Microfinance as an Effective Tool of Urban Poverty Alleviation in Nasik District

DNYANESHWAR N. SONAWANE

INTRODUCTION

According to Adam Smith "Man is rich or poor according to the degree in which he can afford to enjoy the necessities, the conveniences and the amusement of human life. Poverty indicates the condition in which a person is not able to access basic needs of minimum living standards adequate for his/her development.

Urban poor are apparently visible by their peculiar way of living a distinct sub-standard life in extremely deprived conditions with inadequate means of livelihood and insufficient basic amenities. Urban poverty is mostly related to urban woman, because 70 percent of women in total are poor in living standards.

Microfinance has proved to be an effective tool for women's poverty alleviation. Microfinance programmers have been implemented through self-help groups in India since 1992. The Swaranajayanti Shahari Rojgar Yojana is the most effective progrmme launched by GOI for alleviation of poverty through SHGs in urban areas since 1997. The main aims of SJSRY are providing gainful employment to the urban poor through setting up of self-employment ventures, employment promotional training, removal of indebtness through formation of SHGs such as thrift and credit society, thus bringing the urban poor above the poverty line.

In terms of poverty Malegaon city is one of the top most cities in Maharashtra. In spite of various efforts of state and central Government to eradicate poverty the results are not so encouraging.

The present study focuses on urban SHGs of Muslim women belonging to Malegaon city in Nasik District of Maharashtra. It is because 82 percent of the population of Muslim community and 1,50,000 people live under BPL in 34 slums featured with higher density, poverty, violence, *mafiyaraj* along with the impact of Religious fanaticism. This paper makes an attempt to know, to what extend Muslim women's SHG is able to make the poor alleviate them selves from the current economic status to the higher level on the basis of such circumstances.

OBJECTIVE OF THE STUDY

- (i) To study the socio-economic characteristics of the member of SHG.
- (ii) To study the present nature of SHGs and their financial activities.
- (iii) To study the relationship between the participation of SHG Members and the SJSRY program and the benefits exploited/received by them.
- (iv) To suggest measures for further development of SHGs.

METHODOLOGY

This study is based on primary data. A sample survey method has been used. A sample of 50 members has been selected (one member of each group) out of which 50 belong to Muslim SHGs. The SHGs respondents were selected randomly from the places they themselves in engaged different economic activities. However, it was consciously observed to select SHGs having minimum 4 years' existence. Data were collected through a questionnaire and observations.

SOCIO-ECONOMIC CHARACTERISTICS OF SHG MEMBERS

The following are the characteristics of Muslim women SHGs in Malegaon City.

No.	*Characteristics*	*Percentage*	*Observations*
1.	Age Group		It is observed as a result of
	18-30 years	48	study that most of the group
	31-45 years	40	members are from the
	46-60 years	08	more productive age group,
	61-75 years	04	i.e. between 18 to 40 years.
	Total	100	
2.	Education status		88 percent group members
	Illiterate	12	are literate and the rest are
	Primary Education	54	illiterate. 82 percent members-
	High School	28	has education only up to
	Graduates	06	high school levels.
	Total	100	
3.	Family size		It is observed that 54 percent
	1-4 members	16	members live in a joint
	5-8 members	30	family. Only 16 percent
	9-12 members	40	families are "we two ours two"
	13-16 members	14	
	Total	100	

4.	Married status		As expected, 82 percent are
	Unmarried	06	married women who are
	Married	82	in the group while 18
	Widow	10	percent are unmarried but
	Divorces	02	divorces or become widows
	Total	100	
5.	Income source		It is found that 100 percent
	Salary	10	members are earning from
	Wages	32	various sources. Significantly
	Business	52	52 percent members earn
	Agriculture	06	from own business besides involving in SHG movement.
	Total	100	

Source : Questionnaire.

ANALYSIS THROUGH FINANCIAL ACTIVITIES

Self Help Group is the voluntary association of poor people especially women, preferably from the same socio-economic background. They come together with the purpose of solving their common problems through self-help and mutual help. The SHG promotes small savings among its members. The collective savings are kept in a bank. By initially managing their own common fund for some time, SHG members not only take care of the financing needs of each other, but develop their skills of financial management and intermediation as well.

Women are gifted with the quality of being good money savers. Thus, this quality becomes the foundation of SHG's economic transactions taking place through microfinance. The following is the data related to monthly saving pattern of women in Malegaon City.

According to the figures given above 52 percent Muslim women save Rs. 100 every month and collective saving per year of each member is Rs. 1200

It is very clear from the figures give in the table above that 48 percent members mobilize their savings from the income earned by them through their own business. Only 8 percent of

TABLE 1
Saving Pattern of SHG Members

Monthly Savings	*Percentage*
Rs. 50	36
Rs. 100	52
Rs. 150	12
Total	100

Source : Questionnaire.

TABLE 2
Form of Mobilizing Savings

Factors	*Percentage*
Minimizing expenses	32
Family income	12
Doing business	48
Other family members income	08
Total	100

them mobilize savings from the income of the other family members.

SHG provides short-term loan to its members. Collective savings is used through Revolving Fund for the internal lendings. Main purpose of this internal lending is to fulfil various domestic needs.

TABLE 3
Internal Lending (Loans) by Members

Amount of Loans (Rs.)	*Percentage*
500-1000	28
1001-5000	58
5001-10000	14
Total	100

The table shows that 58 percent SHGs providing internal loan per head 1001 to 5000. This amount is utilized for the household needs.

TABLE 4
Loan Uses

Loan Use	*Percentage*
Education	32
Existing Business	26
Household Purpose	20
Health Care	16
Festival	06
Total	100

The table shows that SHG members use most of the Loan for education purpose and the rest in their business.

The main aim of the SHG movement is to make women able, by improving their economical and social status. It is possible only by doing any business activity. Various types of banks are providing loan facilities to SHGs to support women of low socio-economic standard to uplift themselves through their own jenuine efforts by working in SHGs.

TABLE 5
Bank Loan

Amount of Loan (Rs.)	*Percentage*
10000-50000	16
50001-100000	32
100001-200000	42
200001-500000	10
Total	100

The table shows that 52 percent members of SHG have

been offered loan from banks exceeding 1,00,000. This loan is being used in 32 types of the business activities.

According to Dr. Mohammad Yunus, every man has an entrepreneurship skill by birth, only instinct at a proper time is essential.

TABLE 6
Occupation of Beneficiaries

Occupation	*Percentage*
Tailoring	14
Embroidery	14
Xerox	12
Picks, powder mix	10
Foodgrain selling	10
School food	08
Dairy	04
Foot wear	06
Other	22
Total	100

Occupation undertaken by beneficiaries is given in Table 6. It has been found that the beneficiaries are involved in feminine activities rather than commercial activities.

The main aim of all the financial activities is to earn more income. Muslim women are doing various economical activities and 32 types occupation are support from by collective savings, Revolving fund and bank Loan. They have Increased monthly individual income after joining of SHG.

The Table 7 shows that after joining SHG, the income level of SHG members is increased which is presented in the table. Before joining SHG 47 percent of the total members were in the income group of 501-1000. However, after joining SHG the minimum income level has grown up to 501-1000. This is a mark of shift at income level. As the individual members in Rs. 501 to 1000 income group were 50 percent of the total number before joining SHG which is decreased to 22 percent.

TABLE 7
Average Monthly Individual Income of SHG Members

Sl. No.	*Monthly Indidual Income (Rs.)*	*Percentage*	
		Before	*After*
1.	0-500	47	08
2.	501-1000	40	22
3.	1001-1500	13	22
4.	1501-2000	—	34
5.	2001-3000	—	10
6.	3001-5000	—	04
	Total	100	100

The income group of 1001-1500 was 13 percent before and 22 percent after joining SHG. The highest level income of members has gone up from 1001-1500 before to 3001-5000 after joining. This shows that SHG has helped the members in enhancing their monthly income. As monthly income is a yard-stick to measure the economic status which indirectly depicts that SHG has its impact on the socio-economic development of its members and shows the correlationship between these two factors. The highest level income of members has gone up from below poverty line to upper poverty line. It means that most of 70 percent of Muslim women are in the process to be poverty free.

FINDINGS

1. Seventy percent of Muslim women has been made able to alleviate poverty through SHG's microfinances.
2. Increase in the saving habits of the SHG members.
3. Forty-eight percent women mobilize their savings from their own business.
4. Women have been the owners of different 32 occupations who do not have one percent ownership in general society.

5. This study shows that the seventy eight percent of the loan taken is used for existing business, education and house hold purpose.
6. It is also observed that women in SHGs are more aware of the education of their children.
7. Women are being brought into the mainstream of economic development through Microfinance.
8. Illiteracy has made women loose their ability to act, however theyhave regained such ability through Microfinance,
9. Microfinance enables women to fulfill economic needs of their families which results in peaceful atmosphere in the family.
10. Income level has been increased through own business in a respective manner.
11. The beneficiaries are involved in feminine activities rather than commercial activities.

RECOMMENDATIONS

1. Women between the age of 18 to 40 are to be given preference in the establishment of the groups.
2. Educated women in the family are to given preference.
3. There is a need of training to increase employable occupation
4. It should promote the members for commercial business activity.
5. Annual audit of Self Help Group's transactions needs to be done.
6. Gradation of these groups is required to avoid the laziness in the groups.
7. There should be efforts to establish Hindu and Muslim women have mixed groups.
8. There is a need to have special attention to family planning.
9. SHGs shall be offered the works like selling of stamps, preparing telephone, electricity bills, rations cards, etc.

10. All BPL families should be included in Microfinance movement.

CONCLUSION

The microfinance has made significant contribution to Muslim women's empowerment and poverty reduction in Malegaon city. The need of the hour is to devise strategies so as to improve the impact of microfinance and concentrate on specific issues like gender main streaming, products design, delivery systems, value added services, marketing services and group dynamics.

REFERENCES

Bhatia, J.K., 2001, "Census of India", Nasik District Census, Handbook.

Dr. Lazar and Deo, 2009, "Microfinance—Performance Evaluation...." Pondicherry, Allied Publication Pvt. Ltd.

Ganeshmurthy, V.S., 2007, India: Economic Development and Empowerment, New Delhi, New Century Publication.

Mulani, M.V., 2007, "The Role of the SHGs in the Socio-economic Empowerment of Women", Pune.

NABARD Progress of SHGs, Bank Linkage in India.

Progress of SJSRY, Bank Linkages in Maharashtra.

Sahay, Sushama, 1998, 'Women and Empowerment—Approaches and Strategy', New Delhi, Discovery Publication.

27

Women Empowerment Through Micro Enterprises

An Empirical Study

YATHISH KUMAR

INTRODUCTION

Micro, Small and Medium Enterprises (MSME) all over the world have been recognized as the silent drivers of nation's economy. Their enterprise is laudable and their ability to generate pools of growth and employment, invaluable. This is true for most developed as well as developing economies. Next to agriculture, they provide the largest employment in India and serve as a fertile ground for incubating entrepreneurs, who would further create job for others. Their ability to create jobs, foster entrepreneurship, utilize local skills and resources, and provide depth to the industrial base in the economy makes them attractive to policy-makers. As per various estimates available, there are more than 12 million MSMEs in India, out of which about 55 percent are in rural India and balance 45 percent in cities and urban areas. The world of Micro Small and Medium Enterprises are extensive and diversified. It is estimated that they contribute about 8-9 percent of GDP and about 34 percent of total exports (May 2009). In terms of activities, about 40 percent are engaged in manufacturing/ assembly/processing, about 16 percent in repairing and maintenance and about 44 percent in providing various services.

MICROFINANCE AND MICROCREDIT BY SKDRDP

Shri Kshetra Dharmasthala Rural Development Project (SKDRDP) a secular non-political registered voluntary organization is one of the leading NGO in the Country. The Project was started in the year 1982, has celebrated its silver jubilee in the year 2007. As quoted by its president Dr. D. Veerendra Heggade was started as a small experiment with a commitment to do whatever possible to alleviate the poverty in and around Dharmasthala, has grown both in size and coverage. At present SKDRDP is active in the state of Karnataka covering five districts where it is engaged in intensive fight against poverty, illiteracy, alcoholic abuse, and gender discrimination, division of villages on the line of caste, creed and money power.

Microfinance is one of the key areas, which SKDRDP is handling since 1992 and today it is the biggest NGO in the country to provide Microfinance. The microfinance programme has been designed to reflect members' needs. From the beginning there has been a demand for larger, longer-term and lower-cost loans than are normal in microfinance, where short, small, high-interest loans are usually the norm. This was necessary because farmers needed such facilities in order to make the best use of their acquired land.

OBJECTIVES OF THE STUDY

1. To study the various economic activities promoted by SHG members in Micro enterprises.

2. To study the impact of training given by SKDRDP.
3. To study the employment generated and change in the Income of the entrepreneurs after starting the Micro enterprise.

SAMPLE DESIGN AND METHODOLOGY

For the Study of micro entrepreneurial activities, 10 SHGs and 9 micro enterprises promoted by SKDRDP in Belthangady taluk are selected. Each group of activity is selected as a representative unit of that particular category. To study the micro enterprise activities through SHGs, random sampling method was adopted. For this case study 10 SHGs and 9 micro enterprises comprising 10 members each were selected. Hence, total 100 members from 10 units were selected (2 incense stick units). Present study is mainly empirical in nature and has given theoretical framework. The primary data has been collected through a structured questionnaire, by interviewing SHG members. Secondary data were also utilized which includes published and documented sources. The personal observation of the researcher has also formed the basis of analysis wherever necessary.

OCCUPATIONAL BACKGROUND OF THE RESPONDENTS BEFORE JOINING THE SHGS

The study of occupational background of respondents reveals the impact of Micro enterprise activities on their social and economic status. The results of survey data reveal that majority of the respondents in the pre-SHG period were either engaged in beedi or in the wage employment or they were unemployed due to some other reasons (Family restrictions).

The beedi work is considered as a health hazardous occupation. Most of them had given up this and moved to a healthy occupation, which speaks of improvement in the quality of life. Around 25 percent of the respondents were unemployed in the pre SHG are now found their bread by taking up SHGs micro entrepreneurial activities. The proportion of the self-employment is very meager (6 percent) and that too they were engaged in petty individual venture.

Thus occupational background of the respondents and the current status clearly reveals that micro enterprises of SHGs have immensely helped unemployed to earn their income. Shift from hazardous job to healthy occupation, irregular and low-income job to regular income generating job, indicates the qualitative improvement in the employment. The regular employment and enhanced income provided livelihood security to the rural poor through micro enterprises of SHGs initiated by NGOs.

IMPACT OF TRAINING GIVEN BY NGO-SKDRDP

As most of the respondents are illiterates and are not having formal education, they need training on entrepreneurial activities and these trainings are being imparted by the NGO-SKDRDP, based on the preference of the prospective beneficiaries. These trainings had really great impact on the respondents. Based on their satisfaction, conducting of these impact trainings has become the regular feature.

EMPLOYMENT GENERATED: NO. OF DAYS WORKED IN A YEAR AND MONTH

The directors of SHGs and the Government aim at providing more and more employment to the working hands. The number of working days before joining micro enterprises is less, when compared to number of working days after joining micro enterprises. Therefore, the study reveals that there is a significant increase in the number of days available for working and it indirectly increased their income after joining the micro enterprises. In entire units, most of the members get work for 300 to 310 days in a year. Even they have the opportunity to work on holidays. It indicates regular work and guaranteed income. It is the result of collective effort of members and support of SKDRDP for marketing of products through SIRI.

CHANGES IN THE LEVEL OF INCOMES

Formation of SHGs and Micro enterprises aim at enhancing the income level of members and thereby they can improve their standard of living. The Micro enterprises formed by SHGs are focused mainly to eradicate poverty and bring its members to the mainstream of development. The study also reveals that there is a significant improvement in the income level of the members.

FINDINGS

- Major portion of the respondents have joined the SHGs after getting the guidance and information from Self Help Promoting Institution (NGO: SKDRDP).
- Most important determinant of Micro enterprise is the pro-active role played by the SHG organizing NGOs.
- There is an internal stimulus among the individuals who join SHGs to improve their economic status.
- It has been observed that objectives of poverty alleviation programmes can be implemented effectively by providing necessary training and motivation to the rural poor and to start micro enterprises.
- The concept of group enterprises has helped to overcome some of the limitations of individual enterprises.
- The micro enterprises of SHGs have provided regular and gainful employment opportunities.
- SHG members got regular and guaranteed source of income.
- Financial assistance/incentives were provided by the Government to encourage the SHG members to take up Micro enterprise activities through NGO-SKDRDP (Government subsidy).
- Micro enterprises are facing the problem of marketing of their products, as the entire products manufactured cannot be marketed by the group enterprises.

SUGGESTIONS

- There is a need for microfinance regulations about the working of NGOs and the Government bodies and the sponsors.
- Proper linkage shall be created among the similar or different enterprises.
- Members should be educated to realize the importance of savings, and income generating activity and its impact on social and economic empowerment.
- NGOs should help the SHGs in establishing, production and marketing of the products for the sustainability of micro enterprises.
- Skill improvement training programmes should be linked with market analysis, credit provision, income generating activities and market exposure.
- The procedural difficulties are one of the major impediments, which denied women in getting the financial benefits of the banks. Therefore, the procedure for credit access to women should be made more easy and simple.
- Single window system needs to be adopted with specific purpose of women's empowerment. All records keeping are done manually and that is very time consuming. Thus, all these should be computerized and a lady computer programmer has to be recruited for a group enterprise.
- There should be timely release of funds and its channelization to the concerned departments and agencies. The delay in allotment of funds and their release will discourage the members. So there is also a need for timely and quick approval of activities proposed.

CONCLUSION

The study revealed that the majority of the women of Self Help Groups have been able to achieve consciousness about the function of local Self-Government, politics, health awareness, etc. They are also showing a positive attitude towards self-reliance and small family norm as well as acceptance of services provided by development agencies. These women are also gradually taking decision independently in their 'household affairs' economic matters, child education, child health care and family welfare. Thus, they are not only participating in capacity building process but also utilizing their acquired capabilities to improve their quality of life in a holistic manner.

SHGs . . . Pathway to Women Empowerment

K. SIVAKUMAR

INTRODUCTION

In the early decades of planning, the problems of women were redressed through various welfare measures rather than the real development schemes. The poverty alleviation programmes are concentrated in only providing financial assistance to the poor women and others. Since it does not gives any result, certain group activities of women were blossomed in various parts of our country. In 1976, the concept of self-help groups gained significance.

SIGNIFICANCE OF SHG ON WOMEN EMPOWERMENT

This SHG's makes the women to let out from the bondage of male dominance society. One of the best strategies of women empowerment is self-help groups. It brings women in decision making, skill development, self-employment, earnings, etc. of their self and family. Women empowerment is an active multidimensional process which enables women to realize their full identity and powers in all spheres of life. This could be achieved through the SHG which is a best pathway, and it shall be properly utilized to being the women development in India.

MEANING OF SELF HELP GROUP

Self Help Group is a small group of individual members who voluntarily come together and form an Association for achieving a common objective. Self Help Group is small in size with membership ranging from ten to twenty are homogeneous and have certain pre-group social binding factors.

ORGANIZING THE SELF HELP GROUP

The following criteria are to be followed while organizing the Self Help Group:

- Members of the group should be from the same locality.
- All the members of Self Help Group should be equal professional and status. Example: Weavers, artisans, farmers, etc.
- The membership of the member in Self Help Group should be voluntary in nature.
- The members of Self Help Group should have collective responsibilities.

STRATEGY OF MAHALIR TITTAM ON WOMEN EMPOWERMENT

The following strategies have been applied in Mahalir Tittam:

- Strong partnership with banks NABARD/NGOs
- Specific targeting of the poorest poor.

- Planned NGO support and guidance.
- Systematic training for women.
- Financial discipline through internal lending.
- External credit for good groups.
- Experience sharing through federation of SHGs.
- Sustainability through participatory approach.

ROLE OF NGO's ON WOMEN EMPOWERMENT

- To participate in joint selection with potential area, block, clusters, villages along with development of women.
- To conduct survey using techniques like social mapping, wealth ranking and PRA/PLA to identify and facilitate the poorest women to come together for the programme.
- Group formation.
- Monitoring both savings and thrift fund usage.
- Assist in the formation and operation of group Reserve fund.
- Guide the animator, representatives and group in proper book keeping and record.
- Motivation and facilitation for achievement of social development aspects of the project.
- Advisor and facilitator to the groups of various social, economic, problem-solving community action programmes, etc.
- Assist group members in selecting suitable economic/income generation activities.
- Assist formation of federations of women groups at different levels.
- Assisting financial institutions in prompt repayment of loans and recovery camps.
- Evaluate groups periodically and improve performance in all aspects.
- Ensuring and helping in prompt annual audit of books of awareness by each SHG.

KEY ASPECTS CONSIDERED FOR SUCCESS OF SHG FUNCTION

Several factors contribute to group cohesiveness, group size, composition, goals, status differentials, age, caste, and education, etc. of members. Higher degree of group cohesiveness, greater is the group performance, satisfaction and participation. The women also speak with evident pride of the sprit of co-operation and "give and take" that ensures during group discussion on who will be the loan receives of the month. Groups enable the members to share their own views and abilities with each other. The group members are expected to develop the habit of appreciating each others. Further the members of SHG are expected to interact as equals with the little social distance between each other group. This attitude of SHG members provided a sense of safety and security to women who are both psychological and material. The feeling of group solidarity rests on the sense of collective ownership of the group's resources and disbursements of loan among themselves according to group decision based on priority of needs.

ANALYSIS AND DISCUSSION

The study conducted in Keezhavezhi Village Karaikal and the data analyzed. The details are given in table on next page.

It is evident from table that all small SHGs seem to be discussing only personal issue in the meeting (100.0%) while 70.7 per cent of large SHGs have concentrated on economic status of the members. But, only 36.7 per cent of medium-size SHGs are used to discuss the economic status of members and each 28.6 per cent have focused on social issue and women empowerment. Further, the calculated chi-square value, 85.05 is significant at 1 per cent, indicating that the type of issue mostly discussed in the meeting is not the same differ significantly among SHG with difference member size.

Relationship between Member Size and Type of Issue Discussed Mostly in SHGs

Issue	*Frequency*			*Percentage*			*Chi-Square*
	12-15	*16-18*	*>=19*	*12-15*	*16-18*	*>=19*	
Personal Issue	10	3	0	100.0	6.1	0.0	
Social Issue	0	14	7	0.0	28.6	17.1	
Women Empowerment	0	14	5	0.0	28.6	12.2	85.05*** (6)
Economic Status	0	18	29	0.0	36.7	70.7	
Total	10	49	41	100.0	100.0	100.0	

***Significant at 1% level.

Source : Primary Data. Figure in parenthesis is degrees of freedom for chi-square value.

The number of members, who perceive that standard of living in respect of fulfilling basic needs and providing opportunity to grow, are more among respondent groups with age above 50 years, primary and secondary educated, business and housewife, with extended family, belonging to larger families (>8 persons), and among respondent groups with income up to Rs. 2000.

The improvement in standard of living differ significantly only across the groups with different educational status (Chi-square = 15.48, $p < 0.10$).

Hence, it is clearly found that there has been an improvement in the standard of living in respect of developing in the economic status, fulfilling the basic needs and providing an opportunity to grow.

SUGGESTIONS

The Self Help Group member must be trained properly to utilize their leisure time efficiently involving in employment generation programmes. The Government identifies the local resources of the community with the help of Self Help Group members. Based on utilization these resources, the Self Help Group member may start cottage industries. The authorities of

Relationship between Joining in SHG and Improvement in Standard of Living on the basis of their Age Group

Variable	*Frequency*				*Percentage*				*Chi-Square*
	Develop Economic Aspects	*Fulfil Basic Needs*	*Provide Opportunity to grow*	*Leads to better Satisfaction*	*Develop Economic Aspects*	*Fulfil Basic Needs*	*Provide Opportunity to grow*	*Leads to better Satisfaction*	
(1)	*(2)*	*(3)*	*(4)*	*(5)*	*(6)*	*(7)*	*(8)*	*(9)*	*(10)*
Age (in years)									
18-30	16	11	14	4	35.6	24.4	31.1	8.9	
31-40	10	8	4	1	43.5	34.8	17.4	4.3	12.74 (9)
41-50	11	7	4	0	50	31.8	18.2	0	
>51	2	2	3	3	20	20.2	30	30	

Relationship between Joining in SHG and Improvement in Standard of Living on the basis of their Education

Variable	*Frequency*				*Percentage*				*Chi-Square*
	Develop Economic Aspects	*Fulfil Basic Needs*	*Provide Opportunity to grow*	*Leads to better Satisfaction*	*Develop Economic Aspects*	*Fulfil Basic Needs*	*Provide Opportunity to grow*	*Leads to better Satisfaction*	
(1)	*(2)*	*(3)*	*(4)*	*(5)*	*(6)*	*(7)*	*(8)*	*(9)*	*(10)*
Education									
Primary	9	10	7	2	32.1	35.7	25	7.1	15.48* (9)
Middle level	19	12	4	2	51.4	32.4	10.8	5.4	
Secondary	8	3	6	1	44.4	16.7	33.3	5.6	
>Secondary	3	3	8	3	17.6	17.6	47.1	17.6	

Relationship between Joining in SHG and Improvement in Standard of Living on the basis of their Occupation

Variable	*Frequency*				*Percentage*				*Chi-Square*
	Develop Economic Aspects	*Fulfil Basic Needs*	*Provide Opportunity to grow*	*Leads to better Satisfaction*	*Develop Economic Aspects*	*Fulfil Basic Needs*	*Provide Opportunity to grow*	*Leads to better Satisfaction*	
(1)	*(2)*	*(3)*	*(4)*	*(5)*	*(6)*	*(7)*	*(8)*	*(9)*	*(10)*
Occupation									
Self-Employed	8	5	2	0	53.3	33.3	13.3	0	
Labour	15	7	4	4	50	23.3	13.3	13.3	11.27
Business	2	4	3	1	20	40	30	10	(-9)
Housewife	14	12	16	3	31.1	26.7	35.6	6.7	

Source : Primary Data. Figure in parenthesis is degrees of freedom for chi-square value.

Self Help Group members motivate the irregularities to participate enthusiastic in the meeting. The authorities of functionaries arrange periodic meeting of each and every Self Help Group and to review their function.

CONCLUSION

Self Help Group (SHG) is the magic word defines the women development and empowerment. This shows the good pathway towards the goal of developing women in rural areas.

REFERENCES

Aruna Goel (2004), "Educational and Socio-Economic Perspectives of Women Development and Empowerment", Deep & Deep Publications Pvt. Ltd., New Delhi.

Kumar Ronjana (1992), "Women in Decision-making", Allied Publishers; 20-22.

Pillai, Jaya Kothai (1996), "Women and Empowerment", Gyan Publications, 59-89.

Gupta, Kamala, Kishor, Sunita, "Women's Empowerment in India and its States—Evidence from the NFHS", *EPW*, Feb. 14, 2004.

Jesani Amar, "Limits of Empowerment, Women in Rural Health Care", *EPW*, May-19, 1990.

Kaliaperumal, P. (2004), "A Study on the Performance of Self Help Group", 21-26.

Kumar, Ronjana (1992), "Women in Decision-making", Allied Publishers; 20-22.

29

A Study on Performance of Self Help Groups in Keerapalayam Block, Cuddalore

K. SURIYAN

PREAMBLE

"All for all" is the basic principle of Self Help Group concept. It is mainly concerned with the poor and it is for the people, by the people and of the people. The origin of SHG is from the brainchild of Gramin Bank of Bangladesh, which was founded by the Prof. Mohammed Yunus of Chittagong University in the year 1975. This was exclusively established for the weaker sections of the community. The poor people can derive the benefits or linkage with various banking institutions. In India, NABARD (National Bank for Agriculture and Rural Development) has taken interest to translate the benefits derived from the Bangladesh model to develop the poor through SHGs in 1992 which is generally treated as finance to tiny or small industries.[1]

The Self Help Group is an association of people belonging to similar socio-economic characteristic, residing in the same locality. The SHG is a voluntary group valuing personal interactions and mutual aid as a means of altering or ameliorating problems perceived as alterable, pressing and personal is most of its members. They have similar social identity, heritage, caste or traditional occupations and come together to attain some common goals and manage resources for the benefit of the group members. It is an association of poor women who voluntarily come forward to contribute something to the maximum possible level in order to obtain the basic needs of the life. This idea is emerging among the members of Self Help Groups (SHGs) towards the eradication of moneylender's exploitation, obtaining the credit facilities from various institutions and the life; in order to be recognized for this purpose SHGs are formed with fullest cooperation and coordination of its members.[2]

GUIDELINES OF GROUP FORMATION

In the year 1991-92, the Tamilnadu Women's Development project started on an experimental basis in Dharmapuri district with external funding from International Fund for Agricultural Development (IFAD). This project is known as 'Mahalir Thittam' which is implemented with the support of Non-governmental organizations and banks. The Tamilnadu women development project and the Swarnajayanti Gram Swarozgar Yojana (SGSY) scheme of the rural Development Department have been covered for Rural Self Help Groups and common guidelines and norms have been adopted.

All members of the group should belong to families below poverty line (BPL). The group shall not consist of more than one member from the same family. A person should not be a member of more than one group. The group should devise a code of conduct (group management norms) to bind itself. This should be in the form of regular meetings (weekly or fortnightly) functioning in a democratic manner allowing free exchange of views, participation by the members in the decision-making process. The group should be able to draw up an agenda for each meeting and take up discussions as per the agenda. The members should build their corpus through regular savings. The members themselves should decide the quantum of savings. The group should be able to collect the minimum voluntary saving amount from all the members regularly. The savings so collected will be the group corpus fund. The group corpus fund should be used to advance loans to the members. The group should develop financial management norms covering the loans sanction procedure, repayment schedule and interest rates. The members in the group meetings should take all the loaning decisions through a participatory decision-making process. The group should be able to priorities the loan applications, fix repayment schedules, fix appropriate rate of interest for the loans advanced and closely monitor the repayment of the loan instalments from the loanees. The groups should operate a group account so as to deposit the balance amounts left with the groups after disbursing loans to its members. The group should maintain simple basic records such as minute's book, Attendance register, Loan ledger, General Ledger, Cash Book, Bank Passbook and Individual Passbooks.

KEY ACTIVITIES OF SHGs

The main activities of the SHGs is to get self-employment for its individual members of the entire group, (as a whole) by pursuing income generating projects or programmes by following a holistic approach, covering requirements, infrastructure and marketing. The SHGs are stated to be engaged in agriculture and allied activities, various activities relating to non-farm sector, trading or marketing of agricultural products or goods, etc. The activities are pursued based on their skill opportunity and forward or backward linkage available to them.

The Self Help Groups take up economic activity of their choice for income generation. The selection of activity is solely based on the local resources, marketability of the product to be produced, the aptitude and skill of the group. The selection of activity is a participatory process where all the implementing agencies like Bankers, NGOs and Government Officials along with the group members after a detailed discussion identify those activities which would be economically viable and sustainable in respective areas.

Empowerment is a process of awareness and capacity building leading to greater participation to greater decision-making power and control, and to transformative action. "Today the concept of women's empowerment has become the catchword. Women's empowerment appears to be the outcome of several important critiques and debates generated by the women's movement through the world, and particularly by Third World feminists.

Its source can be traced to the interaction between feminism and the concept of "popular education" developed in Latin America in the year 1970's. The concept of empowerment of women as a goal of development projects and programmes has been gaining wider acceptance in the 1990's. Women's participation in grassroots organizations is increasingly as crucial to their empowerment and as a way for them to help shape development policies.

According to Khan and Sinha the Eighth Five Year Plan makes a shift from 'development' to empowerment of women policies, programmes and projects designed, assist and uplift the low-income women have shifted from "welfare approach" to an "empowerment approach". Hence, a number of measures have been taken by the Government in this direction for social and economic emancipation of women".[3]

EMPOWERMENT OF WOMEN

The term empowerment of women has been used at different times under different circumstances to mean different things for some it implied imparting of skills to enable a woman to be economically independent. In other cases it has been taken to mean assertion of her human rights. In yet another situation it has implied political participation for political empowerment.[4]

The draft national policy for empowerment of women 1996 describes empowerment as follows : "A synergy of development measures will be affected and affirmative action designed for the holistic empowerment of women. Women will be given complete and equal access to and control over factors contributing to such empowerment. Particularly health, education, information, life long learning for self-development, vocational skills, employment and income earning opportunities, technical services, land and other forms of property, including through inheritance and matrimony, common property resources, credit, technology and market, etc".[5]

Women Empowerment can be viewed as a continuum of several interrelated and mutually reinforcing components—

- Awareness building about women's situation, discrimination and rights and opportunities as a set towards gender equality. Collective awareness building provides a sense of group identify and the power of working as a group.
- Capacity building and skills developments, especially the ability to plan, make decision, organize, manage and carry out activities to deal with people and institutions in the World around them.
- Participation and greater control and decision-making power in the home, community and society.
- Action to bring about greater equality between men and women.[6]

EMPOWERMENT OF WOMEN AS AN IDEOLOGY

The ways of empowering women is through self-confidence building, increasing social awareness, functional literacy, awareness of legal rights and legal aid access, economic development—consisting of inculcating habit of savings, control over income and better management and change from worker status to work manager status

EMPOWERMENT OF WOMEN THROUGH SHGs

The empowerment of women through self-help groups would lead to benefits not only to the individual woman and women groups but also for the family and community as a whole through collective action for development. These groups have a common perception of need and an impulse towards collective action. Empowering women is not just for meeting their economic needs but also through more holistic social development. Empowerment of poor women is a process that enables individuals and groups to realize their full identity and powers in all spheres of their life. This process provides opportunities for greater access to Knowledge, Skills and Resources. NGOs have the responsibility to build up the capacities of poor women through self-help system, enabling them to graduate from the powerlessness to becoming powerful.[7]

EMPOWERMENT OCCURS AT TWO LEVELS

- At individual level, increase of individual knowledge, competency, skills, resources and opportunities, in which enable more effective action and interpersonal relations. The individual who has become more empowered becomes more human in the fullest sense of the word. From the social point of view it looks at it from individual, group and community levels. Empowerment at individual level is assessed by the increase in knowledge, skills and attitude effecting in better self-esteem and self-confidence. Poor women need more than income to improve the quality of life of their families and community, they need increased information/ knowledge, self-respect, self-confidence, skills and capacities, recognition from their family members and the community act large, their contribution to the family and the community is acknowledge and they be given opportunity to participate in decision-making at various forms.
- At the group level, social empowerment is assessed from the process of participation in discussion and making within the SHG and at the community level is looked into from the point of their involvement and participation in common programmes organized

by SHGs and the social action initiatives by the SHGs.[8]

STATEMENT OF THE PROBLEM

In India there are growing concerns over women empowerment. The reason is that women in Indian society were subjected to various social and economic disabilities for many centuries. However, their status began to change during early part of the twentieth century by the efforts of various social movements, nationalist movements and reform movements. In order to uplift women, our government has introduced women development program in terms of self-help groups.

The dimension of the study relates to the analysis of effectiveness of implementation of women development programme in terms of self-help groups from the point of view of SHGs members. This study analyses various aspects of women empowerment in terms of SHGs women's influence over the economic resources of the household, participation in economic decision-making and influence over other decisions pertaining to general welfare of the family. Further it covers the variables like SHGs women's influence on their own development as an individual, power over local affairs and participation in socio-political decision-making. The women empowerment could be studied from their socio-economic background. The study is partly analytical in nature in the sense of analyses of women empowerment on the basis of some chosen independent variables along with dependent empowerment variables.

OBJECTIVES

In order to study the present status of women and their socio-economic conditions and their problems included in SHGs in the selected villages of Keerapalayam Block the following objectives are formulated such as to study the socio-economic background of the women in the Self Help Groups; to understand the SHGs' influence in women's decision-making process at various level; to assess the level of participation in SHGs' activities towards community activities by the respondents; to identify the problems encountered by the respondents in their day-to-day activities in groups and community as a whole and; to suggest suitable measures to the Self Help Groups for the empowerment of women.

MODUS OPERANDI

Pilot Study

The researcher conducted a pilot study in 10 self-help group members with the help of NGOs who are working there and got permission from that office to meet their organized group members. The pilot study was conducted by using an interview schedule in the month of July 2010. After the completion of this study, all irrelevant questions not pertaining to the objectives of the study were removed from the interview schedule and a final draft was drawn.

Area of the Study

Keerapalayam is located on the way to Pondicherry via Chidambaram and Bhuvanagiri. Chidambaram is famous for the lord Natarajar. Bhuvanagiri is the birth place of famous Maharishi Shri Raghavendra's. In between these two towns Keerapalayam is situated on the main road of Cuddalore, Tanjore. Keerapalayam village panchayat was awarded by the former President of India as one of the best panchayat for its service which was connected with all facilities made by the public themselves. Besides, it is a panchayat reserved for dalit. It is nearer to the famous educational institution called Annamalai University. It is a cyclone brone area which is the centre of earth of the universe. It is connected with Kollidam River and other water source. With this background of the study area the researcher has used descriptive research design for the present. For collecting primary data from 100 respondents a well structured interview schedule was used with the application of cluster sampling procedure from various groups.

Analysis

Analysis of the data is the last and important stage of all

social research. After the collection of data, the next stage is the scrutiny of the collected data. The respondents were classified and tabulated into the master table for analysis. The analysis of data is done throw the application of simple statistical technique namely percentage analysis. The chi-square test was also applied to examine the relationship between predictor variables and dependent variables.

SUMMARY OF FINDINGS, CONCLUSION AND SUGGESTION

Socio-Economic Status of the SHG Members

The majority of the respondents were found to be youth, 59 per cent of them were belonging to Hindu religion, they found to be literates whose education ranged from primary to higher secondary school. The majority of the respondents' family members came under adult working population (21-60 years), they were found to be having monthly income of Rs. 2000-3000.

The majority of the respondents family members were found to be literate whose education ranged from primary to Higher Secondary level, agriculture were the major work for majority of the respondents' family members. More number of the SHG respondents comes under the annual income group of Rs. below 5000 and majority of them were found to be below poverty line 53 per cent, they were living in Kutcha type of houses (57 per cent).

Asset Particular

Almost all the respondents have movable assets of by-cycle, Radio, Television whereas immovable assets such as house 100 per cent. The majority of the SHG respondents were found to be "Daily wage earners" whose Daily income ranged from Rs. 50-75.

Expenditure Particulars

The items of expenditure comprised cloth, fuel, light, ceremonies, medical treatment, entertainment and house maintenance for which the range of monthly expenditure was reported to be Rs. 100-200 for all respondents whereas the monthly expenditure for food items ranged from Rs. 100-600 and above and for more number of respondents' monthly food expenditure was reported to Rs. 300-400. Over 67 percent of the respondents were found to be saving in SHG to the tune of Rs. 40-60 per month.

Indebtedness

All the SHG respondents were reportedly indebted to SHG ranging from Rs. 500-2500 followed by commercial bank Rs. 2000-3000, friends Rs. (500-1500), cooperative bank Rs. (500-2000), relative Rs. 500-1000, 70 per cent of them referred to the NGO namely social awareness and volunteers education (SAVE) which helped the respondents to start SHG on the study area.

Sources of Information

"Self", "NGO" and "BDO" were found to be the sources of information as reported by more number of respondents. The eligibility criteria like "Below poverty line", "Unemployment" and "native of the villager" of becoming members in SHG.

Objectives of the SHGs

The objectives of the SHGs such as "Improve the personal Income" and "Improve the socio-economic status" were reported by majority of the SHG respondents. The place of SHG meeting conducted was reported to be "Village Street", "place of workshop" and "SHG members' house".

Socio-economic conditions of the respondents have improved since there were able to improve educational status as member of SHG groups followed by "Became of aware of Importance of health and sanitation", "Being able increase income level" and "More employment opportunities created".

Role Played by the Animators

The major roles played by the animator of SHGs were conducting group meeting, creating awareness, motivating repayment, training up in banking activities and promoting income generation activity. The reported roles of representatives' were "Trying to solve group problems".

"Mobilizing local resource motivating repayment" and "Convening group meeting". Whereas the roles of representative two were found to be "making necessary efforts in achieving objective" and "using local fund effectively" and "Carrying out decisions of the group". The major roles played by the members of SHG were "Promptly attend SHG meeting", "Create mutual trust among all members" and "Must raise questions in the SHG meeting".

The matters related to "Borrowing loan", "SHG business and production", "group problems such as poor attendance inadequate mobilization of saving" and "Marketability of SHG products" were the matters discussed in the SHG meeting.

The conclusion derived from this is that for majority of the respondents SHG itself was stated to be the place of marketing of the products of SHG followed by "Within group" "Door to Door" and "Weekly market".

SHG members met with problems in the functioning of SHG such as "Casteism in dealing with SHG members" and "intervention of village leaders in the SHG function" "Disbursement of sanctioned loan amount of the banks in many instalments", "SHG members made to visit bank several times by the officials unnecessarily", and "only animators and representatives met with and discussed but not with the SHG members".

CONCLUSION

The socio-economic condition of the SHG members were found to be youth. Literate, agriculture workers, having monthly income of below Rs. 4000. This study reveals that saving habits have been promoted among the SHG members. As for origin and growth of SHGs the local NGOs played vital role in organizing SHG compared to development officials with instruction such as mobilization of village women, enlisting women membership, and identification of below poverty line. The present study concludes that still there is a vast scope for the development of the SHGs through the standard of living of SHG members has been improved. And also self-confidents have been instilled in the minds of the women SHG members.

Since economic empowerment is a major focus of SHG it could be envisaged in the form of greater access to financial resources outside the household, reducing vulnerability of poor women to crisis situation like famine, flood, riots, death, accidents, etc. in the family. This programme is expected to increase the level of women's income and the power to retain such income and use it at their direction. Further, economic empowerment should be assured in the form of equal access and control over various resources at the household level and also the financial self-reliance of women both in the household and in the external environment.

Notes and References

1. World Bank Report, 1991.
2. Bulow, D. (*et. al.*), ' Supproting Women Groups in Tanzania through Credit: Is this a Strategy for Empowerment?', *CDR Working Papers*, 1995, No. 19, p. 14.
3. Rahman, A., 'Women and Microcredit in Rural Bangladesh: Anthropological Study of the Rhetoric and Realities of Grameen Bank Lending', 1999, p. 12.
4. Nandeesha, M.C. (*et. al.*), 'Role of Women in Small Scale Aquaculture Development in South-eastern Combodia', *Naga*, 1994, Vol. 17, No. 4, pp. 7-9.
5. Braimoh, D., 'Integrating Women into Rural Development in Africa by Participatory Research', 1995, Vol. 12, No. 1, pp. 127-33.
6. Devi, L., 'Employment and Income Generation for Rural Women', *National Bank News Review*, Bombay, 1994, Vol. 10, No. 2, pp. 23-27.
7. Rao, D.K. and R. Dasgupta, 'A Study of SHGs and Linkage Programme', 1990, p. 12.
8. *Op. cit.*

30

Problems Faced by Women Entrepreneurs in India

S. RAJAMOHAN AND T. VIJAYARAGHAVAN

INTRODUCTION

Women owned businesses are highly increasing in the economies of almost all countries. The hidden entrepreneurial potentials of women have gradually been changing with the growing sensitivity to the role and economic status in the society. Skill, knowledge and adaptability in business are the main reasons for women to emerge into business ventures. Women Entrepreneur is a person who accepts challenging role to meet her personal needs and become economically independent. A strong desire to do something positive is an inbuilt quality of entrepreneurial women, who are capable of contributing values in both family and social life. With the advent of media, women are aware of their own traits, rights and also the work situations. The glass ceilings are shattered and women are found indulged in every line of business from pappad to power cables. Women Entrepreneurs may be defined as the women or a group of women who initiate, organize and operate a business enterprise. But the Indian women entrepreneurs are facing some major constraints like:

Lack of confidence—In general, women lack confidence in their strength and competence. The family members and the society are reluctant to stand beside their entrepreneurial growth. To a certain extent, this situation is changing among Indian women and yet to face a tremendous change to increase the rate of growth in entrepreneurship.

Socio-cultural barriers—Women's family and personal obligations are sometimes a great barrier for succeeding in business career. Only few women are able to manage both home and business efficiently, devoting enough time to perform all their responsibilities in priority.

Market-oriented risks—Stiff competition in the market and lack of mobility of women make the dependence of women entrepreneurs on middleman indispensable. Many business women find it difficult to capture the market and make their products popular. They are not fully aware of the changing market conditions and hence can effectively utilize the services of media and internet.

Motivational factors—Self-motivation can be realized through a mind set for a successful business, attitude to take up risk and behaviour towards the business society by shouldering the social responsibilities. Other factors are family support, Government policies, financial assistance from public and private institutions and also the environment suitable for women to establish business units.

Knowledge in Business Administration—Women must be educated and trained constantly to acquire the skills and knowledge in all the functional areas of business management. This can facilitate women to excel in decision making process and develop a good business network.

Awareness about the financial assistance—Various institutions in the financial sector extend their maximum support in the form of incentives, loans, schemes, etc. Even then every woman entrepreneur may not be aware of all the assistance provided by the institutions. So the sincere efforts taken towards women entrepreneurs may not reach the entrepreneurs in rural and backward areas.

Exposed to the training programs—Training programs and workshops for every type of entrepreneur is available through the social and welfare associations, based on duration, skill and the purpose of the training program. Such programs are really useful to new, rural and young entrepreneurs who want to set up a small and medium scale unit on their own.

Identifying the available resources—Women are hesitant to find out the access to cater their needs in the financial and marketing areas. In spite of the mushrooming growth of associations, institutions, and the schemes from the government side, women are not enterprising and dynamic to optimize the resources in the form of reserves, assets mankind or business volunteers.

Highly educated, technically sound and professionally qualified women should be encouraged for managing their own business, rather than dependent on wage employment outlets. The unexplored talents of young women can be identified, trained and used for various types of industries to increase the productivity in the industrial sector. A desirable environment is necessary for every woman to inculcate entrepreneurial values and involve greatly in business dealings. The additional business opportunities that are recently approaching for women entrepreneurs are:

- Eco-friendly technology
- Bio-technology
- IT enabled enterprises
- Event Management
- Tourism industry
- Telecommunication
- Plastic materials
- Vermiculture
- Mineral water
- Sericulture
- Floriculture
- Herbal and health care
- Food, fruits and vegetable processing

HOW TO DEVELOP WOMEN ENTREPRENEURS

Right efforts on from all areas are required in the development of women entrepreneurs and their greater participation in the entrepreneurial activities. Following efforts can be taken into account for effective development of women entrepreneurs:

1. Consider women as specific target group for all developmental programmes.
2. Better educational facilities and schemes should be extended to women folk from government part.
3. Adequate training programme on management skills to be provided to women community.
4. Encourage women's participation in decision-making.
5. Vocational training to be extended to women community that enables them to understand the production process and production management.
6. Skill development to be done in women's polytechnics and industrial training institutes. Skills are put to work in training-*cum*-production workshops.
7. Training on professional competence and leadership skill to be extended to women entrepreneurs.
8. Training and counselling on a large scale of existing women entrepreneurs to remove psychological causes like lack of self-confidence and fear of success.
9. Counselling through the aid of committed NGOs, psychologists, managerial experts and technical personnel should be provided to existing and emerging women entrepreneurs.
10. Continuous monitoring and improvement of training programmes.
11. Activities in which women are trained should focus on their marketability and profitability.
12. Making provision of marketing and sales assistance from government part.
13. To encourage more passive women entrepreneurs the women training programme should be organized that

taught to recognize her own psychological needs and express them.

14. State finance corporations and financing institutions should permit by statute to extend purely trade-related finance to women entrepreneurs.
15. Women's development corporations have to gain access to open-ended financing.
16. The financial institutions should provide more working capital assistance both for small scale venture and large scale ventures.
17. Making provision of microcredit system and enterprise credit system to the women entrepreneurs at local level.
18. Repeated gender sensitization programmes should be held to train financiers to treat women with dignity and respect as persons in their own right.
19. Infrastructure, in the form of industrial plots and sheds, to set-up industries is to be provided by state run agencies.
20. Industrial estates could also provide marketing outlets for the display and sale of products made by women.
21. A Women Entrepreneur's Guidance Cell set-up to handle the various problems of women entrepreneurs all over the state.
22. District Industries Centres and Single Window Agencies should make use of assisting women in their trade and business guidance.
23. Programmes for encouraging entrepreneurship among women are to be extended at local level.
24. Training in entrepreneurial attitudes should start at the high school level through well-designed courses, which build confidence through behavioural games.
25. More governmental schemes to motivate women entrepreneurs to engage in small scale and large-scale business ventures.
26. Involvement of Non-Governmental Organisations in women entrepreneurial training programmes and counselling.

CONCLUSION

The challenges and opportunities provided to the women of digital era are growing rapidly that the job-seekers are turning into job-creators. They are flourishing as designers, interior decorators, exporters, publishers, garment manufacturers and still exploring new avenues of economic participation. In India, although women constitute the majority of the total population, the entrepreneurial world is still a male dominated one. Women in advanced nations are recognized and are more prominent in the business world. Independence brought promise of equality of opportunity in all spheres to the Indian women and laws guaranteeing for their equal rights of participation in political process and equal opportunities and rights in education and employment were enacted. But unfortunately, the government sponsored development activities have benefited only a small section of women.

31

Women Empowerment of Marketing for Entrepreneurs

S. JAYASANKAR

INTRODUCTION

The issue of women empowerment has continued to surface time and again, particularly in the last few years. It has been identified that education, government jobs, private jobs, entrepreneurship, reservations, right over property, business process outsourcing, information technology, army, air force, navy, etc., are all means of empowering women in India. However, a more detailed analysis shows that for a vast majority of women, education, government jobs, private jobs, entrepreneurship, etc. would empower, only to add to what the above factors contribute to the creation of property in the form of land, house, gold, etc. This once again points to the high level of correlation between the matrilineal system and the resultant better position of women in India.

Marketing refers to the more than simply advertising or selling a product. Marketing encompasses many more activities than most people realize. It involves developing and managing a product that will satisfy certain needs. It focuses on making the product available at the right place, at the right time and at a price that is acceptable to customers. It also requires transmitting the kind of information that will help customers determine if the product will in fact be able to satisfy their needs.

Marketing has been a perennial problem for the entrepreneur. Most studies on sickness in the small scale sector have identified the lack of marketing skills in the entrepreneur as the major contributory factor. As the business environment is fast changing it is essential that the entrepreneur understands the importance of marketing in the management of a business enterprise. The marketing management process involves the following steps:

1. Analyzing marketing opportunities.
2. Selecting targets markets.
3. Developing the marketing mix.

ANALYZING MARKETING OPPORTUNITIES

The operation of any business enterprise is influenced by the environment in which it operates. The marketing environment consists of six categories of forces: Political, Legal, Regulatory, Social, Economic and Competitive, and Technological. Although there are numerous environmental factors, most operations fall into one of these six categories.

Environmental forces are dynamic. Changes in the marketing environment create uncertainty, threats and opportunities for the entrepreneur. An entrepreneur should be capable of identifying and exploiting opportunities. An opportunity provides an opening for the firm to generate sales from identifiable markets. An entrepreneur who fails to recognize changes in environmental forces leaves her firm unprepared to capitalize on marketing opportunities or to cope with threats created by changes in the environment.

SELECTING TARGET MARKETS

Firms must be customer-oriented in order to succeed in today's highly competitive market. Every customer do not want the same type of product. Markets are made up of customers with diverse product needs. Hence, it is not possible for a firm to satisfy all consumers in a given market. A firm that tries to be all things to all people typically ends up by not satisfying the needs of any customer group at all. It is therefore essential for the firm to divide the total market into a number of market groups or segments having relatively similar product needs. The firm should choose the best segments and focus all its marketing efforts on these chosen segments. The firm should try to serve the chosen segments better than its competitors.

DEVELOPING THE MARKETING MIX

The marketing mix is one of the major concepts in modern marketing. A Marketing Mix is the set of controllable tactical marketing tools that the firm blends to produce the response it wants in the target market. The important constituents of the marketing mix are Product, Price, Promotion and Physical Distribution or Place.

Product

Product is to all activities that deal with researching the consumer's needs and designing a product with the desired characteristics. It also involves the creation and alteration of packages and brand names and may include decisions regarding warranty and repair services. The actual production of the product is not a marketing activity.

Price

Price refers to all activities associated with establishing pricing policies and determining product prices. Price is the amount of money that customers have to pay to obtain the product. The essence of pricing is that the customer should get value for his money, and hence it is a critical component of the marketing mix. Apart from deciding the mode of pricing the product, strategies have to be designed for entering a market, especially with a new product.

Promotion

Promotion deals to activities that advertise the merits of the products and persuade target customers to buy it. Strategies are needed to combine individual methods such as public relations, personal selling, advertising and sales promotion into a coordinated campaign. Strategic decisions must also be made regarding each individual method of promotion. Moreover, there strategies must be adjusted as the product moves from the early stages to the later stages of its life.

Physical Distribution

Place refers to all the activities undertaken by the firm to make the products available to the customers at the right time and in a convenient location. The firm should try to make the products available in the quantities desired to as many customers as possible and to keep the total inventory, transportation and storage costs as low as possible. Hence, the entrepreneur has to design strategies for both the management of channels by which the ownership of the products is transferred from producer to customer as well as the systems by which goods are moved from the place of production to the place of purchase by the final customer.

CONCLUSION

There are four marketing mix elements are interrelated; decision in one area often affects actions in another. The entrepreneur should try to blend these elements into a coordinated campaign designed to achieve the firm's marketing objectives by delivering value to the consumers. The entrepreneur should always ensure that a proper marketing mix is directed towards the target market. The needs of the target market should be continuously monitored. Whenever any shifts are noticed suitable modifications should be made in the marketing mix so that it continues to remain focused on the target market. Marketing the needs of the customers and keeping them satisfied or perhaps delighted alone would ensure an adequate rate of returns to the firm on its investments.

References

Kotler, Philip and Gary Armstrong, Principles of Marketing, Prentice Hall, Englewood Cliffs.

Ramachandran, K., Managing a New Business Successfully, Global Business Press, New Delhi.

32

Women Empowerment Through SHGs in Namakkal District

C. PARAMASIVAN

INTRODUCTION

A woman is a powerful segment of the society who contributes more on the development of civilized society of the country. Women become useful resources; we can achieve the socio-economical goal with sustainable manner. Hence, every part of the world, women issues become popular and concentrate more to their socio-economic, political and legal empowerment. Women development activities are witnessed and implemented with innovative strategies to attain the almost achievement of women society. The country can be full-fledged and independent when the women development programs are successfully implemented and evaluated.

Empowerment of women has emerged as an important issue in our society in recent times. The economic empowerment of women is being regarded these days as a *sine-quo-non* of progress for a country, hence the issue of economic empowerment of women is of paramount importance to political thinkers, social scientists and reformers, women activists, politicians, academicians and administrators.

Empowerment is a process, by which women gain greater control over material and intellectual resources which will assist them to increase their self-reliance, and enhance them to assert their independent rights, and challenge the ideology of patriarchy and the gender-based discrimination against women. This will also enable them to organize themselves to assert their autonomy to make decisions and choices, and ultimately eliminate their own subordination in all the institutions and structures of society

SELF HELP GROUPS

The concept of SHG's evolved to organize the rural people to meet their productive and consumption needs out of the savings supplemented by institutional credit support provided by the rural financing institutions. Thus thrift, self-help, mutual aid and institutional credit support are the main features of the SHGs formed exclusively for the empowerment of rural poor women.

The primary focus of self-help groups is to provide emotional and practical support and an exchange of information. Such groups use participatory processes to provide opportunities for people to share knowledge, common experiences, and problems. Through their participation, members help themselves and others by gaining knowledge and information, and by obtaining and providing emotional and practical support. These groups have been particularly useful in helping people with chronic health conditions and physical and mental disabilities. Traumatic life events such as death and divorce are also the basis for groups. Self-help groups are voluntary, and they are mostly led by members. Generally, groups meet on a regular basis, are open to new members, and do not cost money to join. Traditionally, self-help groups have been in-person meetings, but recently Internet self-help groups have become popular.

Self-help group, non-professional organization formed by people with a common problem or situation, for the purpose of pooling resources, gathering information, and offering mutual support, services, or care.

TABLE I
Growth of SHG in India

(*Nos. in '000*)

Sl. No.	*Year*	*No. of SHGs*	*Bank Loan*	*Refinance*
1.	2002-03	717	2049	1419
2.	2003-04	1079	3904	2125
3.	2004-05	1618	6898	3092
4.	2005-06	2239	11398	4160
5.	2006-07	2924	18041	5459

Source : RBI Annual Report, 2006-07.

Details of the growth of SHGs in India for the year 2002-03 to 2006-07 are shown in the Table 1 for analysis. In the year 2002-03, there are 7,17,000 SHGs and now it has increased to 29, 24,973 SHGs in all over India. Bank loans to SHGs in the year 2006-07 were recorded for Rs. 180,41,000 as against Rs. 20,49,000 in the year 2002-03. Refinance also has increased from Rs. 14,19,000 crore to Rs. 54,59,000 crore in the year 2006-07.

REVIEW OF LITERATURE

Some of the review has collected from various published sources which help to understand the background knowledge previous studies about the SHGs in general and particular.

Ashokan, R. (2005), Women empowerment depends upon the success of women development programmes in terms of women SHGs, David Favachar P. (2005) SHGs movement has made an impact on the lives of a number of individuals and communities, they are many pockets of societies which have not been involved in the movement. Gnanasamuthy, V.S. (2006) position of the women before and after the SHGs after the formation they are economically viable and the living status has improved. Reddy, C.S. (2006) Microfinance through SHG has developed over the past several years as an effective tool to combat poverty, especially in rural areas, and bring about development. Sharma, H.O. (2006) study compared the socio-economic conditions of members in the pre and post-SHG situations and the members have improved the business turnover in the post-SHG situations and in turn the net income. Stephen, J.K. (2005) NGO can play a decisive role as an effective delivery mechanism in rural development they have innate advantage to involve people and ensure their participation in the agencies and fellow NGO is added advantage to them.

Jayaraman (2005) attempted to assess the performance of Fisherwomen's self-help groups (SHGs) in Tamilnadu. Primary data required for the study were collected from 725 fisherwomen SHG members representing 41 SHGs from five coastal villages—Tharuvaikulam, Pazhayakayal and Therespuram in Thoothukudi district and Kootapuli and Uvari in Tirunelveli district—during May-October 2004. The study found the fisherwomen SHGs performing well in availing and repaying microcredit which had contributed to their socio-economic empowerment and to better livelihood conditions.

SCOPE OF THE STUDY

The present study is focus on the growth of SHG and its impact in the rural development in Namakkal district. Role and performance of SHG is an emerging issue to strengthen the concepts of financial inclusion. Namakkal district is being strong rural based poor people with low income groups and women are not awarded about the welfare scheme announced by the government. Hence, this study helps to promote the SHG with innovative and moderate manner and brings valuable suggestions to improve the performance of SHGs in the Namakkal District.

OBJECTIVE

The primary objective of the present study is to measure

the role and performance of the SHGs in Namakkal District, Tamilnadu.

RESEARCH METHODOLOGY

The present study is descriptive in nature and it is based on the secondary data which are collected from government reports, official Gazettes, and RBI annual reports. Collected data has arranged in a systematic manner and some of the statistical tools like percentage, correlation and chi-squire test used for analysis and interpretation.

SHGs IN TAMILNADU

Tamilnadu is one of the developing states in India which consists of organized and regulated social developmental programmes with innovative approaches. Social developmental programmes has been implementing successfully and reached the rural population. The self-help group model has been identified as a potential pathway to alleviating poverty. The number of poor women and men who are enrolling in SHGs all over rural India has been increasing remarkably. They are not only active in thrift and credit management but are also taking up other activities, such as natural resource management and development work, literacy, knowledge management, nutritional security, etc. SHGs lay the foundation for self-reliance through building up of institutions, which have the capacity to generate employment opportunities for the rural poor, and the poorest, and lead to job-led economic growth.

Socio-economic empowerment of women through SHGs has been initiated in Tamil Nadu as early as in 1989 in Dharmapuri district. With this success, Mahalir Thittam, (Women's Scheme) was launched from 1997-98. Mahalir Thittam has facilitated to formation of SHGs in participation with various agencies like rural development department, Banks and NGOs the project has made sustained impact on the status of women. As on March 2008, there are 3,54,148 SHGs with 57,66,743 members in Tamil Nadu.

The Table 2 describes the details of the SHGs in All India level, Southern Region, Tamil Nadu and Namakkal District.

TABLE 2
Number of SHGs

Sl. No.	Particulars	No. of SHG	% to All India Level	% to Southern Region	% to Tamil Nadu
1.	Namakkal District	9418	0.32	0.61	2.66
2.	Tamil Nadu	3,54,148	12.11	23.26	—
3.	Southern Region	15,22,144	52.04	—	—
4.	All India	29,24,973	—	—	—

Source : RBI Annual Report, 2006-07.

12.11 percent of the SHGs in Tamil Nadu and 0.32 percent of the SHGs in Namakkal District to all India level. In Tamil Nadu level, only 2.66 percent of SHGs are in Namakkal District

TABLE 3
Self Help Group's Details

Sl. No.	Particulars	Total
1.	Total blocks	15
2.	Plan Running the block	15
3.	Town Panchayat	19
4.	Plan Running the town Panchayat	19
5.	Total Municipality	05
6.	Plan Running the Municipality	05
7.	Total Self-help groups	9418
8.	Number of Group Members	156368
9.	Groups total savings	Rs. 77.76 crores

Sources : Reports on District Collector Office.

Table 3 indicates the details of Self Help Groups in Namakkal district. All the blocks, town Panchayats, and municipalities in Namakkal District implementing the Self Help Groups Programmes, at present there are 9418 Self Help

Groups with 156368 Members. There Self Help Groups were mobilized Rs. 77.67 Crore as savings in the year 2007.

TABLE 4
Block-wise Self Help Groups

Sl. No.	*Block name*	*SHGs*	*SHG Members*	*Saving*	*Loans*
1.	Sendamangalam	285	4911	54894043	99095000
2.	Erumappatti	426	7256	22788099	63029000
3.	Parmathi	244	4273	16855769	38113900
4.	Mohanur	489	8269	34442951	4542951
5.	Namagiripettai	326	5341	19969425	25851425
6.	Phduchathiram	422	7544	22390430	10550000
7.	Elachipalayam	516	8230	22390430	12900000
8.	Thriuchengodu	402	6361	13660428	10050000
9.	Kabilarmalai	410	6320	14049286	10250000
10.	Mallasamuthiram	286	4498	9469684	7150000
11.	Rasipuram	313	5125	21867629	33625000
12.	Namakkal	728	11138	33548819	42800000
13.	Vennandhur	296	4556	11893005	16400000
14.	Pallipalayam	535	2852	18309294	13375000
15.	Kollihills	362	4756	8394758	9050000
	Total	6180	106380	321405640	442882276

Sources : Reports on District Collector Office.

Table 4 shows the block-wise Self Help Groups in Namakkal Districts in year 2007 there are 6180 groups with 106380 members in all the blocks. The saving of the Self Help Groups were recorded Rs. 32,14,05,640 and they were recovered loans for Rs. 44,28,82,276.

Table 5, Indicates the town panchayat wise details of Self Help Groups in Namakkal Districts. Self Help Groups are implemented in all the blocks in 19 town panchayats of Namakkal District. At present there are 1450 Self Help Groups with 24019 members. The saving some amount is Rs. 58,55,193

TABLE 5

Town-wise Self Help Groups

Sl. No.	Block Name	SHGs	SHG Members	Saving	Loans
1.	Sendamangalam	130	2251	12568864	10750000
2.	Kalappanaickanpatti	57	1017	19761811	1425000
3.	Parmathi	56	950	2242430	1400000
4.	Erumapatti	61	1037	248915	1525000
5.	Vellur	135	2150	2908936	3375000
6.	Mohanur	81	1444	1807186	2025000
7.	Namagiripettai	131	2503	3223640	3275000
8.	Seerappalli	46	970	1885906	115000
9.	R.Pudhupatty	42	894	1322547	1652311
10.	Venkarai	69	1004	764715	1725000
11.	Pothanur	78	1242	812431	1950000
12.	Pandamangalam	60	938	375915	1500000
13.	Mallasamuthiram	110	1893	2204270	2750000
14.	Pillanallur	33	547	1223684	1623850
15.	Pattanam	42	732	654180	1050000
16.	Vennandhur	25	414	778275	625000
17.	Athanur	59	943	1157683	1475000
18.	Alambalayam	66	1140	1423480	1650000
19.	Padavedu	53	950	996445	1325000
	Total	6180	106380	321405640	442882276

Sources : Reports on District Collector Office.

and loan some amount Rs. 4,04,96,161. The highest savings is Rs. 1,97,61,811 in Kalappanaickaanpatti Block and lowest saving in Pandamangalam block Rs. 3,75,915.

Table 6 shows the municipality Self Help Groups in Namakkal District. All municipalities in Namakkal District are implementing the Self Help Groups programs. At present there are 1788 Self Help Groups and 20150 members. There Self Help Groups were mobilized Rs. 5,28,89,464 Crores in the year of

TABLE 6
Municipality-wise Self Help Groups

Sl. No.	*Block Name*	*SHGs*	*SHG Members*	*Saving*	*Loans*
1.	Thiruchengodu	260	4234	12168304	24500000
2	Rasipuram	153	2490	16868545	3485432
3.	Namakkal	262	4043	10153935	65500000
4.	Kumarapalayam	274	4442	9545527	6850000
5.	Pallipalayam	201	3313	4153153	11275000
	Total	1788	20150	52889464	173260432

Sources : Reports on District Collector Office.

2007. Rasipuram is municipality-based Self Help Groups recorded highest saving Rs. 1,68,68,545.

TABLE 7
SC/ST Self Help Groups

Sl. No.	*Particulars*	*No. of SHG*	*No. of Group Members*			
			SC	*ST*	*Others*	*Total*
1.	Village Part	6180	34924	5390	56283	96597
2.	Town Part	3238	6234	125	35212	41571
	Total	9418	41158	5515	91495	138168

Sources : Reports on District collector Office.

Table 7 shows that, there are 6180 SC/ST Self Help Groups in village part, which consist of 34924 groups belongs to SC and 3590 ST, and 3238 SC/ST Self Help Groups in Town part which consist of 6234 SC and 125 ST as against the total number of 138168 members in the Namakkal District.

Participation of SC/ST women in the Self Help Groups significantly more in village than the town part of the Namakkal district. It shows that, SC/ST women has awarded about the Self Help Group.

TABLE 8
Bank Account-wise Position of Self Help Groups

Sl. No.	Name of the bank	No. of SHGs	% to total
1.	SDCCB	223	2.36
2.	Bank of Baroda	99	1.05
3.	Bank of India	40	0.42
4.	Canara Bank	597	6.33
5.	Corporation Bank	294	3.12
6.	FSCB	228	2.42
7.	Indian Bank	3556	37.75
8.	Indian Overseas Bank	758	8.05
9.	Karur Visya Bank	243	2.58
10.	VGB	24	0.25
11.	Primary Agricultural Co-operative	2553	27.11
12.	State Bank of India	448	4.75
13.	Syndicate Bank	107	1.14
14.	Union Bank of India	76	0.81
15.	UCO Bank	95	1.01
16.	Tamil Nadu Mercantile Bank	12	0.12
17.	Urban Bank	44	0.47
18.	Punjab National Bank	5	0.05
19.	ICIC	6	0.06
	Total	948	100

Sources : Primary Data.

Table 8 Display the opening bank account of 9418 Self Help Groups in Namakkal District. Self Help Groups has account with 19 banks in Namakkal District., the majority of the self help groups opening account with Indian bank (37.74%) followed by Primary agriculture co-operative bank (27.11%)

Table 9 reveals that the economic activities involved by the Self Help Groups in the Namakkal District. The major economic activities are readymade, tailoring, computer operation, power looms, rope making, etc. there are 720

TABLE 9
Economic Activities of Self Help Groups

Sl. No.	*Economic activities*	*No. of SHGs*	*No. of SHG Members*	*Percentage to total Member*
1.	Readymade	27	324	1.06
2.	Kalyan Store	24	360	1.17
3.	Petty shop	65	960	3.13
4.	Self Business	640	7680	25.04
5.	Milch Animals	720	9360	30.52
6.	Rope Making	17	255	0.83
7.	Tailoring	250	4000	13.04
8.	Power Looms	10	192	0.62
9.	Computer Operation	32	540	1.76
	Total	2285	30671	100

Sources : Primary Data.

Self Help Groups involved in Milch Animals, 640 Self Help Groups got self business training.

TABLE 10
Nature of Training

Sl. No.	*Training Programme*	*No. of SHGs*	*No. of SHG Members*	*% to total Member*
1.	Readymade	27	320	1.46
2.	Kalyan Store	24	340	1.55
3.	Petty shop	65	820	3.73
4.	Self Business	640	6760	30.78
5.	Milch Animals	720	8980	40.89
6.	Rope Making	17	235	1.07
7.	Tailoring	250	3850	17.53
8.	Power Looms	10	178	0.81
9.	Computer Operation	32	478	2.18
	Total	2285	21961	100

Sources : Primary Data.

Table 10 display that the training programs involved by the Self Help Groups in the Namakkal District. The training programs are readymade, tailoring, computer operation, power looms, rope-making, etc., there are 720 Self Help Groups involved in Milch Animals maintaining 640 self-business training and 10 power looms training activities involves the training programs.

Self Help Group promote the standard of life of the women through the economical activities which will bring the socio-economical status of the women in the society. Income of the Self Help Group members has improved proportionally in the previous years.

SUGGESTIONS

The following are the major suggestions based on the analysis of the data. These suggestions may be used to understand the role and performance of the SHG and gives some suggestions measures to improve the Performance of the SHGs in future.

SHG is one of the emerging concepts which help to promote the rural development through women empowerment. Hence, it is treated as dual benefits mechanism of the society.

SHGs helps to promote the microfinance with the organized from small savings. Hence, the promotion of SHGs indirectly promotes the savings, economic growth and rural development.

Namakkal is one of the famous districts for egg and consists of more rural population. But the number of SHGs is only 9418 which consists of 2.66% to Tamil Nadu level and 0.32% in all India level. Hence, the district authorities should concentrates to promote more SHGs, in the district.

SHGs are mostly promoted by the NGO's for their personal benefits. Most of the members of SHGs are not aware about the Schemes and benefits are available to them. Hence, the government should create the needs and importance of the SHGs with intensive campaign.

Government and district authorities may assigns the SHGs awareness campaign to the educational institutions and teaching faculty because this district consists of large number of level established educational institutions. It is the channels of interaction with the institutes and community development activities.

Monitor and regulate the SHGs activities should by properly maintained and managed. Most of the SHGs are not functioning properly and some of the SHGs functioning only for receiving the grant and aids from the government. So, the district authorities should take serious action to strengthen the SHGs.

CONCLUSION

Financial inclusion and social exclusive schemes can be implemented and maintained only with the help of the active performing SHGs. These sectors are emerging part which are directly related with the society particularly with women. Promote and develop the organized SHGs in large number, the government schemes may be easily canalizes. And above all the government may pass a separate Act to regulate and restructure of SHGs in future. This study concludes that the SHG in Namakkal district is not up to the expectation level of the researchers.

REFERENCES

Ashoka, R., Ponnarasu, S., Kalavathi, M.S. (2005). Inter-district Variations in the Performance of Self-Help Groups in Tamil Nadu, *Cooperative Perspective,* Vol. 40, No. 2, July-Sept.

David, Javachar P., Usha, Nanhini S., and Shivachandran, M. (2005), Women Entrepreneurship Leading to Rural Transformation, *The ICFAI Journal of Enterpreneurship Development,* Vol. 1, March.

Gananasamurthy, V.S., Radha Krishnan; M.K. Bhuvaneswari, Ganesan, A. (2006)., A Study on Thrift and Credit Utilization Pattern of "Self Help Group" in Lakshmi Vilas Bank, Suriyampalayam Branch, Erode, *Indian Journal of Economics,* Mumbai.

Jayaraman (2005), Performance Analysis of Fisherwomen Self Help Groups in Tamil Nadu, National Bank for Agriculture and Rural Development, Mumbai.

Kavitha, K. Ramachandran (2005), Women SHGs in India [A Rural View], Coimbatore.

Ready, C.S. Jennifer Living Stone, and Sandeep Manak (2006), Institutionalizing Support to Self Help Groups, the APMAS Experience, *The ICFAIAN Journal Management Research*, Vol. 5, No. 1, March.

Sharma, H.O., Nahatkar, B., and Minshra (2006). Impact of Microfinance through Self Help Groups on Rural Economy, *Indian Journal of Economics*, Mumbai.

Stephen, J.K., Selian, A. (2005), Role of NGOs in Micro Financing through Self Help Groups, *Indian Journal of Marketing*, Volume 8, August.

33

Role of Self Help Groups in Women Development

R.D. BHOSALE

INTRODUCTION

Indian Society is a male dominated Society. Indian Women's are still socio-economy backward after the 63 years of independence. Women's are the victims of sexual exploitation. Women's face the problem of economic discrimination. In this computer era, they are educationally backward and struggling to get opporunities due to illiteracy, gender discrimination on every front has resulted in the overall backwardness of women in India. There are legal provisions for the empowerment of women but proper implementation and sensitiveness towards this issue is the need of hour. India is emerging as a super power economy in the world but without empowerment of women the task of development is difficult. The Socio-economic and cultural contribution of women should be recognized. To address the problem of women empowerment,

SHG's should get important place on the development agenda of the country.

RESEARCH METHODOLOGY

The paper explains the socio-economic state of women and the importance of SHG's for the empowerment of women especially in rural India. The paper is based on the secondary sources such as periodicals, journals, magazines and references books, research articles on the issue of women empowerment.

OBJECTIVES

- To study the Socio-economic status and problems of women in India.
- To highlight the importance of SHG's for the empowerment of women in rural India.
- To explain SHGs as a movement for Upliftment and leadership development of women in India.

CONCEPT OF SELF HELP GROUP

It is a voluntarily formed group, the members size is 10-20. The group is basically homogeneous in nature. They come together for addressing their common problem. They are encouraged to save in a regular basis. The amount of saving is within the range of Rs. 20-100. They rotate this common pooled resource within the members with a very small rate of interest. Each group has a leader who is called as the president and secretary. They usually maintain records of transaction in daily basis in written format and that has been kept with the president or the secretary. Not only from the internal resources the members also get loan in bulk amount from mainstream banks, different govermental and non-govermental organizations donor agencies through MFIS.

FUNCTIONS OF SHG

Social Identity

Socio-economic Impact through Self-Help Group

Devaluation of women commences at birth with the preference for male offspring and continues through a childhood of conditioning to the submissive and later on, the subservient role required of them in the marital home. A woman is never viewed as a person in her own right but always as someone's daughter,. wife or mother especially in rural areas.

Platform

SHG's have an in-built mechanism where emphasis has been given over capacity building of women through its regular meetings, where members perform transactional activities and discuss over different related issues. This discussion among the group members is the means through which they give voice to their needs and it proves to be a platform for addressing their social and economic problems and enlightening their inner selves as well.

Social Status and mobility

Social mobilization through 'Self Help Groups' is ineuitable for economic empowerment and poverty alleviation. The concept of Self Help Group exists prior to any intervention. The members are linked by a common bond like caste, blood, community and place of origin or activity in these natural groups of affinity groups. It is imperative that the self-help group should be promoted in the way the facilities, a cooperative, participative and empowerment culture.

Economic Status and Benefits

The 'Self Help Groups' provide economic benefits in certain areas of production process by undertaking common action programmes, like cost-effective credit delivery system generating a forum for collective, learning with rural people; promoting democratic culture, fostering an entrepreneurial culture, providing a firm base for dialogue and cooperation in programmes with other institution possessing credibility and power to ensure participation and helping to assess an individual member's management capacity.

Enhance Equality

Self Help Groups enhance the equality of status of women

as participants, decision-makers and beneficiaries in the democractic, economic, social and cultural spheres of life, the SHG's have inculcated a great confidence in the minds of rural women to succed in their day-to-day life.

ASSISTANCE BY GOVERNMENT FOR WOMEN EMPOWERMENT

There is a constitutional provision under Article 16 about male-female equality which has still not a practical thing. Women empowerment is the need of hour for the family, society, country and the world. Women's are still get ill-treatment from the society except Sweden in the world. Indian Government has initially taken some efforts for the betterment of women.

CENTRAL GOVERNMENT EFFORTS

Indian Government has given reservation in Panchayat Raj System for the women through 73rd and 74th Constitutional amendments. Considering the Socio-economic and political state of women, the Government has introduced various legal provisions for the social justice for women in India. Proper and effective implementation of these legal provisions is necessary for the removal of injustice and atrocities against the women in India.

STATE GOVERNMENTS EFFORTS

Maharashtra Government has introduced new a innovative policies towards social reforms. Economic investment, educational progress and women empowerment in the golden jubilee year. Government has introduced strategy for the social justice of women and other weaker section of the society. Government has increased Financial assistance for various schemes such as free education to girls, Dalit *vasti* reforms, scholarships and inter-caste marriages. Government has given preference for the Self Help Groups of women's in the state especially residing in rural area.

Self Help Groups have helpful for the empowerment of women. Nationalized banks, Economic finance and development corporation and NGO's have contributed in the movement of women empowerment. Business run by women such as cloth-making, tailoring, agricultural marketing, milk dairy, goat farming, electric items. Agriculture service centre have increased and created economic reliance for them. State Government has encouraged the movement of Self Help Groups through rural development ministry and its associate institutions at tahsil and village level. The Government is funding Rs. 25 lakhs for the building of training for SHG members.

CONCLUSION

Women play the role of invisible hand of Indian economy. Illiteracy, social status and gender discrimination are the main hurdles of women empowerment in India. As per the construction and its amendments they got equal opportunities for eco-economic reliance. Contribution of women through SHG's is noteworthy especially for the women in the rural area. Government policies and role of banking is vital for the overall development of India and especially women empowerment. The picture of social status of women is changing due to economic contribution through various activities of SHG. Women's should get the representation on the political and economic dias. The efforts of Government are effective but needs to be properly implemented. The banking sector should act towards SHG as a social business instead of modern moneylenders. Panchayat Raj System has provided leadership opportunities at local level for women but the loopholes and leucocratic hurdles should be removed. Women should get representation in national politics as per the legal provisions. They should become part of the decision-making system. Women should get equal opportunities in education and the process of economic development. SHGs are the proper stage for their upliftment. Govt., NGOs and SHGs should share the stage with co-ordination for the empowerment of women in India.

References

Yojana, Marathi Monthly Magazine, Vol. 4, November 2010.

2008, Indian Economy, Datta, Sundraram, S. Chand Publication, New Delhi.

2005, S.B. Varma and Y.T. Pawan (edited), 'Rural Emprovement through SHGs, Deep and Deep Publications Pvt. Ltd., New Delhi.

NABARD Reports specially on Bank linkages of SHGs.

2001, Satish P., 'Some issues in the formation of Self Help Groups', *Indian Journal of Agriculture Economy,* Vol. 4.

1999, Karamakar, K.G., 'Rural Credit and Self Help Groups : Microfinance Needs and Concept in India', Sage Publication, New Delhi.

Government of India, Economic Survey, 2009-10.

Constitutional Amendunent Act, 73rd and 74th.

Journal of Rural Development, National Institute of Rural Development, Hyderabad, Oct., Dec. 2007.

Womens and Social Justice, Dr. Shubhangi Gogate (Marathi).

34

Self Help Groups and Women Empowerment

B. Rajamani and M. Julius Prasad

INTRODUCTION

It is not surprising that the development of women in India has been the centre stage of its development planning since independence through the concept has been evolving from plan to plan. In most south Asian countries, the status of women is low and their socio-economic conditions are much more depressed than that of men. In India, while the constitutional and legal status of women is equal to that of men in all respects the reality is that they suffer in all spheres of social and economic life. Poverty, in fact, is one of the aspects of their deprived condition. Low earning, lower wages, low level of skills, limited access of the factors of production, low literacy, malnutrition, poor standard of health, and greater exposure to domestic violence are the causes for the sufferings of the women in India.

Self-help groups have emerged as a popular method of working with people in the recent years. Power to the people signifies a new social movement, which has probably has born out of the realization that society's traditional arrangements for solving their problems. This movement stems from the people's desire to meet their needs and determine their own destinies though the principle of "by the people, for the people, and of the people". Ordinarily self-help refers to provision of aid to self, but here self is also taken to mean internal. Self-help emphasizes self-determination, self-reliance, self-production, and self-empowerment by mobilizing internal resources for the persons, the group, or the community.

MEANING OF SELF HELP GROUPS

Self Help Groups (SHGs) is a small voluntary association of poor people, preferably from the same socio-economic background. They come together for the purpose of solving their common problems through self-help and mutual help. The SHGs promotes small savings among its members. The savings are kept with a bank. This common fund is in the name of the SHGs. Usually, the number of members in one SHG does not exceed twenty.

WOMEN'S EMPOWERMENT

Women's empowerment is a process whereby women become able to organize themselves to increase their own self reliance, to assert their independent right to make choices and to control resources which will assist in challenging and eliminating their own subordination. The goal of women's empowerment is to address issues relating to women's subordination, inequality and inequity. Hence it is a process where women are able to change from a state of powerlessness (I cannot) to a state of collective self-confidence (we can).

Moreover, the poor can benefit from financial services such as savings, credit and insurance, such services can help smoothen consumption pattern, take up economic activities, manage risk and enable growth. This can be effectively done through SHGs.

EMPOWERING SELF HELP GROUP WOMEN

1. Imparting knowledge, creating awareness about the government and bank procedures.
2. Helping women to read and write.
3. Taking them to visit outside.
4. Developing the capability to manage a mini bank with ledgers and passbooks.
5. Aiming at the total abolition of over interest rate (Kandhu Vatti).
6. Enhancing their knowledge and skills to undertake economic activities.
7. Motivating them to increase their incomes by undertaking successfully economic activities as individual or groups.
8. Providing good marketing outlets for their products.
9. Encouraging their participation in the Gram Sabhas, panchayat level, federation clusters, Block Level Federations.
10. Creating the confidence and courage to address and take up varied issues concerning themselves and the community.
11. Creating more awareness on health care activities.
12. Getting recognition from the society and family.
13. Taking part in the decision-making of her family.
14. Increasing the capacity of independency.
15. Encouraging them to take active participation in Panchayat election and subsequent responsibilities.

SUCCESS OF SHGs STRATEGY

Training can contribute significantly to the success of the SHGs. Appropriate training (formal or informal) at each stage of SHGs' growth is one of the essential inputs required. The State of Tamil Nadu has a successful record of consistent growth in Self Help Groups. (See Table 1)

Kancheepuram district has more number of Self Help Groups followed by Coimbatore and Chennai districts in Tamil Nadu. Andhra Pradesh state has taken number one place with regard to the volume of Self Help Groups at the National

TABLE I
Growth of SHGs in Tamil Nadu

Sl. No.	District	No. of SHGs	Percentage
1.	Kancheepuram	20,551	5.77
2.	Coimbatore	19,430	5.46
3.	Chennai	16,596	4.66
4.	Erode	16,005	4.49
5.	Thirunelveli	15,678	4.4
6.	Salem	15,592	4.38
7.	Viluppuram	15,248	4.29
8.	Thanjavur	14,866	4.18
9.	Cuddalore	14,337	4.03
10.	Other Districts	2,07,656	58.34
	Total	3,55,959	100.00

Source : TNCDW Interim Report (2007-08).

Level. If we assume the strength of a Self Help Group is 15 members, the total strength of the beneficiaries through SHG schemes may be around 53, 39, 385 in Tamil Nadu. It is a marvelous achievement. If these group, are functioning efficiently our economic growth will attain a considerable level.

Now-a-day SHG has achieved a tremendous growth all over the country. Our government as well as voluntary organizations may utilize these groups for implementing various rural development as well as social service schemes.

WOMEN ACHIEVEMENT THROUGH SELF HELP GROUPS

1. They have provided them with a sense of security, confidence and encouragement to overcome misfortunes and contingencies. This resulted in elevated status of women in family, community and society at large.
2. The family expenditure has been increased due to positive change in the SHGs members' income. The incremental income not only enhances the

expenditure of the family but also promote the savings of the family after they join in the SHGs.

3. This is an achievement of the women SHGs, usually working women are being respected by the household members and the society. Now-a-days the women in the SHGs are also respected by the others, because they are independent in earning the income and they are contributing to household income, expenditure and savings.
4. The SHG realized that a job centered socio-economic development, which had faith in social justice and equality, would provide self-respect faith in social justice and equality, would provide self-respect to women, initiate and strengthen the empowering of women and the resultant sustainable development.
5. Today women are in the process of enriching themselves through Self Help Group.
6. The Self Help Group has concentrated on social mobilization of women giving them awareness of their legal and political rights.
7. Now-a-days women got health care awareness. They are regularly visiting the hospital for medical treatment.
8. They have got the capability of opening bank accounts and paying insurance premium independently.
9. Their bargaining power is also increased considerably in all respect.

Even though Self Help Groups have attained the above said benefits for the rural women, there are some drawbacks in the functioning of the Self Help Groups.

1. *Burden of meeting:* Time consuming meetings, in particular in programmes based on group lending, and time consuming income generating activities without reduction of traditional responsibilities increase women's work and time burden.
2. *New pressures:* By using social capital, in group lending/group collateral programmes, additional

stresses and pressures are introduced, which might increase vulnerability and reflect disempowerment.

3. *Reinforcement of traditional gender roles:* Lack of economic empowerment; microfinance assists women to perform traditional roles better and women thus remain trapped in low productivity sectors, not moving from the group of survival enterprises to micro-enterprises.
4. Lack of knowledge of the market and potential profitability, thus making the choice of business difficult.
5. Many members feel that the interest rate charged by the SHGs is higher than agricultural lending.
6. Most of the members are using the loan only for consumption purpose rather than productive.
7. They could not sell the products at the right time since they face heavy competition from the large scale producers.
8. They could not spend enough amounts for promotional activities hence they depend on government and other organizations for promotional activities.
9. Because of SHGs' liberal finance, many members spend more money beyond their capacity. Thus their financial burden ultimately will be increased.

CONCLUSION

SHGs are a media for the development of savings habit among the women folk. It mobilizes a large quantum of resources. It is a window for better technology and skill up-gradation. It helps to increase an income of the family. The SHGs' collective action and solidarity are important empowering mechanisms, moreover, the Government and bankers are giving whole-hearted support for providing credit either directly or thoroughly NGOs. This helps to develop the entrepreneur skill of the women in our country. The women members should come forward to utilize this opportunity to stabilize their economic growth and empowerment.

REFERENCES

Khari, D.S., "Women Empowerment for Sustainable Development Through Self-Help Group, ALB Books, New Delhi, 2009.

Sugana, B., "Women's Empowerment: Dimensions and Directions", *Social Welfare*, Vol. 55, No. 12, March 2009.

Vanitha, B., "Micro-Credit and Women's Empowerment with Special Reference to Swarnajayanthi Gram Swarozgar Yojana", *Social Welfare*, Vol. 56, No. 12, March 2010.

Index